CYBERIDENTITIES

CANADIAN & EUROPEAN
PRESENCE IN CYBERSPACE

The International Canadian Studies Series
La Collection internationale d'études canadiennes

The *International Canadian Studies Series* offers a unique collection of high-quality works written primarily by non-Canadian academics. The Series includes conference proceedings, collections of scholarly essays, and other material (including poetry, novels, plays, and monographs). The Series publishes works written in either English or French.

La *Collection internationale d'études canadiennes* présente des ouvrages de premier ordre, rédigés surtout par des universitaires non canadiens. Elle comprend des actes de colloques, des séries d'articles et d'autres formes d'écriture comme des recueils de poésies, des romans, des pièces de théâtre et des monographies. La collection publie des ouvrages en français et en anglais.

Editorial Committee/Comité éditorial:

Guy Leclair
Chad Gaffield

International Canadian Studies Series

Collection internationale d'études canadiennes

CYBERIDENTITIES

CANADIAN & EUROPEAN
PRESENCE IN CYBERSPACE

Edited by Leen d'Haenens

A. L. Cobb, M. J. Edwards, P. van Eecke, N. H. Faraqui, S. Garipis,
L. d'Haenens, C. J. Hamelink, C. Haythornthwaite, N. Jankowski,
D. Johnston, R. Kroetsch, C. Leeuwis, P. Martin, M. Noordhof,
S. Proulx, J. van Rossum, L. Roth, I. Shubert, P. Timmers,
K. Uyttendaele, L. Van Fleteren

International Council
for Canadian Studies

University
of Ottawa Press

Institute
of Canadian Studies

University of Ottawa Press gratefully acknowledges the support extended to its publishing programme by the Canada Council and the University of Ottawa.

We acknowledge the financial support of the Government of Canada through the Book Publishing Industry Development Program for this project.

Canadian Cataloguing in Publication Data

Main entry under title:
  Cyberidentities: Canadian and European presence in cyberspace

(International Canadian studies series = Collection internationale d'études
  canadiennes)
Includes bibliographical references.
ISBN 0-7766-0493-7

  1. Information technology—Canada.   2. Information superhighway—Canada.
3. Internet (Computer network)—Canada.   4. Information technology—
European Union countries.   5. Information superhighway—European Union
countries.   6. Internet (Computer network)—European Union countries.
I. d'Haenens, L. (Leen) II. Cobb, Alan L. III. International Council for
Canadian Studies.   IV. Series: International Canadian studies series.

ZA3225.C92   1999   303.48'33   C99-900510-3

 UNIVERSITY OF OTTAWA
UNIVERSITÉ D'OTTAWA

Cover Design: Robert Dolbec

ISBN 0-7766-0493-7
ISSN 1489-713X

© University of Ottawa Press, 1999
  542 King Edward, Ottawa (Ont.), Canada K1N 6N5
  press@uottawa.ca   http://www.uopress.uottawa.ca

Printed and bound in Canada

CONTENTS

Preface

Part One: Stationary Travelers?

Part Two: Cyberlaw

Part Three: Communities in Cyberspace

PREFACE

BEYOND INFRASTRUCTURE:
CANADIAN AND EUROPEAN IDENTITIES IN CYBERSPACE

by Leen d'HAENENS

The Canadian discourse is neither the American way nor the European way, but an oppositional culture trapped midway between economy and history. This is to say that the Canadian mind is that of the in-between: a restless oscillation between the pragmatic will to live at all costs of the Americans and a searing lament for that which has been suppressed by the modern, technical order. The essence of the Canadian intellectual condition is this: it is our fate by virtue of historical circumstance and geographical accident to be forever marginal to the "present-mindedness" of American culture (a society which specializing as it does in the public ethic of "instrumental activism" does not enjoy the recriminations of historical remembrance); (...) At work in the Canadian mind is, in fact a great and dynamic polarity between technology and culture, between economy and landscape. And this dialectical movement between the power of American empire and our bitter historical knowledge that the crisis has its origins much deeper in European culture is the gamble of the Canadian discourse on technology. (Kroker, 1984: 7-8)

What do car enthusiasts, compulsive hardware upgraders and gun nuts have in common? Aside from the fact that they are usually men, their respective fetishes confine them to a static world in which tools verge on the transcendental and their own selves become identified with the objects of their affections. Which can more or less be said of long-serving public servants as well... For all such people, the medium truly IS the message.

This book is an attempt to go beyond such mechanistic and conveniently reductive thinking, and face the fact that what is but a toy in the hands of a few can only come into its own as a potentially world-changing tool if access to it is both consensual and universal. In other words, people do not only need to know that the tools are out there – they need access to the tools and they also need to WANT to take advantage of them, which they only will do if they are allowed to see current uses for such tools, and to invent new ones as well.

So infrastructure is clearly not the focal point of this book. Although necessary, strong capital investment in infrastructure is not enough: if we are to reap the full benefits of the world's emerging cyberculture and take advantage of its major vehicle – the Internet – developing low-cost and widely accessible content, services, and applications must be a priority.

The EU minister conference in Bonn, July 1997, was attended by ministers and corporate figures, mostly from Europe, but also from the US, Japan and Canada. One thing everybody agreed on was that Europe is trailing far behind the US and Japan: North-American companies and governments spend twice as much money on information technology as their European counterparts. The Bonn partners are aiming to bridge this gap. For the very first time a unanimous European position has been achieved in this field. I refer to the Bonn Declaration on the protection of data, electronic commerce, and penal liability related to Internet use. At the next such conference, worldwide agreements are expected to be discussed.

Ensuring that the Internet becomes a more accessible, more reliable, and self-regulating tool is a task that primarily falls to industry. Governments, on the other hand, can contribute to the education of "virtual citizens" and provide security and safety through regulation. In Europe, policy-making about the Internet remains largely incidental. Moreover there is no unanimity among EU member states concerning the regulation issue. The Netherlands and Germany do not favour special regulatory measures targeted at the Internet. Self-regulation is the keyword here: Internet providers can police their own sites and provide parents with the software tools they need to select or filter Web pages based on their views of what their children can and should not view. At the other end of the spectrum, countries such as France, Italy, and Belgium have strong regulatory instincts.

Interesting against this background is the fact that in the US the *Communications Decency Act*, passed on February 1996, was struck down in June 1997 by the Supreme Court, which deemed it incompatible with the First Amendment. The ruling states that Government should not interfere with Internet content, not even with a view to preventing children being exposed to porn, violence, or indecent language. It cannot be mere chance that only 4 days after the ruling, on July 1st, President Clinton introduced a far less controversial, and therefore safer text establishing a framework for worldwide electronic commerce while favouring limited government intervention and aiming at a harmonization of commercial rules.

Canadian policy options are often overshadowed by US positions. Nevertheless, Canada has a high *telecompetitivity index* with regard to the US, Europe, and Japan – 7.6 per cent of its GNP already derives from trade in information technologies. Moreover, Canadian companies are often mistaken for US firms. To name a few, such Canadian companies as Cognos, Mitel, Newbridge, Hummingbird, Corel, and Nortel are all at the top in their respective fields. In and around Toronto, Ottawa, Montréal, and Vancouver (itself a city many Americans seem to think of as a suburb of Seattle), small and mid-size high-tech companies have been flourishing. While Canada has no Silicon Valley, one positive consequence is the fact that development costs are half as high there as in the US.

The computer departments of several Canadian universities have excellent reputation. The *University of Waterloo* seems to be Bill Gates's absolute favourite, and many US companies regularly scour Canadian universities in search of the talent they need. The *University of Waterloo* has developed a co-op program to provide graduating students with four months of experience in industry while working on their research project.

Canada is facing the same problem as European countries: training and keeping qualified personnel. The biggest threat comes from California, where taxes are lower and salaries around 30% higher.

This book looks at Canada's policy options, since these can be usefully pondered by European Union officials. Apart from the necessary technical infrastructure, one cannot ignore the fact that the Information Highway's vitality will be directly dependent on the content on offer – we hardly need to point out that in the past many promising technological achievements disappeared because they failed to fire the imagination of the buying public. So, beyond financial and technological issues there is a need for basic principles governing content supply, such as the following: content should reflect the international diversity of perspectives and languages for the benefit of a majority of users. The emphasis in the supply must be on openness instead of concentration; on diversity rather than one single perspective.

What is on offer on the Information Highway should not be dictated by the G7 countries' narrow and often protectionist self-interest. According to the Canadian vision, what is interesting about the Information Highway has more to do with communication than information: this is the basic difference with the American stance, which emphasizes infrastructure and raw data sharing. Canadian government documents indicate that the World Wide Web should not be a mere hub regulating the flow of data crisscrossing the globe, but that it should be promoted as the meeting point for those various dynamic communities that make up McLuhan's global village – a space where creative minds cross-fertilize each other...

In accordance with its chosen cultural policy, it is the Canadian government's objective not to accept any expression of cultural hegemony or cultural monopoly on the Information Highway. Until now, a whole slew of governmental measures – financial compensations in film production and quota in radio and television – has contributed to the protection of Canada's cultural identity. These policy options, together with active support of local creative production, proved quite effective. The arrival of the Information Highway, however, is considered a potential threat. An initial, probably impulsive response could then be to clutch at the protective measures taken in the audio-visual sector and amplify them. Precisely because of the open character of the Information Highway, the question remains whether the options chosen by the Canadian government to protect Canadian culture (mostly in the field of radio and TV) will prove applicable and effective with regard to the Information Highway.

Because governments indeed do have a role to play still: above all they must strive to put to right the infrastructure situation, which is currently characterized by the emergence of mega-mergers among suppliers. Furthermore, governments must ensure that power, currently in the hands of a few, is better distributed among larger groups of actors.

Otherwise the only force in operation will be the market, which means that too many people may be left behind once and for all.

At least one government is determined to do something about it: the Canadian government has invested heavily, and successfully in technology to assist in the creation of a new style of government which is more concerned with values such as open access and strategic partnerships with industry, universities and other non-governmental organizations than with control and ownership. The Canadian government is taking steps to prevent the Information Highway from becoming a vehicle for cultural homogenization or an outlet for monopolies. Canadian policy makers want to make sure that their opinions on content issues are heard on the international scene, which means that Canadians may become more actively involved in the global co-ordination of the Information Highway. A lot of other regions, including the European Union, have also been looking for an approach which is more strategic and user-friendly. And most of them agree that the United States is never more aggressive in international matters than when it sees in them a means to boost its economy. What all parties really need to strive for is the establishment of a set of long-term, realistic and useful objectives: technology as a tool must be used to recognize and stimulate creative activities (so that anybody who wishes to produce and distribute new products and services, from electrical cars to electronic music, may do so), to make institutions more flexible, to eliminate market boundaries and expand horizons and perhaps – less realistically, but then the need is commensurate to the difficulty – ultimately to help draw humankind together (d'Haenens, 1999).

Canadians are already massively plugged in: 98.5 per cent of households have a phone; 95 per cent have access to cable TV; cellular services are available to 90 per cent of Canadians, and satellite services connect high arctic and remote Aboriginal communities. According to the Spring 1997 ACNielsen Canadian Internet Survey, over 30 per cent of Canadians are on-line: the amount of people aged 12 and over who are currently on-line in Canada amount to 8 million and this figure is growing at a rate of 50 per cent. Heavy users, who access the Internet on a daily basis, represent 35 per cent of Internet users, while frequent users, who log on at least once a week, account for 34 per cent and casual users, logging on less than once a week, represent 31 per cent. Further the survey finds that more females are joining the on-line community than males and that male dominance is gradually being reduced. Through the *SchoolNet* program 16,500 schools, 3,400 public libraries and 450 Aboriginal schools will be connected to the Internet by the end of 1998. The *Community Access Program* (CAP) will connect 5,000 rural or remote communities to the Internet by 2000. Other programs have been designed to help Canadians learn about, and take advantage of, Cyberspace. One such program is the *Student Connection Program*, which will hire 2,000 students over a three-year period to connect 50,000 small businesses and non-profit organizations to the Internet and train them in the use of business applications. The Information Highway Advisory Council

(IHAC) has made over 300 recommendations to the Government since its creation in 1994. More than 90 per cent have been, or are being, implemented.

This book's five sections shed light on initiatives taken by Canadian government and industry in order to provide "open access" in a wide variety of user contexts (community nets, freenets, school nets, intranets). Major issues discussed include: the role of Government, the role of the private sector and the place of the "virtual citizen." Of supplementary interest in the debate will be the extent to which Canada's IT initiatives can be adapted and implemented in a European – that is Flemish or Dutch – context.

In the first part, **Stationary Travelers?**, *Shubert* and *Kroetsch* show that cyberspace and the Information Highway can be approached in a metaphorical way: Shubert's parallel between the Trans Canada Highway and the Information Highway allows him to trace the spatial history of one of Canada's national icons and compare its development to that of the Information Highway. In so doing, the author asks whether the Trans Canada Highway will become the road less traveled, or simply one thoroughfare no one has any use for any more? Kroetsch also places emphasis on the notion of travel when dealing with the Information Highway: he sees the sequential delivery of bits of information as a narrative pattern in which users become involved in a manner similar to that of a conventional reader or traveler. Kroetsch wonders what other changes cyberspace has in store for us. He shapes his ideas around two of Aritha van Herk's most challenging texts: her novel, *No fixed Address*, and her "geografictione," *Places Far From Ellesmere*.

In part two, **Cyberlaw**, *Hamelink* explores the application of the international human rights regime to the governance of cyberspace. The proliferation of cyberspace technologies inevitably implies a confrontation with moral issues such as the unequal distribution of harm and benefit of applications among social actors; control over technology and its administration; and the uncertainty about the future impacts of technology. Looking into control over the Internet, *Garipis* confronts Internet use with legal rights and freedoms; which legitimate institution is entitled to regulate abuses deemed incompatible with the national public order? Should this regulatory institution be found on a national or international level? Or, put differently, can the notion of national public order justify *de facto* restrictions imposed to citizens of other States? *Van Eecke* looks into European initiatives in electronic commerce and the crucial need for legally accepted digital signatures within the Single Market. Issues at stake here are the legal recognition of digital signatures, the set-up of certification authorities, legal acceptance in the various EU member states as compared with guidelines for the introduction of digital signatures in Canada.

Part three, **Communities in Cyberspace**, starts off with *Roth*'s article on the several ways in which Canada's First Peoples may gain equitable access to the Information Highway. Although distance is and remains a major obstacle, it can be made less significant thanks to several recent projects and plans for extending the Information Highway into the North. *Leeuwis* investigates, irrespective of a given geographical context, the potential of electronic forms of debate in governmental policy processes and their advantages over conventional forms of debate. He concludes that electronic forms of debate may have various advantages over conventional forms. *Cobb* brings us back to the Canadian context with recent experience with two models of communities on the Net: SchoolNet and Community Access, in which through volunteer effort and limited government funding, schools across Canada are being linked in an enormous network. By 1999, 16,500 elementary and secondary schools will be linked through Internet connections. Community Access will create similar links between several thousands smaller rural and remote communities with populations larger than 400.

With the popularization of the Internet, discussion around forms of teledemocracy has gained a new lease of life. *Jankowski et al.* assess an experiment which took place in the Dutch province of North Brabant. Residents and interest groups were invited to participate in a month-long public debate conducted on an Internet site established for this purpose. More than a dozen interest groups and political parties contributed position statements related to the central issue of the debate: "Is space running out in North Brabant?" A research team monitored the personal assessments of the participants in this teledemocracy experiment.

In part four, **(Business) Opportunities on the Net – Case-studies**, *Haythornthwaite* sees computer-supported social networks (CSSNs) at the core of virtual communities, allowing for a wide variety of co-operative work and friendship relations, connecting workers within and between sites that are often physically dispersed. *Uyttendaele* promotes the use of the Internet and of electronic commerce for small and midsize businesses: accelerated introduction of information and communication technologies will stimulate economics growth and enable SMEs to become "virtual giants." Away from the business environment, *Edwards* describes the ways in which the Centre for Editing Early Canadian Texts (CEECT) at Carleton University has been preparing scholarly editions of major works of early English-Canadian prose with the help of computers. The pros and cons of mounting these editions on the Internet are evaluated. At stake are the wish to protect both the integrity of the work of the authors and the reliability of the editions as well as the desire to distribute these as cheaply, conveniently and widely as possible.

Part five, **The Role of Government**, looks into some Internet-related initiatives taken by the Flemish, Québec, Canadian governments, as well as the European Commission. *Van Fleteren* points out that the Flemish government is determined to make Internet access available for the widest possible audience. From 1997 on, free access to the Internet was made available in all Flemish libraries, schools of higher education, and a first group of 150 secondary schools. In the medium term all primary and secondary schools will be connected. The most ambitious plan is Telenet Flanders, whose goal is to convert the existing cable networks into an interactive broadband network which, apart from the existing broadcasting services, will also offer telephone, Internet access, and other multimedia services. The complete network overlay will be finished by 2002. Telenet Flanders already delivers fast Internet access in some areas and started with telephony services on January 1, 1998.

Proulx describes the intentions of the Québec government to assiduously pursue three essential objectives: (1) increasing the productivity of its own ministries and organisms; (2) supporting that part of the private sector interested in positioning itself on the world market for electronics (the government favours projects with pay-offs in the industrial environment as a whole rather than supporting projects that are exclusively aimed at the development of one particular firm); (3) supporting the production and on-line dissemination of contents and services in the French language (undoubtedly to be understood as an element of the Government's sovereignist project). On the other hand, the objectives concerning universal access and its integration in educational contexts seem to be long in coming. *Johnston & Faraqui* outline those areas in which further efforts are needed in order to fulfill the promise of a knowledge society in Canada. Government has a responsibility to take the lead role in developing this knowledge society by positioning itself as a model user of information and communications technologies. Access to the Information Highway is critical to Canada's future, as the economy becomes more dependent on information. Reinforcing Canadian sovereignty and protecting Canada's cultural identity continues to be a major public policy mandate. Thanks to information technology, there are now new ways to create, produce, market and distribute content. Sectoral areas such as health, education, and small business represent significant opportunities for the development of content, applications, and services. In each of these sectors, the potential benefits of the Information Highway are considerable. Finally, *Timmers* explores one crucial policy area for the European Commission within the context of the promotion of the Information Society: creating a framework which will encourage the sound development of electronic commerce.

This book is an offshoot of a conference (*Beyond Infrastructure. A Conference on Entrepreneurship, Communication and Culture*) held in Antwerp (September, 11-13, 1997) by the Association for Canadian Studies in the Netherlands and Flanders. The personal and professional support of a few special people has been especially important to me during the preparation of the conference and the compilation of this book. I have benefited from the advice and experience of the doyen of Canadian Studies in the Netherlands, Professor Cornelius Remie. My special thanks go to Robert Todd, Counselor in Communications and Culture at the Canadian Embassy in Brussels and Josiane Boone, Assistant for Academic Relations, whose support and expertise were invaluable for me.

Working with them is always a pleasure. I am also grateful to Philippe Sailler, of STS Communications, who proofread the book and designed the cover image, and did both with an extraordinary eye for detail and high quality. Last but not least, this publication came into being thanks to the financial support of the International Higher Educational Division of the Department of Foreign Affairs and International Trade, the International Council for Canadian Studies, the Canadian Embassy in Brussels (Communications and Culture), and the Association for Canadian Studies in the Netherlands and Flanders.

Part One:
Stationary Travelers?

THE TRANS-CANADA HIGHWAY VS THE INFORMATION HIGHWAY: THE ROAD LESS TRAVELED?

by Irwin SHUBERT

I perceive communication to be the value of Canada, a state where understanding and misunderstanding, where constant negotiation and the limits of language, coexist. We have had to learn how to contact one another over an enormous land space, across five and a half time zones, in what was a wilderness of scattered settlements. Technology forges connections and disconnections here. (B.W. Powe, 1993)

Montréal. Monday, May 3, 1971. Steve and I leave on our cross-Canada odyssey that will take us from a quiet suburb of Montréal to the "exotic" West Coast and Vancouver. We have been planning this trip for over a year, poring over maps, plotting mileage and side trips, saving money, and trying to figure out if there will be room for my guitar in the already-too-packed back of my 1965 VW Bug. Our parents have spent the year worrying about two twenty-year-olds traveling the Trans-Canada highway in what Steve's father called a "death-trap on wheels." Granted, the car was nothing to look at, but it was mechanically sound even though the tires were suspect. I can remember quite vividly the looks on their faces as we pulled out of the driveway – our fathers' stern smiles seeming to say: "I wish I had done this at your age," our mothers' bold attempts not to convey the "I'll-never-see-them-again-look" – pointed the car west, and slowly eased our way onto the Trans Canada. First stop, North Bay.

Just east of Ottawa, for some still unknown reason, the radio just quit playing. We drove in silence for a few miles not wanting to acknowledge this omen of things to come – the words muttered by my father under his breath as we left reverberating louder and louder in our ears: "They won't make it past Ottawa" – then, spontaneously bursting into laughter, as if someone had just lifted this great curse off of our shoulders, we looked at each other and resolved, in the true bravado that only a twenty-year-old can muster: "Well, I guess we just had our first and last breakdown;" (this, of course was not to be the case) "Here's to the rest of the trip," Steve said, popping a *Grand Funk Railroad* tape into the eight-track, the speakers bursting with sound. The silence was broken, the radio forgotten. It was us and the highway, as we chugged our way west.

Ottawa. Thursday, May 5, 1994. The newly formed *Information Highway Advisory Council* (IHAC), holds its first of 15 monthly meetings to discuss a Canadian strategy for the information highway. The council was guided by three objectives: 1) creating jobs through innovation and investment in Canada; 2) reinforcing Canadian sovereignty and cultural identity; 3) ensuring universal access at reasonable cost; and five principles: 1) an interconnected and interoperable network of networks; 2) collaborative public and private sector development; 3) competition in facilities, products and services; 4) privacy protection and network security; 5) lifelong learning as a key design element of Canada's Information Highway (Information Highway Advisory Council, 1995).

The term itself: *Information Highway*, denotes the "advanced information and communications infrastructure that is essential for Canada's emerging information economy. Building on existing and planned communications networks, this infrastructure (...) will [link] Canadian homes, businesses, government and institutions to a wide range of interactive services from entertainment, education, cultural products and social services to data banks, computers, electronic commerce, banking and business services (Industry Canada, 1994).

So, what does a rite-of-passage trip across Canada 26 years ago have to do with the development and exponential growth of Canada's Information Highway? In a word, everything! Consider this: In 1971 there were 50,000 computers in the world. In 1997 there are 50,000 computers sold every day (Graham, 1993). In 1971 the Trans-Canada Highway was 9 years old, the last sections having been paved the previous year. In 1997 the Information Highway is approximately 26 years old, having cut its teeth on the Advanced Research Projects Agency network (ARPAnet, the precursor to the Internet), developed by the US Defense Department as a "fail-safe" communications network capable of surviving a nuclear attack.[1] At around the same time Steve and I, wide-eyed and naive, were discovering the *links* of the Trans Canada Highway, places like Blind River, Wawa, Indian Head, Swift Current, Salmon Arm, and Hope, places as diverse in geography as they are in people, the US government was creating their *links*, seemingly unconcerned about geography or people.

There has been much written to support the metaphor of the highway being used to describe this massive undertaking to "wire" the world. Headlines such as: "Information's brave new road," "Information highway or hypeway?" "300 rules of the road posted for high-tech highway," or, "The Information Highway – From Public Thoroughfare to Private Road," to name but a few, all serve to solidify in our minds the link between transportation and telecommunications. As the authors of *Getting Canada Online* state:

> There are both similarities and distinctions between traditional transportation systems and the I-way, the contemporary metaphorical equivalent. Both require substantial capital investment. Both provide a basic infrastructure for modern society. But the term "I-way," drawn from the more understandable transportation highway, is imprecise in several respects. First, I-way ownership will be less public, more private and more varied. Second, its creation will engage

---

[1] Although the *Internet* is actually a component of the *Information Highway*, the words have become interchangeable as descriptors for telecommunications technology. In this paper I will also use both terms to describe the same thing, understanding fully their distinctive differences, while acknowledging their common usage.

a substantial number of technological systems. Third, it will be interactive, with intelligence and flexibility. (Johnston & Handa, 1995)

While I would agree that the metaphor is flawed in some respects, I also have my doubts about the so-called "intelligence" of the "I-way." But, before we go on to examine other such prophetic announcements, a closer look at both highways is needed.

Attributing highway status to the light-speed communication systems criss-crossing the globe may be a relatively new phenomenon, but the idea of transportation as a means of communication is not. Marshall McLuhan (1965) broached the subject over thirty years ago in *Understanding Media: The Extensions of Man*, in particular his chapter entitled "Roads and Paper Routes." Here McLuhan ruminates about the "speed-up" of transportation systems (roads, bridges, canals, sea routes, etc.), and their impact on cities and what economists refer to as the *center-margin* structure. As McLuhan writes:

> Great improvements in roads brought the city more and more to the country. The road became a substitute for the country by the time people began to talk about "taking a spin in the country." With superhighways the road became a wall between man and the country. Then came the stage of the highway as city, a city stretching continuously across the continent, dissolving all earlier cities into the sprawling aggregates that desolate their populations today. (1965: 94)

Falcon Lake, Manitoba. Thursday, May 6, 1971. Steve and I have spent the last three days crossing the province of Ontario. We have driven over 1,100 miles (this was a pre-metric trip!) and passed through more than 100 cities, towns, villages, and outposts. Although our grade-school geography classes and our trusty maps told us just how big the province was, none of this fully prepared us for the experience of driving across Ontario from border to border. At our campsite that night, in Whiteshell Provincial Park just west of the Ontario/Manitoba border, we retraced our route along the Ottawa River and over the top of Lake Superior. We babbled endlessly about the scenery and landmarks that we had passed, but saved our most fervent praise for the highway, each twist and turn unfolding new vistas, another Kodak moment. We realized how fortunate we were to be able to cross the country this way, familiarizing ourselves with places we had only heard about. As the miles clicked away, the highway infused us with a sense of awe; and of course, we had no idea at the time what a huge undertaking building this highway had been.

The Trans-Canada Highway is the longest national highway in the world. As if this fact were not significant enough, in *The Road Across Canada*, Edward McCourt (1965: 2) embellishes slightly when he writes: "No doubt we on this continent have always tended to exaggerate the importance of mere size; none the less, it is gratifying to know that the 5,000-mile Trans-Canada Highway is the longest continuous road on earth." McCourt's trip across Canada was not the first. That distinction belongs to Thomas William Wilby who, along with his wife, "motored" across the country in 1912, taking 52 days as well as a few barges to complete the trip (Wilby, 1913). The first authentic crossing of Canada, in which all four wheels were in constant contact with the road, excluding of course the crossing of two oceans, was not until 1946 by one Brigadier R.A. Macfarlane. The official opening of the Trans-Canada Highway, the first all-weather road to link all of the provinces, came on June 30, 1962. This momentous occasion took place at Rogers Pass where highway crews had to literally blast their way through the Selkirk Mountains of British Columbia. It wasn't until 1970 that the highway was completely paved, and the final cost was over one billion dollars. The highway successfully surmounted two of the greatest barriers nature has flung across this nation: The Canadian Shield and The Rockies. Nearly 1,300,000 cubic yards of rock and dirt were displaced; 25 major bridges were constructed – one of them 200 meters long; the tunnel under the St. Lawrence River in Québec cost 75 million dollars and it is a little over one kilometer long; and, 31 (over 6.5 kilometers) snow-sheds had to be built over the highway through Rogers Pass to contend with avalanches and an annual snowfall of 15.2 meters.

It is not surprising, given the incredible feat of building this highway, that it quickly assumed the role of defining our nationalism. Then Prime Minister John Diefenbaker, who presided over the opening ceremonies, uttered these words (quoted in McCourt, 1965: 196): "This event has generated a renewed sense of national unity (...) It has brought about a sense of oneness from the Atlantic to the Pacific Ocean comparable to that which moved Canadians when the first transcontinental railway was completed (...) It is a day when another landmark is met and passed in the building of a strong Canadianism."

Ottawa. April, 1994. Industry Canada (1994: 8) publishes yet another paper on the Information Highway: *The Canadian Information Highway: Building Canada's Information and Communications Infrastructure*. In the chapter entitled, "National Vision and Strategy," the authors lay out their nationalist agenda:

> The goal for Canada is to build the highest-quality, lowest-cost information network in the world, in order to give all Canadians access to the employment, educational, investment, entertainment, health care and wealth-creating opportunities of the Information Age. In short, the vision is to make Canada number one in the world in the provision and utilization of the information highway, creating substantial economic, social and cultural advantage for all Canadians.

There is a difference, albeit a subtle one, between this vision of the Information Highway and the vision for the Trans-Canada Highway. The builders of the concrete road were simply trying to physically unite the nation from the Atlantic to the Pacific;

the builders of the fiber-optic road are competing with other nations to develop the best communications system in the world. The Information Highway's nationalism is being built by design, the Trans-Canada Highway's nationalism was built by default.

The amount of noise being created by Canada's newest national highway is deafening. Barely audible above the din of this traffic in information, are those who would dare to be skeptical about Canada's transformation into an "information" economy. Just what is an information economy? How does it differ from a manufacturing economy? What are the natural resources of an information economy, and are they different from those of a manufacturing one? Perhaps these questions are best left for economists to figure out, but I have always been struck by how quickly some people tend to forget that Canadians are still consumers of products, products made from raw materials that, although they may not be made in Canada anymore, are definitely being made somewhere. The long list of these consumer products includes the cars needed to travel the Trans-Canada Highway as well as the computers needed to travel the Information Highway.

While the car and the computer are both tangible products, their respective thoroughfares are very different. Roads, like the Trans-Canada Highway, are very visible components of the landscape. They take up a vast amount of space in their attempt to shorten distance, and their impact on cities has been monumental. On the other hand, telecommunications networks tend to be invisible, their impact on city landscapes only recently being explored. There is no denying that the Internet, as Stephen Graham (1997: 33) suggests in *Imagining Cities*, is "beginning to make telecommunications more visualizable," however, it has a ways to go before it is seen in the same light as Canada's roads and highways.

Rogers Pass. Friday, May 21, 1971. We were just approaching the summit of Rogers Pass, following the twisting road that seemed to be carved out of the rock beside us, when the "Bug" died. It was a slow death. The road was steep and the car started to lose speed. I kept down-shifting to compensate, but this had no effect and the car finally stalled as I steered to the side of the road. We were, as the cliché goes, in the middle of nowhere. Steve got out of the car to have a look at the engine – not because he knew how to fix it, but because it seemed like the thing to do – while I sat in the car looking at the maps wondering if this was the end of the line. For some reason we had taken to waving to truck drivers who passed us going the other way. Many of them responded in kind, perhaps thinking that they might know us, or, perhaps curious about the little black "Bug" with the Canadian flag attached to its aerial. In retrospect, I think we started this salute out of respect for these drivers who spent hour after hour traveling the highway, secretly envious of the trucker-bond and what it represented. In the end, it was one of these truck drivers that finally came to our rescue, but not before the car had somehow miraculously healed itself. We landed in Vancouver May 25, the first half of the trip over.

Vancouver. August 29, 1997. I now live in the city I first visited in 1971. I have traveled across Canada three times since that trip, each time being guided by the memories of that first voyage. The Trans-Canada Highway has improved tremendously since then, so too has the Information Highway. The headlines continue to herald the I-Way as the road to the future, and more and more people are spending their time plugged into their computers, traveling all over the world form the comfort of their homes. There are, of course, many benefits to this shrinking world and enhanced communication, but there are drawbacks as well. As far as Canada goes, time will tell if telecommunications technology will forge more "connections" than "disconnections." Perhaps McLuhan (1965: 105) had it right when he stated: "Our electric extensions of ourselves simply by-pass space and time, and create problems of human involvement and organization for which there is no precedent. We may yet yearn for the simple days of the automobile and the superhighway." As for myself, the next trip is in the works!

ON THE (INFORMATION) HIGHWAY:
SO IS THIS A JOURNEY OR WHAT?

by Robert KROETSCH

". . . reading is a new act here, not introverted and possessive but exploratory, the text a new body of self, the self a new reading of place." (Aritha van Herk, *Places Far From Ellesmere*)

◎

Many years ago, one afternoon in Upstate New York while I was attempting to reprimand my very young daughter Megan for something – I forget what – she looked up at me and said, "Dad, don't get hyper." Unbeknownst to me I was at that moment commencing a paper, for delivery in Antwerp, to the Association of Canadian Studies in the Netherlands and Flanders. I was entering into the world of hypertext.

"Hyper" implies versions and visions of excess. The hyper-textual implies an excess of all the complexities that come together, or appear to come together, simply and reassuringly, in a traditional text. As we go from the bound and bounded book to the technologies that give us hypertext, we move from containment to expansion. The debate about what we call postmodernism focuses on that alteration. Those who criticize the postmodern fear the implications of excess. Those who favor postmodernism celebrate the potential of that alteration – even while admitting to anxiety. I number myself among those anxious celebrators. We are moving fast. Are we going somewhere?

◎

Last month I delivered a manuscript of a novel to my publisher in Toronto. The novel is about a group of people who travel from Seattle, up the Northwest coast to Skagway, then over the Chilkoot Pass and down the Yukon River to the Klondike goldfields. It is, in a basic sense, a treasure hunt. And yet the story is a (rather strange) love story. Somehow for me those two master narratives of western culture – the treasure hunt and the love story – are intertwined. When I finished my novel, instead of going out and buying a bottle of scotch, I went out and bought a new computer. I am suggesting that contemporary technological change is of life-altering consequence.

◎

In Canadian literature it is the work of Aritha van Herk that represents one of the most daring and insightful looks of the implications of hypertext for the writer of books. Aritha van Herk is a distinguished Canadian novelist and essayist whose parents emigrated from The Netherlands to Canada in 1949. Her three novels are *Judith*, *The Tent Peg*, and *No Fixed Address*. I will make mention of the third novel only. Aritha van Herk published *No Fixed Address* in 1986. That novel is full of kinds of restlessness, as announced by the title, and as enacted by the story. In that story a man stays at home, in Calgary, minding the house, while his girlfriend travels in circles around the prairies, selling panties to general merchants in small towns. That is, she upsets the traditiona' narrative that goes back at least to Homer's *Odyssey*, the narrative that has the woman at home while the man roams the world. *No Fixed Address*, adding defiance to subversion, has as its subtitle: An Amorous Journey.

Aritha van Herk, after publishing that novel, began to write and publish a series of highly speculative, and some would say difficult, essays. She began more intently to examine the conventions of the novel and, metaphorically at least, the implications the hypertextual as they might influence a writer of books.

◎

Her volume of essays, *Places Far From Ellesmere*, published in 1990, most clearly prophesies the effect of hypertext on traditional literary texts. I read that book as a kind of fable that tells us, obliquely, where we might be going.

◎

The impulse of the hypertext, for all its ability to digress, and to summon up specters of the past, remains powerfully prophetic – it looks longingly, not to the past, but to the future. Perhaps the basic impulse operating at this conference is the impulse toward prophecy. Prophets tend to come in from the desert to the city, bearing word of change, of transformation, of condemnation, of repentance and penance. Of revitalization.

Aritha van Herk grew up in a kind of desert. She grew up on a wheat farm south of Edmonton, on the border where the treeless Canadian prairies become parkland – that is, the bald or short-grass prairies begin to be clumped over with groves of poplar. *Places Far From Ellesmere* is in many ways a bringing into the city of the prophetic demand for change and rejuvenation. It is a collection of four essays. Each essay takes its title from a geographical place in Canada.

The first is the Alberta prairie town called Edberg, the town (or technically, village) near which van Herk grew up. The second is Edmonton, the city in which she received her university education. While there she wrote her MA thesis, *Judith,* a prize-winning novel about a young woman growing up on a pig farm. The third is about Calgary, the city in which she works as a professor of literature.

Those three essays are full of what an older discourse might call sin. All three echo, obliquely and profanely, ideas of death and damnation. Graveyards abound. The fourth and culminating site is Ellesmere. Ellesmere Island is the most northerly island in the Arctic Archipelago, and also the most northerly point of land in Canada. It is on Ellesmere that the narrator – let us call her Aritha van Herk, to distinguish her from the novelist, Aritha van Herk – encounters, along with a violent sense of death, a sense of hope.

Each of the four essays is a meditation on a place, even a description; yet each, while describing a particular place, becomes autobiographical narrative. The four pieces together constitute a single narrative. They might be read as the education of the artist – a *Kunstlerroman*. The education of the artist toward hypertext. Or they might be read as departures from a narrative that has been too long in place. The book, after all, is resolutely not a novel. I am reminded of Wallace Stevens's poem, *Metaphors of a Magnifico*:

> *Twenty men crossing a bridge,*
> *Into a village,*
> *Are twenty men crossing twenty bridges,*
> *Into twenty villages,*
> *Or one man*
> *Crossing a single bridge into a village*
>
> *This is old song*
> *That will not declare itself . . .*

Aritha van Herk's book teases us with an old narrative: we are assuredly crossing a bridge. Where to?

◎

Let me begin again, this time by getting as far as the title page. In a certain way, hypertext is composed entirely of digressions. It raises the question: does the center exist at all? Places "far from Ellesmere" van Herk tells us. She says this to an audience that has always insisted that Ellesmere is far from us. Her title dislocates us. We are made to feel uneasy. But we also feel a kind of liberation. The field begins to open. Circumference and center threaten to trade places. Or they are encouraged to trade places. Or they lose the sense of difference, based on the assumption of center and circumference, that has traditionally given them identity.

The condition I'm describing bears a curious resemblance to the mysterious condition called falling in love. We enter into the erotics of hypertext. I'm thinking of the ways in which the intellect is so open to seduction by the technological invitation – but I'm getting ahead of myself. And even to say I am getting ahead of myself implies the existence of a vestigial narrative. A progression from "then" to "and then" to "and then."

◎

Beneath van Herk's disturbing title we read a sub-title: "a geografictione." The mating of two words. Geography. Fiction. The making of a new word that contains in its middle a reminder at a third word – graphy. That is: writing, description, representation. Geografictione: a writerly version of virtual reality.

Aritha van Herk's text begins:

> Home: what you visit and abandon: too much forgotten/too much remembered. An asylum for your origins, your launchings and departures, the derivations of your dream geographies. Where you invented destinations. Always and unrelentingly (home) even after it is too late to be or to revert to (home), even after it pre/occupies the past tense.

Place and story, immediately, become lost in each other. We cannot begin to guess which was seduced by the other. This opening is the writer's instructions to the reader. Instead of orientation, we are offered the risk and the exhilaration of disorientation. Too much forgotten/too much remembered. An asylum for your origins, your launchings and departures. The derivations of your dream geographies. Where you invented destinations.

We are in the erotic world of travel – and surely travel is a socially acceptable version of the erotic. Reading that first paragraph, we experience the rub and touch, the distance and desire that, named variously, incline us always into the subterfuge of a four-letter word. Love.

That first essay has as its full title: "EDBERG, coppice of desire and return." That essay's second paragraph begins: "A welt in the parkland between Dried Meat Lake and Meeting Creek, just off the Donalda/Duhamel trail . . ."

The sheer erotics of places named. The lovers, naming and renaming. Repeating. As you can see, I have been seduced by van Herk's version of the hypertextual. It turns out that I too grew up on a wheat and cattle farm, only a few kilometers from the Battle River. From Dried Meat Lake. That lake's name, translated into English from Cree, denotes a place where the Blackfoot and Cree killed buffalo at various buffalo jumps, butchered the animals, and dried the meat in the hot summer sun. When I was a boy a trace and extension of the cart and wagon trail to which she refers – a trail that in an earlier manifestation was no doubt a buffalo and then a horse trail – was still to be found in a patch of prairie on my father's homestead. That is, looking for a goal, we came only to signs of journey.

Aritha van Herk's home town, Edberg, was already, before her birth, she tells us immediately, a marker on a trail. That is, it was a marker on a journey. She was born into a journey, this writer who sets out so willfully to deconstruct the traditional idea of journey. She authenticates this in the traditional manner by referring to the travels of the geologist and explorer J. B. Tyrrell and his own written text of 1887. Joseph Burr Tyrrell was one of the truly great explorers of the Canadian West. Working for Geological Survey of Canada (1881-98), he traveled into huge blank spots on the Canadian map. He is credited with discovering the dinosaur beds that lure thousands of tourists into the badlands of Alberta. He had, unwittingly I suppose, a hand in my writing a novel called *Badlands.*

It is from Tyrrell's texts, we guess, that van Herk draws the unlikely term, coppice – a word in turn whose usage shows us now (it seems to me) that Tyrrell the geologist, the explorer, the historian, was as homeless in this terrain as van Herk is at home. She and I would call such a coppice a bluff. Again, there is a kind of misnaming in this, because the bluffs of poplars in the parklands of the Battle River country are not always located on hills or headlands. A bluff for us might well stand on perfectly flat land. Aritha van Herk's "geografictione" insists on the connectedness of landscape and story. It insists also that the relationship is always shifting direction, changing definition.

Traditional narrative is a means of dealing with the ingredients that constitute a text – or, more radically, I would argue, the elements that constitute a life. Narrative enables us to live our lives. Hypertext puts that narrative under revision. It questions our very perceptions of what a life – individual or collective – might be. I keep offering you what this paper is not about. Given another hypertextual shift, I might suggest that the hypertextual marks the end of the Romantic [capital R] self. Or self as hero. Or self as something independent, self-made, marked by clear boundaries. We too become geografictiones.

Aritha van Herk's title, *Places Far From Ellesmere,* calls our attention to a prior narrative, a narrative that has served as a master narrative from the beginning of European expansionist exploration into present times. I am referring to the quest for the Northwest Passage. The quest for a passage through ice and cold to the silks and tea and spices of the Indies. Why does the European imagination insist that to get to spices you must past through ice?

In this age of excess, be it an excess of information, or, more problematically, an excess of accessibility, it is especially the traditional journey that comes under question. The traditional journey was based on inaccessibility. The hero faced many trials, many tests. The journey, or quest, was based on an absence of information, whether being acted out by Christopher Columbus, setting sail westward for the Indies, or by John Franklin, sailing northward, but seeking the same goal – the Indies. Or Cathay.

The goal was absolutely clear, but sort of vague. Columbus believed all his life that he made it – that he got to the Indies. Sir John Franklin and his ships and crews disappeared into the ice. To this day they still occasion the annual launch of a search expedition.

The narrator in van Herk's book journeys North with an awareness that there is no cornucopia at the far end of the trip. There is, she says with a vengeance, no horn of plenty – at least not for the female traveler. Aritha van Herk, setting out, carries along her own ambiguous treasure. She takes with her on her trip to Ellesmere one book and one book only – Tolstoy's *Anna Karenina.*

The phallic confidence of traditional narrative, be it that of Franklin or Tolstoy, comes under debilitating scrutiny. Going up north – by brazen implication a question of "getting it up" – this time, explicitly, announces the feminine subtext that was disguised by earlier explorers as spices and silk. Aritha van Herk's vision of the feminine is not so benign. And never so safely distant.

I would venture that, in hypertext, the traditional male journey is feminized. Geograficitone and the hypertextual allow for no essentialism, no purity of intent, no assurances. In a geograficitone, the supposed spatial certainty of geography and the willfulness of fiction (that is, our unpredictable movement through time) meet in erotic play. [And I am thinking of the high seriousness granted to play in the book *Homo Ludens,* written by the cultural historian who was Rector of Leiden University, Johan Huizinga]. To put it another way, love is a messy business. But it beats being frozen in the ice.

◎

In *Places Far From Ellesmere,* Ellesmere Island itself is mysterious and largely unknown. Ellesmere, itself a geograficitone, is for van Herk a representation of the presence and absence of woman. The full title of the fourth essay is: "ELLESMERE, woman as island." Aritha van Herk, to elaborate her own geograficitone, takes with her to the geographical and female island a novel – a patriarchal novel.

◎

George P. Landow, that very helpful theorist of the hypertextual, tells us that "linking is the most important fact about hypertext (...)" (Landow, 1994: 6) The train (speaking of technologies) is one of the principal linking images in van Herk's book. The train that killed Anna Karenina in Tolstoy's novel is present in the opening essay, announced with the sentence, "The train went through." Through Edberg, that is. But through Edberg to implications and stories of sex and violence and death. Aritha van Herk reminds us that in Tolstoy's novel, Anna must confront that grandest and most romantic of endings in the western narrative tradition: she must die because of love.

Aritha van Herk cannot help but read and cannot help but disagree. As an ending – as one of the endings – in *Places Far From Ellesmere* – the narrator and her husband finally walk as far as the Abbe Glacier and the Seven Sisters. And as they turn away from their apparent goal we are in for a linguistic surprise. "I" turns to "you":

> The day you return from the glacier, you realize that Anna is condemned because she reads. 'You are astonished to discover this in the novel, waiting there, your

own addiction so carefully prepared for on this trip where you have lost libraries and bookstores, where only the jaegers and the arctic hares bounce between lines. Your pages flutter in the wind that funnels from the glaciers above, from the glaciers to the north, from Russia just over the flat top of the world.' (van Herk, 1990: 130)

The reader in the last pages is addressed as you. But that you is also the writer addressing herself. In hypertext the distinction between writer and reader begins to slip. Returned from the mountain, having learned a new reading, you abandon the traditional linearity of the book. You enter into hypertext. More than that, you can now survive the death that is the necessary consequence of linearity.

In the word "Ellesmere" we hear mother and sea. The life-giving and life-taking mother of traditional mythology. The life-giving and life-taking sea. We also hear "she" in the plural. In Ellesmere as site/sight – in its immense whiteness – we see plurality. We see, and experience, not simply a desert of snow, but also what van Herk calls "white nights." In the Ellesmere summer, the sun does not set. We experience the color that contains all colors. We have gone beyond Ellesmere as an image of the blank page. We have recognized Ellesmere as an image of the computer screen. That change of perception allows a revision of the story. Ellesmere becomes for us as readers the image of cyberspace itself.

I am reminded of two lines from a W. B. Yeats poem:

> *And therefore I have sailed the seas and come*
> *To the holy city of Byzantium.*

We have indeed set sail. In the past we set sail for Byzantium. For Cathay. For the Indies. We set sail with a ruthless will to possess, to destroy, to colonize. You might begin to think I have come before you, after all, as the prophet out of the desert, to scourge you for your sins. But not so. Setting sail with van Herk, going down the information highway with her, into hypertext, we come to the harsh, blank, full, and beautiful island of Ellesmere. We come to an abundance that is disorienting. We are instructed to engage in linkage.

I am not quite persuaded that we have come to a new paradigm. We are travelers still, on a journey; we go on searching. But now we do not say we are searching for spices or silks or exquisite porcelain. Linkage is a barren word. And yet that word encodes our longing for a transformation into a fullness of the imagination. What is linkage, at its best, but love: a geografictione that acknowledges place, time, paradox, change, desire, imagination and the real.

Aritha van Herk has other and more explicit terminologies. She says of Anna Karenina:

Anna holds her red bag as talisman, she carries its ubiquity, daring to know her cunt, its lust for reading. Anna trusts her reading and her body: all other persuasions are traducer's inventions, excuses. She reads toward her own capitulation: her lover/her killer? her necrophiliac scribe. (van Herk, 1990: 142)

To enter into the hypertextual is to risk all. The journey toward the unpredictable discovery remains the paradigm. But, to make that journey now we must, like Aritha van Herk, reread the old texts, then re-imagine the journey even as we make it. The old map, existing as a trace, as a palimpsest, is unreliable, even deceptive. We must not only cross boundaries; we must proceed even while boundaries change, fade, disappear. We must re-imagine the linkage; we must, as van Herk shows us, make linkages that are not suggested by any map. Encountering myriad pathways, we still desire to connect.

And so I am suggesting that we, having traveled across oceans and through train stations, must now, exhausted as we might be, write a love story. It must be a new version – a very new version of that old story. And believe me, for your sake, for mine, for all our sakes – I wish us the best of luck. Because luck too is part of the journey. And part of love. And, while I hesitate nowadays to disagree with my grown daughter, I must suggest that we, contrary to her sage advice, "Get hyper."

**Part Two:
Cyberlaw**

HUMAN RIGHTS IN CYBERSPACE

by Cees J. HAMELINK

I   INTRODUCTION

This essay explores the application of the international human rights regime to the governance of cyberspace. Cyberspace is the virtual communicative space created by digital technologies. It is not limited to the operation of computer networks, but also encompasses all social activities in which digital information and communication technologies (ICT) are deployed. It thus ranges from computerized reservation systems to automated teller systems and smart cards. With the "embedding" of digital facilities in more and more objects (from microwave ovens to jogging shoes), these acquire intelligent functions and communicative capacities and begin to create a permanent virtual life-space.

The issue of the governance of cyberspace emerges in many current ICT debates at different levels. There is the staunch anarchistic position that considers cyberspace a totally new and alien territory where conventional rules do not apply. For those holding this cyber-libertarian view (represented by visionaries like John Perry Barlow) no governance is the best governance. But, however attractive this approach may seem, if more people are to use cyberspace this is likely to need public and corporate policymaking. This is equally the case if cyberspace is to be protected against unprecedented opportunities for criminal activity. Moreover, cyberspace technology does create a virtual reality, but this is not altogether de-linked from politics in the real world.

Opposed to cyber-anarchy are those governments who would want a strict regime for activities in cyberspace in order to control not only the pornographers, and neo-Nazis but also the copyright pirates or just anybody who holds politically subversive aspirations. Then there are the cyberspace citizens who feel they can best police themselves and who discuss among themselves a variety of forms of self regulation ranging from Parent Control software to CyberAngels, Codes of Conduct and Netiquette.

Cyberspace is perceived by the digital settlers as the last "electronic" frontier, but cyberspace also colonizes our non-virtual reality and lest it totally controls daily life it needs to be governed by norms and rules. A recurrent question is whether cyberspace gives rise to new forms of democratic [electronic] governance, which are less-territory based, less hierarchical, more participatory, and demand new rules for political practice.

Whatever position one may take regarding future governance of cyberspace, it cannot be denied that in any case (moral) choices have to be made and are being made since, like all technological developments, the proliferation of cyberspace technologies inevitably implies a confrontation with moral issues on different levels. These relate to – among others – choices about the way the technology will be designed; choices among possible applications and the responsibility for certain applications; choices about the introduction and the use of applications. They also address issues such as the unequal distribution of harm and benefit of applications among social actors; the control over technology and its administration; and the uncertainty about the future impacts of technology.

The specific question that concerns me here is whether the current international human rights regime can provide us with meaningful moral and legal guidance in addressing these moral choices.

II   THE INTERNATIONAL HUMAN RIGHTS REGIME

In response to the assaults against human dignity during the Second World War, the United Nations began to develop a universal framework of moral standards. This was to become the international human rights regime. Before 1945 there were human rights declarations, such as the Magna Charta of 1215, the British Bill of Rights, the American Declaration of Independence and the French Déclaration des droits de l'homme et du citoyen. In 1945 this long history of the protection of human dignity acquired a fundamentally new significance. The novelty of the international human rights regime – as it was established after 1945 – was the articulation of the age old struggle for the recognition of human dignity into a catalog of legal rights. Moreover, the political discourse shifted from "rights of man" to the more comprehensive "human rights."

The protection of human dignity (earlier on mainly a national affair) was put on the agenda of the world community. Herewith, the defense of fundamental rights was no longer the exclusive preoccupation of national politics and became an essential part of world politics. The judgment whether human rights had been violated was no longer the exclusive monopoly of national governments. More importantly yet, the enjoyment of human rights was no longer restricted to privileged individuals and social élites. The revolutionary core of the process that began at San Francisco – with the adoption of the UN Charter in 1945 – was that "all people matter." Basic rights were to apply to everyone and to exclude no one.

The new regime would evolve around a set of basic texts (some codified as legally binding instruments and some adopted as customary law) and mechanisms for their enforcement. The foundation for the regime was laid down in the United Nations Universal Declaration of Human Rights (adopted on December 10, 1948 by the UN General Assembly) and the two key human rights treaties, the International Covenant on Economic, Social and Cultural Rights (in force since January 3, 1976) and the International Covenant on Civil and Political Rights (in force since March 23, 1976). In these three documents (commonly referred to as the International Bill of Rights) one finds seventy-six different human rights. If one were to take into account all of some fifty major international and regional human rights instruments the number of rights would obviously increase even further. There is also a current tendency among human rights lobbies to put more and more social problems in a human rights framework and thus to add to the number of human rights.

Since this proliferation of rights does not necessarily strengthen the cause of the actual implementation of human rights, various attempts have been made to establish a set of core human rights that are representative for the totality. One effort concluded to the existence of twelve core rights (Jongman, A.J. & Schmid, A.P., 1994: 8).

These are:
1. The right to life
2. The right not to be tortured
3. The right not to be arbitrarily arrested
4. The right to a fair trial.
5. The right not to be discriminated against
6. The right to freedom of association
7. The right to political participation
8. The right to freedom of expression
9. The right to food
10. The right to health care
11 The right to education
12. The right to fair working conditions

These rights are the legal articulation of fundamental moral   principles and their implied standards of human conduct. These principles and standards are:
• Equality and the implied standard that discrimination is unacceptable.
• Security and the implied standard that intentional harm against human integrity is unacceptable.
• Liberty and the implied standard that interference with human self-determination is unacceptable.

The universal validity of the human rights regime and its basic moral categories has been a contentious issue for some time. However, the United Nations World Conference on Human Rights (Vienna, 1993) stated the following in its unanimously adopted declaration: "The World Conference on Human Rights reaffirms the solemn commitment of all States to fulfill their obligations to promote universal respect for, and observance and protection of, all human rights and fundamental freedoms for all in accordance with the Charter of the United Nations, other instruments relating to human rights, and international law. The universal nature of these rights and freedoms is beyond question." This recognition of universal validity does not mean that all local forms of implementation will be similar. A variety of cultural interpretations remains possible. This has raised the question of the degree to which local cultural interpretations can be accepted. There is increasing support for the view that culturally determined interpretations reach a borderline when they violate the core principles of human rights law. Moreover, this view holds that the acceptability of the interpretation should be judged by the international community and not by the implementing party.

III   HOW ARE THE BASIC HUMAN RIGHTS STANDARDS RELEVANT TO CYBERSPACE?

A first issue concerns the observation that the human rights regime is firmly embedded in modernist, Enlightenment thought that seems to collide with the view that cyberspace is "a manifestation of the postmodern world." (Loader, 1997: 8) Characteristic of the modern world are the physical categories, such as location, gender, ethnicity, appearance, from which cyberspace seems to liberate us. There is a pragmatic answer to this question. Even if the international human rights regime is affected by the flaws of modernity in today's reality the regime is more noted for its violations than its respect, and the world would undoubtedly be a safer place for the world's majority if its provisions were implemented. Moreover, cyberspace itself it solidly rooted in and connected with the forces of modernity. It originates with the military establishment (that created the predecessor of the Internet) and is strongly promoted by the world's leading financial and industrial corporations.

It seems however necessary to expand the discussion with a conceptual critique of the conventional human rights discourse. The real significance of human rights standards can only be uncovered if a number of theoretical inadequacies are addressed and remedied. Conventional theories on human rights imply limitations to the understanding of human rights that erode the effective implementation of the very basic claims they enunciate. These theories are characterized by their exclusive emphasis on individual rights; their limited interpretation of the concept *freedom*; their limited understanding of the concept *equality*; their limited scope for *horizontal effect*; and their lack of institutional consideration.

IV   INDIVIDUAL AND COLLECTIVE RIGHTS

Human rights have both individual and collective dimensions. "There are also rights which present individual and collective aspects. Freedom of religion and freedom of expression are cases in point." (Van Boven, 1982: 54) Rights to language and religion are enjoyed in communities. They cannot be implemented by protecting individual rights only. Also the right to development demonstrates this relationship. UNGA Res. 34/46 of 1979, states that "the right to development is a human right and that equality of opportunity for development is as much a prerogative of nations as of individuals within nations." As a result, in the discussion on the locus of human rights the individual and the community cannot be separated. Individuals do not exist in isolation and are members of communities. Communities do not exist outside the individuals that make up the collective. Sanders concludes that "individual rights and collective rights are distinct ideas, they are separate categories. Some individual rights can be vindicated without reference to collective rights (...) But other basic rights – such as freedom of religion – cannot be effectively vindicated without the recognition of collective rights." (Sanders, 1991: 383)

This does not exclude that in different cultural and ideological traditions there are conflicting emphases on the individual versus the collective. There may be conflicts between individual and collective rights. This needs careful balancing. A case in point is the collective right to cultural autonomy of a group that practices sexual discrimination through the practice of "female circumcision."[1] A guiding principle here is the provision of Art. 5 of ICCPR and ICESR which prohibits any collective to engage in acts that are "aimed at the destruction of any of the rights and freedoms" recognized in the Covenants. The exercise of collective rights cannot imply the destruction of individual rights. In international law there has been a remarkable evolution from an exclusive emphasis on sovereign nation-states, to individuals, to non-state social groups (peoples) and to humankind. There is still a strong tendency to give priority to individual rights, and states tend to be inclined towards the recognition of the collective rights of minorities and usually favour assimilation over cultural autonomy.

Even so, there is increasing recognition of collective rights. Following Sanders (1991) collective rights are claims on behalf of communities (for example ethnic minorities) that seek to protect their specific features, such as cultural or linguistic characteristics. Sanders distinguishes collective rights from group rights, "the major limitation of group rights is that they only exist while the discrimination continues." (Sanders, 1991: 369) Groups are joined because of external discrimination, whereas collectivities are joined by internal cohesiveness. "Collectivities seek to protect and develop their own particular cultural characteristics." (Sanders, 1991: 369) For example, "cultural minorities seek more than the right of their individual members to equality and participation within the larger society. They also seek distinct group survival." (Sanders, 1991: 370)

V   NEGATIVE AND POSITIVE FREEDOM

The basic assumption of conventional human rights thinking regarding freedom of information is that freedom of expression as such is a given and that there should only be protection against the danger of interference by the state. This assumption glosses over the fact that in unequal societies this freedom does not exist for everyone. In almost every society individuals and peoples are silenced. Therefore, promoting freedom of expression would require focusing upon the provision of access to the public expression of opinions rather than on restrictions to freedom of expression. Moreover, the concept of freedom is usually construed in a negative sense only. The classical right to freedom of expression is a good illustration of this. It calls for freedom from interference in the expression of opinions, ideas, and information.

---

[1] Female circumcision: a genteel euphemism for the genital mutilation of young girls (ripping out the clitoris and scraping off the labia minora, then stitching the labia majora together, all done in non sterile conditions and without benefit of anesthetics).

Complete freedom, however, also encompasses emancipation and self-development. It implies a process of human emancipation.

Conventional human rights concepts do not provide this positive extension of the basic norm of freedom. The "freedom to" (positive freedom) points to a process of empowerment through which people liberate themselves from all those forces that hinder them in taking decisions concerning their own lives. This interpretation of freedom implies a process of emancipation that should be guided by the basic norm of the sovereignty of individuals and peoples. The liberal right to freedom of expression does not imply that everyone acquires equal access to the means of expression. Another important element is that the freedom of information in the liberal tradition is not directly linked with the principle of equality. As a result it offers insufficient support to the "information-poor" who claim that their freedom of information can only be realized if adequate means of expression are available. The liberal interpretation does not favour the use of preferential measures ("positive discrimination") in situations of social inequality.

5.1   Equal entitlement

Conventional human rights theories are biased towards a European tradition in which it is assumed that all human beings are equally capable to assert their rights and in which the legal system is formally based upon the assumption of the initiative by free citizens intent on defending their rights. These liberal foundations of human rights law tend to neglect the reality of widely varying abilities to take such initiative. It is a truism that the powerful are always better at asserting their rights through litigation than the less powerful. Whenever the concept of equality is used this usually pertains to the Lockean interpretation of "one rule for rich and poor" or to the Kantian interpretation of non-discrimination: the law should treat all citizens as equals.

In these interpretations the law recognizes a formal concept of equality that is related to the perception of inequality as a form of social differentiation which can and should be corrected. Law is anti-discriminatory in the sense of repairing social disadvantage by the equal treatment of unequals. This however does not change the structurally unequal relations of power. The equal treatment can even reinforce the inequality. In other words, providing equal liberties to unequal partners favours the most powerful. In a more adequate interpretation of "equality," the concept means equal entitlement to the social conditions that are essential to emancipation and self-development.

5.2   Horizontal effect

Conventional human rights thinking mainly focuses on the vertical state/citizen relation, while the basic moral standards almost exclusively focus on the political sphere. This ignores the possibility that concentration of power in the hands of a few individuals can be as threatening as state power. Whenever citizens pursue different economic interests, individual human rights can be under serious threat. Citizens also need to be protected against each other. A concept like that of equality should therefore be extended to all those (socio-economic and cultural) spheres that are essential to human emancipation and self-development. Beyond the concern to achieve equal voting rights in democratic societies, for example, the need to create equal participation in cultural life should receive similar emphasis.

5.3   Institutions

Human rights cannot be realized without involving citizens in the decision-making processes about the spheres in which freedom and equality are to be achieved. The idea of human rights has thus to extend to the social institutions (the institutional arrangements) that would facilitate the realization of fundamental standards. This moves the democratic process beyond the political sphere and extends the requirement of participatory institutional arrangements to other social domains. It claims that culture and technology should also be subject to democratic control. This is particularly important in the light of the fact that current democratization processes (the "new world order" processes) tend to delegate important areas of social life to private rather than to public control and accountability. Increasingly large volumes of social activity are withdrawn from public accountability, from democratic control, and from the participation of citizens in decision-making.

VI   HOW DOES THIS APPLY TO CYBERSPACE?

6.1   Collective claims

Human rights in cyberspace should not only be articulated as individual rights, but should be recognized both as individual and as collective rights.

To place human rights exclusively in either category unduly limits the rights of individuals as members of a community or the rights of the collectivity. Collective claims to cyberspace communications require provisions for access to public communication on behalf of all social groups. This is particularly important as so many social groups, such as women, ethnic minorities, or poor communities tend to be excluded from cyberspace communications. In addition to this right of access for communities, collective claims also include the right to development, and the recognition of communal knowledge resources. The recognition of the development principle in world communication politics implies an entitlement to the development of communication infrastructures, procurement of adequate resources, sharing of knowledge and skills, equality of economic opportunities, and correction of inequalities. The communal claim to intellectual property recognizes that knowledge resources are often a common good owned by a collective. Knowledge as common heritage should be protected against its private appropriation by knowledge industries. Collective claims also imply provisions on cultural identity, on the recognition of cultural diversity and linguistic variety, or on the cultural autonomy of communities.

6.2   Liberty

What does the positive interpretation of "freedom to" imply for cyberspace? Following Bourdieu's use of the terms "cultural" and "social" capital). "The position of a given agent within the social space can thus be defined by the positions he occupies in the different fields, that is in the distribution of the powers that are active within each of them. These are, principally, economic capital (in its different kinds) cultural capital and social capital, as well as symbolic capital, commonly called prestige, reputation, renown, etc., which is the form in which the different forms of capital are perceived and recognized as legitimate." (Bourdieu, 1984) Information capital refers to the motivation and the interest to be informed, the capacity to process and apply information resources, the technical skills to manipulate ICT and the financial means to secure access to and use of digital networks. In national and global social realities the distribution of information capital is highly skewed. This is reinforced by growing income inequalities across the world (by what could be termed the "globalization of poverty") and the concurrent lowering of educational standards (and decline in status and salaries of teaching staff) and shifts in educational programs from critical reflection to training for economic productivity and the dramatic loss of credibility political institutions face almost everywhere. The "freedom to" implies the entitlement to those socio-economic conditions that support the development of "information capital."

6.3   Equal entitlement

This principle implies that "all people matter" and that no person should be excluded. The cyberspace project of a Global Information Superhighway could exclude vast numbers of people. The norm of equal entitlement to cyberspace resources is deeply threatened by the current disparities in access to the uses of ICT. This gap is for example illustrated by the fact that 77% of the world population has only 5% of the world's telephone lines. The communication gap in the world is not decreasing. On the contrary, it is widening. There are no indications that the international donor community or national governments are making a serious effort to change this. Rather the opposite is happening. The UNDP support to telecommunications in the developing countries, for example, went down from US $ 27 million in 1990 to US $ 2.2 million in 1995. Without major public efforts in this field, the global super information highway is not likely to include the two billion people who live on less than $300 a year, or the more than 1 billion people who are illiterate and some 500 million children for whom there are no schools.

When he launched the Global Information Infrastructure project in a 1994 speech at the conference of the International Telecommunication Union in Buenos Aires, US Vice President Al Gore spoke very movingly about the creation of this mother of all networks. "The development of the GII (...) must be a democratic effort (...). In a sense, the GII will be a metaphor for democracy itself (...). I see a new Athenian Age of democracy forged in the fora the GII will create. (...) The Global Information

Infrastructure (...) will circle the globe with information superhighways on which all people can travel. These highways – or, more accurately, networks of distributed intelligence – will allow us to share information, to connect, and to communicate as a global community." Vice President Al Gore referred to a New Age of Athenian democracy. He may well be right since Athens had a highly discriminating political arrangement. Athenian democracy excluded slaves and women. Women are likely to be excluded from the global electronic democracy unless current female disadvantages in computer access, use and skills are drastically changed. If the tradition of women's use of new technologies continues, women will have little chance of defining their role in cyberfuture. "The users of the Net are predominantly male, white, young and university-educated." (Smith, 1995: 22)

A form of governance for cyberspace that takes equal entitlement to its resources seriously requires far-reaching changes in the current political practices in such areas as development assistance, transfer of technology, intellectual property protection, and space cooperation. These practices all reinforce the inegalitarian character of the present global order. Changes would include a drastic increase in overseas development assistance in the field of communication and under conditions more favourable to recipient parties, the adoption of the UNCTAD Code of Transfer of Technology on the terms proposed by developing countries, a revision of provisions on the protection of intellectual property in the GATT/WTO multilateral trade accord so as to take the interests of less powerful countries and small producers into account, and the adoption of a multilateral accord on space cooperation and equal benefits.

6.4   Security

The moral standard of *human security* tends to receive a limited interpretation in the individualistic legal and biological sense. Article 3 of the Universal Declaration of Human Rights ("Everyone has the right to life, liberty and security of person") has to be read in the context of Articles 5 and 9 which protect people's moral and physical integrity against interference from state and non-state actors. This implies protection against torture, cruel, inhuman, and degrading treatment, and against arbitrary treatment in the form of arrest, detention, or exile on grounds not established by law. The International Covenant on Civil and Political Rights provides for a similar protection of personal security in Article 9.

In the International Covenant on Social and Economic Rights (Article 9) security is broadened to social security, inclusive of social security. However important this is, it reflects the common one-sided view in which human rights are almost exclusively understood to mean civil and political rights. Processes of economic growth that pauperize ever larger groups of people are usually not perceived as a gross violation of human rights by most Western governments, donor institutions, or as a matter of fact, by many human rights organizations. If in the normal course of free market operations, World Trade Organization rules, or IMF conditionalities, millions of people are uprooted, impoverished, or unemployed, this is usually not seen as human rights violations. Human rights advocates usually attack murder and torture, but not poverty. The exclusive perception of human rights as civil and political rights is dangerously shortsighted. It creates explosive contradictions between political criteria that press for good governance, democracy, and respect for human rights on the one hand, and on the other, economic criteria that impose measures so harsh that the resulting inequalities can only be controlled by highly undemocratic policies! Throughout the Third World, IMF policies have undermined the economic conditions for democracy, such as education, social equality, and reduction of poverty. The structural adjustment programs of the IMF have in fact in many countries weakened the ability of governments to meet international human rights obligations. The neglect of basic social and economic rights undermines such civil and political rights as freedom of expression and freedom of association.

In view of the increasing vulnerability of contemporary societies to a broad range of social risks, including the possibility of total human extinction, the human rights regime needs to incorporate a broader concept of global human security. (Beck, 1992; Leslie, 1996)

Human security today is jeopardized by fundamental risks induced by the process of modernization and its global spread. There are risks related to economic maldistribution – the growing income disparities throughout the world and the globalization of poverty entail lethal risks for increasingly large numbers of people on Earth. There are risks related to environmental disasters (desertification, the depletion of the ozone layer, deforestation, the Greenhouse effect). There are industrial risks which may lead to many Bhopal-style catastrophes. There are risks related to the proliferation of nuclear and conventional (e.g., biological and chemical) arms. There are risks related to bio-technological experimentation and genetic engineering. There are also social risks related to cyberspace technology. These include nuclear warfare triggered off by computer malfunctions, large-scale financial frauds, technological addiction, and aviation disasters. Intentional harm is easily inflicted in cyberspace. Computer networks enable people to communicate in anonymity. Anonymity brings out the worst in people. Under the cloak of anonymity people engage in harmful acts against others through abuse and deceit. Apparently, anonymity creates a "moral distance" to the victim which makes it easier to commit harmful acts. It is the classical case of the bomber pilot who pushes the button and never knows who was hit.

The Information Superhighway creates enormously attractive opportunities for "digital crooks" and "cybersnoopers." Such crimes and misdemeanours, which range from copyright infringements to electronic surveillance, pose serious threats to people's moral and physical integrity. Cyberspace-related social risks to human security are also induced by increasing dependence upon vulnerable and error-prone digital systems. A risk factor is also the "cyberization" of daily life, which reinforces current trends towards high-speed, robot-centric societies.

6.5   Horizontal effect

Human rights should have a horizontal effect: they should not only apply to state-citizen, but also to citizen-citizen relationships. In the case of information provision there should be protection against information oligopolies set up by fellow citizens. This so called "Drittwirkung," or third party effect of human rights means, for example, that information rights of people should be free from interference by public as well as by private parties. Already in the discussions leading to the human rights Covenants it was proposed that interference by private parties should be banned. The proposal did not acquire the status of legal provision. "An individual has the right to freedom of opinion without interference by private parties as well, and the state is obliged to ensure that freedom. (...) It is doubtful, however, whether the complex problem of protecting a person's opinion against interferences by other individuals can be solved in this global and absolute manner." (Partsch, 1981: 218)

In spite of these reservations, the defense of freedom of expression should go beyond state interference and incorporate the reality of situations in which private parties exercise power equivalent if not exceeding that of the state.

The right to freedom of expression goes beyond this negative freedom from interference, however, and includes the recognition of positive free speech rights. If freedom of expression is interpreted in more than the classical negative sense, the positive interpretation makes it necessary to define this right not merely as unconstraint, but as a right. A positive freedom to communicate implies the right to express opinions and the related entitlement to facilities for the exercise of this right. The recognition of freedom of expression as a positive right is particularly important in situations where the voices of some people are systematically excluded. In such situations mere freedom from interference does not enable people to participate in public communication (Barendt, 1985: 86).

It is becoming increasingly clear that cyberspace needs defense against attempts to impose censorship. This defense should not only be directed against governmental actors. Informational self-determination (encompassing free speech, freedom to receive and seek information, the right to control person-related information, the right to confidentiality of communication, and the right to refuse information) is threatened by the fashionable Information Superhighway project. This happens for example as a result of the potential and highly likely censorship exercised by mega gatekeepers. In fact, at the gateway to the Information Superhighway stands a shadowy figure looking oddly like Rupert Murdoch (Winsbury, 1995: 8).

As the Information Superhighway project is to be privately funded and commercially driven by the market there needs to be a system that defines what services the consumer will get, that charges consumers for what they get and shuts out those who cannot pay. If major companies invest billions of dollars in the Information Superhighway they will want control of access to consumers so they can recoup these investments. The freedom principle should offer protection against control of information and media by a limited group of citizens. Beyond freedom to be protected from state interference, the right should also address the restrictions that fellow-citizens can pose upon access to information.

6.6   Institutional consideration

This notion has two dimensions. It proposes to involve all people into decision-making that affects their lives and to extend such participation beyond the political realm. Maximum participation and extended equality call for the participation of people in decision-making in former elitist fields such as technology and culture.

Especially in the light of the increasing privatization of the production of technical knowledge and cultural expressions, these social spheres should also be subject to democratic control. This requires that affected citizens have a right to participate in decisions about its development and utilization of technology and culture.

This is undoubtedly a complex proposition, since technology and culture are related to special requirements of expertise, skills, and creativity. It will therefore be necessary to explore introducing forms of democratic control that do not constrain the essential input of individual expertise and creativity. The individual scientists, engineers, and artists may resist the notion of technological and cultural democracy, but it would be fallacious to believe that they are fully autonomous today. They may stand to gain more than to lose if their creativity is subject to common good considerations rather than to corporate profit motives.

6.7   Cyberspace and public accountability

The implementation of human rights, as Hossain rightly observes (1997: 20) requires "good governance." "Governments as well as powerful corporations must adhere to respect human rights and be accountable for their conduct measured by human rights standards." The serious obstacle here is that increasingly governments are (often voluntarily) losing regulatory instruments through which to exert control over powerful corporations, and global governance is increasingly the arena of private business actors. The trademark of these actors is a rejection of public accountability. This principle makes the key players in world communication accountable for their decision-making on behalf of others. Decisions that affect people's daily lives are made in such fields as quality of information, diversity of cultural products, or security of communications. Decision-makers are increasingly private parties which are neither elected nor held accountable. As a matter of fact the worldwide drive towards deregulation of social domains tends to delegate important areas of social life to private rather than to public control and accountability. Increasingly large volumes of social activity are withdrawn from public accountability, from democratic control, and from the participation of citizens in decision-making.

The global corporations that control ever more facets of people's daily lives have become less accountable to public authorities everywhere in the world. "Most corporate leaders, while proudly exercising their constitutionally protected right to influence elections and legislation, deny that they are making public policy merely by doing business. They do not accept responsibility for the social consequences of what they make or how they make it." (Barnet & Cavanagh, 1994: 422) The key issue is therefore the establishment of public accountability of the most powerful private players.

It would seem however that the adoption of strict rules of public accountability of private players is highly unlikely in the first place and that their enforcement would probably be beyond the power of public authorities. The only effective pressure could come from the main constituencies of these players, the customers on their markets. Ultimately they are dependent upon the people who buy their goods and services and for whom they decide such matters as the quality of their food, clothing, entertainment, work, environment or health care. The establishment of accountability therefore demands a massive mobilization and politicization of consumer organizations around the world.

6.8   Implementation

International human rights law remains a weak and largely non-enforceable arrangement. It should not be ignored that this is a conscious political choice. Most nation-states have shown little interest in interference with their human rights record. The state-centric arrangement of world politics in which states are unwilling to yield power over their citizens is still dominant and stands squarely in the way of universal respect for human rights. In current world politics states still maintain a considerable measure of sovereignty in the treatment of their citizens. Yet, the United Nations World Conference on Human Rights of 1993 has reaffirmed that "the promotion and protection of all human rights is a legitimate concern of the international community."

The real significance of these standards will depend upon the degree of their enforcement. Present remedial procedures are mainly based upon the Optional Protocol (OP) to the International Covenant on Civil and Political Rights (ICCPR, 1966) and Resolution 1503 adopted by the Economic and Social Council of the UN (ECOSOC) in 1970. The Protocol authorizes the UN Human Rights Committee to receive and consider communications from individuals subject to its jurisdiction who claim to be victims of a violation by that State Party of any of the rights set forth in the Covenant. Individual complaints can only come from nationals of states that are party to the OP (presently 75 states). The OP provides for communications, analysis, and reporting, but not for sanctions. Resolution 1503 recognizes the possibility of individual complaints about human rights violations. It authorizes the UN Human Rights Commission to examine, "communications, together with replies of governments, if any, which appear to reveal a consistent pattern of gross violations of human rights." The 1503 procedure is slow, confidential, and provides individuals with no redress. In addition to the UN Human Rights Commission and the Human Rights Committee to monitor the ICCPR, institutional mechanisms for implementation are the Committee on the Elimination of Racial Discrimination, the Committee on Economic, Social and Cultural Rights, the Committee on the Elimination of Discrimination against Women, the Committee against Torture, and the Committee on the Rights of the Child. However important the work of these bodies, their powers to enforce human rights standards are very limited. The UN Human Rights Commission is a permanent body of ECOSOC. Its members are state representatives. Commission recommendations have a certain significance but are not binding.

The Human Rights Committee consists of eighteen experts supervising the implementation of the ICCPR. The work of the Committee covers only those parties that ratified the covenant (presently 129 states) and provides international monitoring on the basis of reports provided by states. The Committee's monitoring does not imply any sanctions, but it can generate some negative publicity about a country's human rights performance. For the implementation of the Race convention the Committee on the Elimination of Racial Discrimination has been established. The Committee can receive complaints among states, but only fourteen states authorize the Committee to receive communications from individuals. The implementation body for the 1979 Convention on the Elimination of Discrimination Against Women is the Committee on the Elimination of Discrimination Against Women. The Committee is not allowed to receive individual communications.

Whatever may be the case, it is clear that the worldwide lack of implementation of human rights standards poses the most serious challenge to the human rights regime. It is also obvious, but worth stressing again and again, that the world would be a different and far more humane place for many people if human rights standards were respected. The most important issue for the significance and validity of the regime then is the implementation of the standards it proposes. There is abundant evidence that these standards are being almost incessantly violated throughout the world, by actors with very different political and ideological viewpoints. Usually, in wars of liberation, for example, one finds gross violations both by the oppressors and the liberators. And if one studies the depressing reports from such bodies as Amnesty International, there appear to be no countries where human rights are not violated. For moral philosophers this is actually not a terribly surprising problem. It concerns the classical gap between the moral knowledge human beings possess and their intention to act morally.

6.9   The People's Communication Charter

The recognition of individual rights under international law was thus linked with the notion that individuals also have duties under international law. This was eloquently expressed in 1947 by Mahatma Gandhi in a letter to the director of UNESCO about the issue of human rights. Gandhi wrote, "I learnt from my illiterate but wise mother that rights to be deserved and preserved came from duty well done."

The People's Communication Charter articulates essential rights and responsibilities that ordinary people have in relation to their cultural environment. It represents an attempt to redress some of the weaknesses inherent in the conventional human rights regime. It aspires to a democratic and sustainable organization of the world's communication structures and information flows. It is abundantly clear that these great ideas cannot be simply implemented by drafting and revising a text. The text constitutes merely a point of reference for a much needed civil activism that targets a very central social domain.

The People's Communication Charter is an initiative of the Third World Network (Penang, Malaysia), the Center for Communication & Human Rights (Amsterdam, the Netherlands), the Cultural Environment Movement (USA), the World Association of Community Radio Broadcasters (AMARC), and the World Association for Christian Communication. The Charter provides the common framework for all those who share the belief that people should be active and critical participants in their social reality and capable of governing themselves. The People's Communication Charter could be a first step in the development of a permanent movement concerned with the quality of our cultural environment.

The movement should not be seen by those who work in the mass media as a populist intervention with their professional independence. It should rather be welcomed as a creative alliance between media producers and consumers against those commercial forces that are more intent on generating profits than informing people properly. Applying human rights standards to relations in cyberspace requires active responsibility on behalf of all concerned.

From the beginning it was clear that the Charter should not be seen as an end in itself. It intends to provide the basis for a permanent critical reflection on those worldwide trends that will determine the quality of our lives in the third millennium. The Charter has now been adopted by a growing number of organizations and individuals around the world and several activities inspired by the Charter are planned for the coming years. Among them an international tribunal on violations of the Charter's rights. In August 1997, for example, the Charter was displayed at the famous Dokumenta exhibition at Kassel, Germany. The text was discussed and signed by many visitors. Today the Charter's Web site is the place where such events and the progress in widening support for the PCC are made public.

The core themes of the movement concern:
1. Communication and human rights
Communication and information services should be guided by respect for fundamental human rights.

2. The public domain
Communication resources (such as airwaves and outerspace) are the common property of all human beings; they are public domain and should not be appropriated by private parties.

3. Ownership
Communication and information services should not be monopolized by governments or business firms.

4. Empowerment
People are entitled to the protection of their cultural identity and to the development of their communicative capacities.

5. Public accountability
Providers of communication and information services should accept public accountability for the quality of their performance.

The cultural environment is ultimately not only shaped by governments and media moguls, but in important ways by the clients of the system. We need a critical debate on the use of the international human rights regime as instrument of moral guidance. Ultimately, all depends upon the commitment of people themselves to shaping a humane governance for our future in cyberspace.

INTERNET AND PUBLIC ORDER

by Stylianos GARIPIS

Although in the post-modern era deregulation has become the rule in Western jurisdictions, attempts at regulating the Internet reality demonstrate a reverse orientation. Should we consider such attempts as contradicting the current trend? Or should we view them as the expression of a general bewilderment due to the fact that humanity is standing on the threshold of virtuality? Anyway, if we accept, as we should, that the use of the Internet is related with the existence of several constitutional rights and liberties (right of expression, communication, publication, advertisement and so on) we then need a legitimate regulatory institution in this field. Should this regulatory institution be found at a national or international level? The answer to this crucial question is strongly related to the impact of Internet use on public order. If certain uses – or abuses – are not compatible with the national public order, are the national institutions competent to limit these uses? Then, of course we should answer the following question: can the notion of national public order justify restrictions de facto imposed to citizens of other countries?

According to a technical definition, "the Internet is a collection of packet-switched computer networks, glued together by a set of software protocols. These protocols allow the networks and the computers attached to them to communicate and (using a common address system) to find other computers attached to the Internet." (Smith, 1996: 1) According to an utilitarian definition, the Internet is a means to transfer information between millions of computers and their users in different countries around the world. This aim is achieved through several Internet applications such as the World Wide Web, which has made on-line content (real-time or downloadable) accessible to the average user and has facilitated the tasks of exploring and obtaining information on the Internet or through Usenet, which is a system of discussion groups to which anyone can post a public message.

If we combine these two approaches we could conclude that the Internet is a network with roots in over 160 countries but without physical boundaries, center, direction, owner, established structure, or administration, where everyone has the ability not only to access information by hopping from one site to another around the world using one set of Internet-compliant software, but also to create one's own information. It is in this virtual universe that the rights and freedoms of users seek to be exercised. Due to the nature of the Internet these freedoms and rights concern principally expression through speech rather than expression through conduct. Unlike other kinds of expression, expression via the Internet is pure speech involving no kind of conduct whatsoever. This is why any restriction can be justified only based on content of expression, rather than, for example, because of the location of the individual or group, or the undesirability of extremist demonstrations. So, before examining how limits can be legitimately imposed on these rights and freedoms, we should examine, from a comparative point of view, on which grounds they could be restricted.

In the United States, the State of Georgia has enacted a statute prohibiting computer transmission of bomb-making instructions.[1] In Germany, neo-nazis have been allegedly using the Internet in order to keep in touch, to set up databases of targets such as immigrants' addresses, to send out hate material and Holocaust denial material, and to organize activities (Oppenheim, 1995: 112). This is why bavarian prosecutors, while trying to keep users from reading neo-nazi propaganda on the Internet have notified America Online Inc. that it may be charged with inciting racial hatred. For years the Chinese government has been prohibiting Internet use for anything other than academic pursuits, with national authorities seeking to block access to "objectionable" material.

What we could conclude from these selected examples is that expression through the Internet is being restricted by many jurisdictions for reasons of public order. Without entering into problematic issues such as whether the Internet facilitates communication between terrorists or on the contrary their localization by the police or other national authorities, we could simply state that the Internet can facilitate many offenses against public order (Gerard & Willems, 1997: 140-1) and that any attack on public order that can be committed through information dissemination can be committed via the Internet.

The threat to public order is therefore one of the most significant issues created by the appearance of the Internet. However, in order to combat this threat one has to confront the libertarian foundation of western societies, where expression is considered to be free. Thus, in 1995, a Michigan court, based on First Amendment protections[2] dismissed a criminal case against a student charged with transmitting threatening communications (a combination of postings to a newsgroup and private E-mail communications fantasizing about kidnapping and torturing a fellow student) in interstate commerce in the US.

The notion of public order provides many jurisdictions with an obvious reason to seek to suppress freedom of expression. Thus, prior restraint could be permitted where there is a clear and present danger to the public order that cannot retrospectively be remedied and posterior restraint could be permitted if it is shown that a specific harm has been committed. Public order *ab definitio* has as a consequence the prevalence of the public interest over the interests of the individuals. By public order we mean a harmonious society, a situation without social troubles. Although its normative content is defined as an objective or as a motive of a legal system, the concept of public order as such is a principle that prevails within a legal system. This means that we should not accept an instrumentalist approach of public order. Public order should not be

---

[1] 1995 Georgia Laws 322 (April 12, 1995).
[2] United States v. Baker, 890 F. Supp. 1375 (E.D. Mic. 1995), cited by Perritt (1996).

considered a means to ensure the exercise of rights or freedoms of the collectivity. Certainly, the rights of others can constitute a limit to rights and freedoms, but public order should be considered a distinct kind of restriction.

According to a maximalistic approach, public order is a flexible concept which depends on the facts, the circumstances, the social context, the values, the fundamental institutions, norms and objectives of the collectivity, the needs for stability and public peace. Therefore, it expresses an axiological content, which represents the subjective, changing, evolutive values (Vimbert, 1993: 701). According to a minimalistic approach, public order is the security of persons and goods and the security of the State.[3] National security is the collective and abstract security of the public domain. It should not be confused with government security, especially that of the government of the day. Otherwise, restricting a number of liberties and rights in ways which protect the interests of the governing party rather than the public should be considered as contradictory with the democratic and libertarian tradition. This is why we should draw a distinction between an expression which necessarily endangers public order and an expression that is intrinsically undesirable to a political group. In this sense publication on the Internet of the numbers and location of troops of a national army could be considered a breach of public order but not the expression of a radical political opinion.

If we accept a maximalistic approach of public order in the frame of the Internet issue we face a serious problem. Public order could express either an existing social or an ideal order. However, when talking about social order we should refer to a specific society. Therefore, we need to define the society in which we want to avoid disorder. At this point many could say that the Internet is a "distinct society" which should be ruled by its own principles and values. This is why we could not impose the needs of a specific society to the cybersociety or the so-called "cybernation." According to this point of view, surfing the Internet means entering a different society, where a new kind of mass interaction is taking place.

In order to solve this problem we should answer the following question. "When speaking about legal rules in cyberspace who do we want to protect? Internet users, or the status quo in a given national society?" It is this crucial question that the notion of public order seeks to answer. What we want to protect when imposing public order as a restriction of expression via the Internet is to protect the national societies from the users of the Internet. This is because of the presumption that users of the Internet may a) be incited to crime, b) obtain certain hazardous information, or c) develop an awareness which is not desirable.

a) In 1969, the Supreme Court of the United States held that free speech could not be punished unless it was "an incitement to imminent lawless action.[4]" The consequence derived from such an approach is that expression via the Internet could be restricted when it consists of an incitement to commit a crime or to disturb public order. The role

---

[3] Constitutional Council Decision 91-294 DC of July 25, 1991, Schengen Convention.
[4] Brandemburg v. Ohio, 395 US 444, 1969.

of the restriction in this case is to enforce public order by preventing users from being exposed to such an incitement. The reasoning here is that the less citizens are incited to disorder the less they are likely to provoke it. The fact is that even if we accept that certain kinds of expression may inspire or incite public disorder, the nexus between the words and subsequent action is far more attenuated on the Internet than in any other case. Many kinds of expression which may be provocative in the physical world are far less threatening when appearing on the Internet.

b) Let us take now the famous example of crazed extremists who exchange nerve-gas recipes via the Internet. If such instructions are available on an Internet newspage which is open to an unspecified number of users, this does not necessarily satisfy the conditions of intention to incite a threat to public order. Such recipes may be considered to serve only informative purposes. Nonetheless, downloading such noxious information could be considered an act leading to an offense. In this sense, we should distinguish between the mere possession/consumption of a specific material and the storage, further transmission or the use of it. Furthermore, we should distinguish between the users who know where to find specific information and the users who do not. For the former what has changed with the Internet is the means of getting the information. For the latter one could argue that search engines have made it easier to fulfill their desires. However, even in the latest case, one could argue that the need to protect users from information found in the Internet is not bigger than the need to protect them from any other kind of published material. Hence, public order considerations are not legitimate when citizens of one jurisdiction are permitted to obtain the same kind of information in other types of printed texts.

c) The third eventuality derives from the State's preoccupation to ensure a "healthy" conscience of its citizens. It is widely known that public order restrictions have been used by totalitarian regimes in order to justify State interference with the citizens' minds. The intrinsic contradiction in such kind of "protection" is that it seeks to regulate the inner world of the citizens despite the fact that the scope of the public order restriction is to regulate the relations between people and the type of interaction between them, in order to ensure a certain level of social harmony. Therefore, even if we accept a maximalistic approach of public order we cannot use it to limit the development of the people's personal world.

As we have seen, although the State's preoccupation is to enforce public order by protecting users of the Internet, it cannot impose any kind of restrictions on them in order to avoid the breach of public order, unless determined to eradicate the libertarian and democratic features of its regime. The dilemma of modern democratic states is the following. In order to preserve national public order, a legitimate concern of every regime, they have to protect the national societies from noxious information circulating via the Internet. The legitimate way of achieving this aim is to protect the national societies from the users of the Internet. However, governments cannot impose legitimate restrictions on the Internet users who are nothing more than recipients of Internet information.

The other way is to impose restrictions on those who post the information on the Internet. In this case, national authorities have to face two problems. The first problem is that posting information on the Internet means expressing oneself, a fundamental freedom or right. The second problem is that most of the times national authorities have not the competence to impose such restrictions since the posting of information is taking place in another country. In order to solve the first problem we have to answer a variety of questions. Should the freedom of or right to expression be interpreted to encompass a right to post anonymous or radical political messages across Usenet groups, or even a right to send encrypted messages that are, for all intents and purposes, immune to eavesdropping by law enforcement agents? Or, according to a reverse way of thinking, should we restrict a specific type of expression because it causes greater harm than other types of expression, because there is a clear evidence of a causal link between this kind of expression and a specific harm or because this expression undermines principles which are contrary to the ones contained in the notion of public order?

In every human society there is a tension between the need for public order and the need of citizens to bring to the attention of their fellow citizens matters considered to be important. "The way in which any legal system resolves the tension, and the balance which it strikes between the competing interests, is indicative of the attitude of that society towards the relative value of different sorts of freedom. A society which tolerates a good deal of annoyance or disorder so as to encourage the greatest possible freedom of expression, particularly political expression, is likely to be one in which the public, political activities of citizens are regarded as making a useful contribution to the health of a democratic system (...) The job of the lawmakers is to decide when the interests of society in being free of unwanted persuasion or disorder outweighs the interest in free expression of opinions and persuasion." (Feldman, 1993: 782)

Therefore, a balancing approach should be adopted in order to reconcile the interests in freedom of expression and in public order. According to this balancing approach a variety of criteria should be taken into consideration. Thus, the strictness of limitations of the liberties of expression should vary, depending on the specific kind of expression involved. Freedom of political debate is at the very core of the concept of a democratic expression and should, therefore, remain unlimited. As the European Court of Human Rights has argued, speech involving political issues and political figures serves a fundamental role in the function of democratic societies and consequently, any arguments that a restriction of such discussion is necessary in such a society will be harder to sustain.[5] Another criterion could be the fact that when expression through the Internet reaches a variety of potential audiences. "It is surely correct to take into account the character of the audience in determining the likelihood" of a breach of public order (Barendt, 1996: 201). In addition to these we could mention the vital distinction between the right to hold an opinion, which cannot be restricted, and the right to express that opinion, which can be restricted. In this sense, restrictions in the name of public order can be justified when the release of information would cause a

---

[5] E.C.H.R. Lingens v. Austria, judgment of July 8, 1986, 103, 8, E.H.R.R. 407.

clear and present danger. Anyway, any restriction of freedom of expression must meet the principles of proportionality and necessity.

The second problem is related with the imposition of public order restrictions on the way citizens of another country express themselves. We cannot but consider as a paradox the enforcement of the public order exigencies of the country of access to the foreign citizens of the country where the transmission originates. It is well known that input into network triggers a chain of events which are not confined to the place where the offender happens to be. Thus, one could justify the limitations by the argument that all logging-on points where information is made accessible to users constitute places of commission of offenses against public order. However, according to the existing technology infrastructure the sender of information has no control over countries from which the information can be accessed (Central Computer and Telecommunications Agency, 1996: 143). Anyway, the sender cannot be aware of the public order exigencies of every country around the world. If a kind of expression is considered legal in his country he is not expected to know, or even imagine, that this same expression can provoke public disorder in another country. In consequence, and leaving aside the impracticability of the very notion, there is no legitimacy in attempting to preserve public order in one country by imposing restrictions to the fundamental rights and liberties of the citizens of another country.

This is why many jurisdictions have put forward legislation prescribing certain obligations for access providers to the Internet. An on-line service provider could be an academic institution, a government body or a commercial outfit selling Internet access to various users. The justification of such a public policy is that it has been considered that only through this way national authorities can prevent offenses against public order. Making access providers responsible for the content of the Internet information seems to be the only practical means of control since the provider is better situated to prevent or control an initial transmission. The legal prescriptions concerning service providers could be of two categories. The first category is the prescription of the obligation of a service provider to assist the enforcement of public order exigencies. In this sense, according to the new Information and Communication Services Bill in Germany, service providers have a duty to assist in tracking down criminal material on the Internet. According to another category of prescriptions, national jurisdictions go further and accept that on-line service providers are liable for the content of information on the Internet. Nonetheless, in order to accept this kind of liability we should answer a preliminary question. Should the access provider be considered a publisher or a distributor? This question was examined in the Cubby Inc. v. CompuServe Inc. case.[6] The difference is that the distributor does not know and has no reason to know the content of the information. The distributor is a passive recipient for information and cannot be held liable in the absence of actual knowledge. The Court found that "CompuServe has no more control over such a publication than does a public library, book store, or newsstand, and it would be no more feasible for

---

[6] 776 F. Supp. 135 (S.D.N.Y. 1991).

CompuServe to examine every publication it carries for potentially defamatory statement than it would be for any other distributor to do so." On the other hand, the Supreme Court of New York found Prodigy liable as a publisher since it held itself out to the public as a service which controlled the content of its bulletin board postings.[7] The consequence of such a judgment cannot be other that to discourage providers to control the information disseminated through their services in order to reduce their potential liability.

We consider that the responsibility of service providers adopted by several jurisdictions in their effort to protect their public order does not go without serious problems. The first problem is that if we accept a legal obligation of the provider to investigate the entire content of the network for perilous content we are probably facing a contradiction with the principle of inviolability of telecommunications or privacy. If such an infringement in personal communication between users could be accepted in the case of a public authority, it is not so easy to accept it for an individual. The second problem is based on considerations concerning the political and economic dimensions of the question. The obligation of on-line service providers to conduct spot checks, would wipe out smaller providers with insufficient personnel to carry out such checks, and thus market dominance would go to a few major providers. Small providers provide a few local telephone numbers and a single connection into someone else's network and they are nothing more than local resellers of capacity on a large access provider's network. In addition to this, freedom of expression protects small providers themselves as the conduits for expression, by protecting them from any kind of burdens that would make it difficult to keep running on-line systems (Rose, 1995: 7). Last, but not least, control of Internet content exercised by access providers would amount to *a priori* censorship. Any legitimate case for attempting to protect public order through restrictive measures could be made only in highly specific and documented instances. Otherwise there is the danger of discriminatory treatment of specific social groups or political parties. Moreover, permanent restrictions would be very rightfully construed as attempts to curtail freedom of expression.

As is very well known and legitimate, many countries are determined to protect their cultural and political heritage against onslaughts from the outside. This is exactly what is happening with the Internet. The notions of public order and morals, as well as the competence of the national authorities to define them, are the only means of national resistance to the omnipotence of those who control some specific networks. Through the concept of morals, national societies seek to protect their cultural heritage; through the concept of public order, they try to preserve their social and political structure.

In any case, State intervention is compromised by the existence of a global network environment and the decentralized design of the Internet based on the scattered locations of individual network users. In order to respond to these difficulties many authors have proposed the adoption of international legislation. We consider that this proposition cannot solve the problem without creating new ones. Regulation by an

---

[7] Stratton Oakmont, Inc. v. Prodigy Servs. Co, N.Y. Supreme Court, May 25, 1995.

international body is inconvenient inasmuch as it cannot express any national definition of public order. What is needed for cyberspace would be an international social contract, a contract which respects the diversity of national societies. We consider that it seems utopic to expect an international agreement spelling out those types of expression which could be considered dangerous for national public order, in the light of the social and political diversity between countries around the world. In consequence, what we propose is the adaptation of national regulations concerning the protection of public order for the needs of cyberspace in a frame of international cooperation in order to suppress offenses against national public order.

THE LEGAL ASPECTS OF DIGITAL SIGNATURES

by Patrick van EECKE

I INTRODUCTION

In its recently adopted Communication "A European Initiative in Electronic Commerce" the European Commission announced its intention to come forward with a specific initiative on digital signatures (EC, 1997). This initiative will aim at ensuring a common legal framework encompassing the legal recognition of digital signatures in the Single Market, the setting up of minimum criteria for Certification Authorities, as well as pursuing worldwide agreements. In its communication the European Commission expresses the need for a sound and flexible regulatory framework which would generate *confidence* for both business and consumers and ensure full and unlimited *access* to the Single Market. Such a regulatory framework would be an essential key to Europe's success and a major competitive advantage in itself (EC, 1997: 13).

In this respect the following study seeks to describe and analyze the legal situation in the different EU member states and the main contracting countries regarding the use, the implementation and the legal acceptance of digital signatures and Certification Authorities. Furthermore, the study seeks to define the legal obstacles to the Internal Market, and advocates the need for a European legal initiative.

II THE EC COMMUNICATION ON ELECTRONIC COMMERCE

This chapter briefly describes the Communication from the European Commission announcing a Community initiative in the field of digital signatures:[1] "A European Initiative in Electronic Commerce."

2.1 Electronic commerce – A need for trust

2.1.1 What is electronic commerce?

Electronic commerce is about doing business electronically. It is based on the electronic processing and transmission of data, including text, sound and video. It encompasses many diverse activities including electronic trading of goods and services, on-line delivery of digital content, electronic fund transfers, electronic share trading, electronic bills of lading, commercial auctions, collaborative design and engineering, on-line sourcing, public procurement, direct consumer marketing and after-sales service. It involves both products (e.g., consumer goods, specialized medical equipment) and services (e.g., information services, financial and legal

---

[1]The complete text of the communication is available at
[http://www.cordis.lu/esprit/src/ecomcomx.htm].

services); traditional activities (e.g., healthcare, education) and new activities (e.g., virtual malls) (EC, 1997). Electronic commerce is not a new phenomenon. For many years companies have exchanged business data over a variety of communication networks. But there is now accelerated expansion and radical changes, driven by the exponential growth of the Internet.

Until recently no more than a business-to-business activity on closed proprietary networks, electronic commerce is now rapidly expanding into a complex web of commercial activities transacted on a global scale between an ever-increasing number of participants, corporate and individual, known and unknown, on global open networks such as the Internet (EC, 1997, {par. 6}).

The pace and the extent to which Europe will benefit from electronic commerce greatly depends on having up-to-date legislation that fully meets the needs of business and consumers. The objective of the Commission is to implement the appropriate regulatory framework by the year 2000. The existing Single Market regulatory framework has proved its worth for traditional forms of business. It must now be made to work for electronic commerce by achieving two complementary objectives: building trust and confidence and ensuring full access to the Single Market.

2.1.2 Electronic commerce: Need for trust and confidence

Every form of trade needs trust and confidence between the participants. The ability to be sure who is your contracting partner, what is exactly agreed upon (what is the exact content of the transaction), when the transaction takes place, creates trust between the partners. As we move towards the use of electronic forms of communication and documentation, this ability to trust must be maintained. Building such trust and confidence is indeed the prerequisite to win over businesses and consumers to electronic commerce.

Building trust and confidence among businesses and consumers implies the deployment of secure technologies (such as Digital signatures, digital certificates and secure electronic payment mechanisms) and of a predictable legal and institutional framework to support these technologies. In order to allow electronic commerce operators to reap the full benefits of the Single Market, it is essential to avoid regulatory inconsistencies and to ensure a coherent legal and regulatory framework for electronic commerce at EU level. This should be based on the application of key Internal Market principles (EC, 1997: 5).

2.1.3 Electronic commerce: Ensuring full access to the single market

Given its size, the Single Market potentially offers businesses a "critical mass" of customers before addressing further global markets. However, faced with the new challenges posed by electronic commerce, member states are responding in different ways. The development of divergent legislative approaches is not only ineffective given the transfrontier nature of electronic commerce, but it also may result in fragmenting the Single Market and thus inhibiting the development of electronic commerce in Europe. The proposed Transparency Mechanism Directive[2] is precisely targeted at reducing the danger that new measures, by being different from one member state to another, may restrict the free movement of Information Society services (EC, 1997).

However important it is to avoid regulatory inconsistency by discouraging divergent actions at national level, the Union must also ensure that a coherent regulatory framework for electronic commerce is created at European level. Such a regulatory framework will inevitably be built on existing Single Market legislation which already largely creates the right conditions for on-line businesses. As part of that framework, specific measures have already been taken to respond to new developments. They include the recently adopted directives on data protection,[3] on the legal protection of data bases[4] and on contracts negotiated at a distance;[5] and the proposed revision of the "Television without Frontiers" Directive.[6] In addition, a number of consultation or policy documents have been issued to stimulate debate on various policy areas including the legal protection of encrypted services,[7] copyright and related rights,[8] industrial property,[9] commercial communications,[10] public procurement[11] and the protection of children and human dignity in audio-visual and information services[12] (EC, 1997).

---

[2] Proposal for a European Parliament and Council Directive, third amendment, Directive 83/189/EEC laying down a procedure for the provision of information in the field of technical standards and regulations, COM (96) 392 final, 30.08.1996.

[3] Directive 95/46/EC of the European Parliament and the Council on the protection of individuals with regards to the processing of personal data and the free movement of such data. OJ L281 23.11.1995, p.31.

[4] Directive 96/9/EC of the European Parliament and of the Council on the legal protection of databases OJ L77 27.03.1996, p.20.

[5] Directive 97/7 of the European Parliament and the Council of 17.2.1997 on the protection of consumers in respect of distance contracts.

[6] Proposal for a European Parliament and Council Directive amending Council Directive 89/552/EEC on the coordination of certain provisions laid down by law, regulation or administrative action in member states concerning the pursuit of television broadcasting activities, COM(95) 86 Final of 31.05.1995, OJ C 185 of 19.07.95, p. 4.

[7] Commission Green Paper "Legal Protection of Encrypted Services in the Internal Market", COM (96) 76 final. 06.03.96.

[8] Communication from the Commission "Follow-Up to the Green Paper on Copyright and Related Rights in the Information Society", COM(96)568 final, 20.11.1996.

[9] Questionnaire on "Industrial Property Rights in the Information Society". Version 5.0. September 1996. DG XV/E/3.

[10] Green Paper on "Commercial Communications in the Internal Market", COM (96) 192 final. 08.05.1996.

[11] Green Paper on "Public Procurement in the EU: Exploring the Way Forward", COM(96) 583 final. 27.11.1996.

[12] Green Paper on the "Protection of Minors and Human Dignity in Audiovisual and Information Services". COM (96) 483 final. 16.10.1996.

2.2   Digital signatures as a tool to ensure trust and confidence

Secure technologies – such as Digital signatures and digital certificates – go some way to meeting these challenges. Digital signatures enable the unambiguous confirmation of the identity of the sender and the authenticity and integrity of electronic documents. Unique to the sender and unique to the message sent, Digital signatures are verifiable and non-repudiable. Similarly, the exchange of digital certificates ("Internet ID cards") through an automatic "digital handshake" between computers provides assurance that the parties are who they say they are, and helps to assess whether the service provided and the goods or services delivered are genuine (EC, 1997).

Copyright protection mechanisms, also based on secure technologies such as cryptography and smart cards, ensure the protection of digital material and are a crucial factor in the emergence of a mass-market in electronic content. Also based on cryptographic methods, secure electronic payment mechanisms provide the final element of trust: the ability to pay and to be paid. Such secure technologies are for the most part fully operational and commercially available.

Digital signatures will be the driving force behind the development of many new services, which vary from certification (i.e., linking identity with a public key) to fully-fledged digital notary services, like adding a time stamp to a electronic document, electronic archiving, etc. These service will play a dominant role in the Information Society, particularly in electronic commerce.

However, the necessary regulatory and institutional framework supporting such technologies is not yet complete, particularly in areas such as interoperability and mutual recognition across borders.

III   CURRENT INITIATIVES WITH RESPECT TO DIGITAL SIGNATURES

This chapter shortly describes some practical and legal initiatives which are taken on national, international and Community level regarding the introduction of digital signatures and CA services.

3.1   Practical initiatives

Especially in the banking sector, the tax administration and the social security field, electronic communication authenticated by digital signatures is or is being put in use. Electronic shopping malls, introducing electronic commerce in the real sense, have been appearing on the Internet.

The **Belgian** Isabel network allows the customer to communicate in a secure way with most of the Belgian financial institutions and some private enterprises by making use of digital signatures and smart-card technology.[13] The Chambers of Commerce

---

[13] [http://www.isabel.be/].

initiative "BelSign" operates as a Certification Authority (CA) and offers on-line certificate management services to issue and manage digital certificates.[14] In **Scandinavia** the Nordic Post Security Service (NPSS), a joint venture of the Finnish, Danish, Swedish and Norwegian postal authorities, is testing its first service using digital certificates and cryptography keys – a secure electronic mail system that will soon be launched. **Sweden** already has various digital signature initiatives, in the private as well as in the public sector. In **France** the Banque Nationale de Paris (BNP) and Société Générale, together with Visa International, France Télécom and Gemplus, are working together to develop a secure way of buying goods and services over the Internet, using chip card technology. In **Germany**, within the scope of their *Banking Communication Standards,* banks offer their clients the use of a digital signature for secure electronic banking. The *Teletrust Deutschland e.V.*[15] projects create public-domain application solutions for secure electronic communication. The two biggest **Irish** banks have set up Internet "shopping malls" making use of digital signatures. The **Dutch** I-pay project implements a trustworthy and secure electronic payment system, including the use of digital signatures and a Certification Authority function. Also the PTT Post – a private company in the Netherlands – is planning to offer secure e-mail services, using digital signatures and cryptography. PTT Post will act as a Certification Authority/Trusted Third Party. In **Spain** "Telefonica" is planning to create, in co-operation with the most important banking associations in Spain a certifying authority regarding electronic banking transactions using credit cards and being carried out through Internet.[16] Another application concerns the Banesto bank. This bank has created a CA which is presently operating through Internet.[17] In the **United Kingdom** the Certification Authority Eurosign is offering its services to the Internet public.[18] Also in the public sector an infrastructure is being developed for the transmission of intergovernmental secure electronic mail to be used by the British Government (Communications Electronic Security Group, 1996). In **France** an electronic professional health card will be introduced before 1999 enabling professional users and health insurance organizations to send, sign, receive and process electronic care documents. Also Spain and Belgium are implementing electronic social security cards based on smart cards and digital signatures. In **Luxembourg** "Healthnet" is an already partly operational value added network which offers all kinds of telematic services to all the professionals working in Healthcare and Social Security. To provide security, digital signatures will soon be utilized.

Also on a **European Community** level, diverse applications of electronic communication are in a project phase, or already implemented. Most of them are tending to introduce digital signatures for authenticating the electronic messages. The electronic tendering procedure in the public procurement field (SIMAP)[19] and the

---

[14] [http://www.belsign.be/].

[15] [http://www.teletrust.de].

[16] [http://www.ncr.es].

[17] [http//www.banesto.es].

[18] [http://sest.mkn.co.uk].

[19] See also *Green Paper on Public Procurement in the European Union: Exploring the Way Forward,*

electronic request procedure for a Community trademark (OHIM-RESMA)[20] are only two examples. Diverse pilot projects and studies are currently being carried out for encouraging electronic commerce, such as SEMPER (Secure Electronic Marketplace for Europe)[21] and ICE-TEL (Interworking Public Key Infrastructure for Europe).[22]

Especially in the **United States**, but also in **Canada** and **Japan** the development of electronic commerce in both the private and public sector is booming. Internet shopping malls, and electronic communication between the government and citizens are in full operation. The use of digital signatures in these countries is recognized as one of the most important tools to produce technically and legally secure electronic documents. Well-established certification authorities provide for identification and issuance of digital certificates. Legislation has been or will soon be enacted to provide for a legal framework eliminating existing legal obstructions and regulating the new services.

3.2   Legal initiatives

The **Council** has requested the member states and the Commission "to prepare consistent measures to ensure the integrity and authenticity of electronically transmitted documents."[23] Also the **European Parliament** has invited the Commission to prepare as soon as possible legal provisions concerning information security and digital identification.[24]

At the end of March, the **OECD** has adopted Guidelines for Cryptography Policy, [25] setting out principles to guide countries in formulating their own policies and legislation relating to the use of cryptography. These Guidelines make recommendations on several aspects of cryptography, including Digital signatures and international service provision.

The European standardization body (**ETSI**) is in the process of drafting a report[26] on the requirements for so-called Trusted Third Parties (TTPs). This report, once finalized, will serve as the basis for the European standardization process concerning TTP services, including those related to Digital signatures. The draft report explicitly

---

Communication adopted by the Commission on 27th November 1996 on the proposal of Mr. MONTI, [http://europa.eu.int/en/comm/dg15/gpentoc.htm].

[20] See also Office For Harmonization In The Internal Market (Trade Marks And Designs), [http://europa.eu.int/agencies/ohim/ohim.htm].

[21] SEMPER is part of the European Commission's ACTS program, [http:/www.semper.org].

[22] ICE-TEL is funded by the Telematics for Research Initiative within the Euopean Telematics Applications Program, [http://www.darmstadt.gmd.de/ice-tel/].

[23] Council Resolution Nr. 96/C 376/01 of 21.11.1996 on new policy-priorities regarding the information society, OJ C376 of 12.12.1996.

[24] European Parliament Resolution A4-244/96 of 19.09.96, OJ320, p.164 of 28.10.96.

[25] Recommendation of the OECD Council concerning Guidelines for Cryptography Policy, 27.03.1997; http://www.oecd.org/dsti/iccp/crypto_e.html

[26] ETSI Technical Committee Reference Report, Requirements for Trusted Third Parties, Vs. 0.0.7 of 26.03.97.

recognizes the impact of the commercial and legal environment on the technical standardization process. At the global level, the **IETF** (Internet Engineering Task Force),[27] **ISO/ITU**[28] and the **W³C** (World Wide Web Consortium)[29] are working on standardization relevant for Digital signatures.

In its recently adopted Communication "A European Initiative in Electronic Commerce" the **Commission** responded by announcing its intention to come forward with a specific initiative on Digital signatures (EC, 1997, {par. 51}). This initiative will aim at ensuring a common legal framework encompassing the legal recognition of Digital signatures in the Single Market, the setting up of minimum criteria for Certification Authorities, as well as pursuing worldwide agreements.

EU member states are preparing their national regulatory framework. **France** has already adopted a new Telecommunications Act,[30] implementation legislation has been announced. In **Germany** a law on digital signatures was approved by the German Bundestag on June 13, 1997.[31] The **UK** Government has launched a Public Consultation on the regulation of TTPs.[32] The **Dutch** Government has created an inter-departmental task force.[33] Also **Denmark** is developing a draft law on digital signatures. **Sweden** organized a public hearing in June. **Belgium** announced a legal initiative with respect to Digital signatures and electronic documents.[34] **Italy** has recently approved the legal equivalence of electronic documents, and TTPs is expected as an application of the general principle stated by the new law.[35]

Other countries are also implementing national legislation allowing the use of electronic documents and setting the rules for the delivery of relevant services. In some of the **United States**, digital signatures are already accepted as legally valid mechanisms. Of 33 state laws that have been enacted, proposed, or drafted, 23 of them are technology neutral, and 10 call for the use of digital signatures (Drolte, 1997; Horning, 1997). **South Korea** recognizes the legal validity of digital signatures.[36] Also **Malaysia** has drafted a bill seeking to make provision for, and to regulate the use of, digital signatures and to provide for matters connected therewith.[37] In **Japan** the Electronic Commerce Promotion Council has published Certification Authority

---

[27] Public-Key Infrastructure (X.509) (pkix) Charter:
[http://www.ietf.cnri.reston.va.us/html.charters/pkix-charter.html]
[28] X500 and ISO9594 series; ftp://ftp.bull.com/pub/OSIdirectory/ITU
[29] W³C Digital Signature Initiative:
[http://www.w3.org/pub/WWW/Security/DSig/DSigProj.html].
[30] Loi N° 96-659 du 26.07.1996 de réglementation des télécommunications.
[31] Informations- und Kommunikationsdienste-Gesetz - IuKDG, Article 3.
[32] Licensing of Trusted Third Parties for the provision of cryptography services - Public Consultation Paper on detailed proposals for legislation, March 1997.
[33] Staatscourant nr. 54, 18.03.1997.
[34] Press release, Council of Ministers, 30.05.1997.
[35] Law of 15 March 1997, n° 59, Article 15, § 2 Supplemento Ordinario alla Gazzetta Ufficiale della Republica Italiana n.63 del 17.03.1997.
[36] South Korean Act on Promotion of Trade Business Automation.
[37] Digital Signature Bill 1997 [http://www.geocities.com/Tokyo/3399/digisign.html].

guidelines.[38] Also the Canadian government is currently developing guidelines for the operation for all CAs in **Canada**. The **Australian** government is considering issues associated with establishing a public key authentication framework as well.

International **regulatory co-operation** relating to digital signatures is still in its infancy, but will mature rapidly in the coming months. Initial bilateral (EU/US, EU/Japan) and multilateral (UNCITRAL)[39] discussions have started. National security and law enforcement issues are dealt with in other fora (G7-P8).

IV   BRIEF OVERVIEW OF CONCEPTS AND TERMINOLOGY

This section briefly describes the most important concepts and terminology which are used in the report.

4.1   What is a digital signature?

Several different methods exists to electronically sign documents. These electronic signatures vary from very simple methods (for example, inserting a scanned image of a hand-written signature in a word processing document) to very advanced methods (using cryptography). The subset of electronic signatures based on public key cryptography, is often called digital signatures. The basic nature of digital signatures is that the author of an electronic document can sign his electronic document by using a secret cryptography key. This key must be kept private at all times by the user. The signature can only be verified with the associated public key of the author. This public key is widely known.

The idea behind this authentication is the confirmation of identity by proving the possession of a secret key. The author encrypts the message or a part of it with his secret key. The recipient of the message can check the identity of the author by decrypting the information with the public key of the presumed author. If the decryption is not successful the recipient will not validate the message. This process of authentication relies on the public keys of the users that are accessible to all the communication partners and on a trusted relationship between the identity of the users and their public key.

In this sense, a digital signature can be described as a piece of data that has been extracted from the electronic message itself, made unforgeable by the use of public key cryptography and consequently attached to the message.

---

[38] Certification Authority Guidelines (Alpha version), April 1997, Electronic Commerce Promotion Council of Japan (ECOM), Certification Authority Working Group, Certification Authority Guidelines Special Working Group, [http://www.ecom.or.jp/eng/output/ca/ca-eng-guideline.htm].
[39] Working Group on Electronic Commerce:
[http://www.un.or.at/uncitral/sessions/wg_ec/index.htm#TOP]

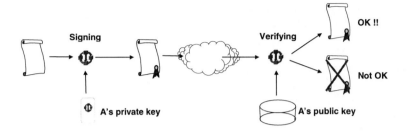

Like the signature you use on written documents today, digital signatures are now being used to identify authors/co-signers of e-mail or other information objects electronic data. Digital signatures can provide three important functions:

- **Authentication**: To authenticate the identity of the person who signed the data – so you know who participated in a transaction.

- **Integrity**: To protect the integrity of the data – so you know that the message you read has not been changed, either accidentally or maliciously.

- **Non-repudiation**: To allow you to prove later who participated in the transaction – so someone may not successfully deny having sent or received the data.

It is important to know that in order to create a signed message, it is not necessary to send the message itself in encrypted form. The digital signature will be appended to the message and can be verified irrespective of the form (clear/encrypted) of the message itself.

Digital signatures: step by step

A digital signature is created as follows:

The *first step* is to create the *data unit* that is to be signed, e.g., a precisely delimited information object in digital form. This can be a text document, software, or any other digital information.

The *second step* will be to create a *hash value*, often called a "message digest" or a "fingerprint" of the message. That is the result of a mathematical process based on the data unit and an algorithm which creates a compressed digital representation. If the data unit is changed the hash value will no longer correspond to this data and this will generate an error message.[40] This technique will enable the signature software to operate on small and predictable amounts of data.

As a *third step* the signer will encrypt the hash value with his private key. **The checksum** — *the digital signature* — will be unique to both the data unit and the private key used to create it, and it has to be attached or appended to the data unit.

---

[40] There must be only a negligible possibility that another data unit could result in the same hash value, and these routines must also be secure against any attempt to try to achieve this.

As a *final step* the digital signature will be verified by regenerating the hash value on the basis of the same data unit and the same algorithm. This hash value will be computed with the public key to once again produce a checksum, which should be compared with the checksum/signature attached to the data unit. If the result is identical it will verify that the signer's private key was used to sign and that the data unit has not been altered.[41]

4.2   What is cryptography?

Cryptography is a highly important instrument for achieving secure electronic commerce. By encoding or scrambling the data of an electronic message, it is possible to protect the information from being disclosed or modified. The encoding and decoding of the message is performed by using a key which is only known to the communicating partners. The main advantage of encoding the message is that the partners can be sure nobody can read the message. Furthermore, since only the contracting partners know the secret key, every encrypted message which can be decoded by that secret key can only originate from the other party, and thus authenticates the message. This system of sharing one secret key is called **symmetric or secret key cryptography**. Before the partners start to communicate they, of course, have to exchange the secret key. This creates both practical and security problems: the communicating parties have to contact each other before they start the encrypted communication, and the secret key can be intercepted during its transmission. Furthermore, since the receiver is also in the possession of the secret key, he is able to sign as well The main problem, however, is that you cannot communicate with partners you have never contacted before. This creates difficulties in an open electronic environment, such as the Internet, in which electronic commerce will mostly take place between partners who do not know one another.

Symmetric cryptography, however, is not the only type of cryptography. The encoding and decoding of the message can also be performed by using two keys: one public key which is publicly known, and one secret key, which is only known by the entity. This cryptography technique is called **asymmetric or public key cryptography**. The public key can be used by anyone to encrypt a message. Only the owner of the secret key can decrypt it. Thus, if two entities want to send information to each other, they exchange their public keys. The public keys could also be retrieved from a database which is open to the public. When A sends to B a message, A encrypts the message using the public key of B. Only B can encrypt the message using his secret key.

The primary advantage of public-key cryptography is increased security. The secret keys do not have to be transmitted or revealed to anyone. Another advantage of this system is that the public key and the secret key can both be used for encoding as well as for decoding. Their functions are interchangeable. This means that A can encode a

---

[41] See also, LegSec WP3 Report Security Issues, *ENS Legal and Security Issues,* E2307, Deliverable 3, p.30.

message with his own secret key, which B can decode by using A's public key. On the face of it, this seems a silly method, because everybody has access to A's public key and can thus decrypt and read the message. This is, indeed, true. On the other hand, B can be sure that the message can only originate from A, since he is the only one who knows the secret key. Without having contacted A before, B can trust on the authenticity of the message. It is on this technology of sharing a public key that digital signatures are based.

4.3   Where does the user get his keys from?

The key pair can be generated by the user himself by running specific cryptography software. Even the recent versions of the most popular Internet communication software, such as Microsoft Internet Explorer and Netscape Communicator, allow the user to create its own key pair. The key pair can also be generated by a third party. This is, for example, the case in the electronic banking sector. For security reasons, the secret key can immediately be destroyed by the third party.

4.4   How does the user store his private key?

Temporarily, secret keys are being stored on the hard disk of the user's computer. The user gains access to the secret key by entering a password or pass phrase. This type of storage, however, has the disadvantage of non-mobility. The user always needs his own computer in order to put his digital signature on an electronic file. Therefore, the storage of the secret key on a removable carrier, such as a smart card is getting more popular. The user simply inserts his smart card into a reader by which he can sign digitally.

4.5   Can the private key not be stolen?

Once a person has generated or received his public and private key, it is extremely important to keep the secret key free from access by others. If somebody gains access to the secret key, that person will be able to counterfeit the key and, thus, to create digital signatures. Protection of the secret key is, however, for the user a local matter under his control or the control of a responsible site security officer. Every person bears responsibility for his own signature and should protect it from lost, theft or illegal use. Neither should the user forward his secret key to other people such as a secretary or colleague.

4.6   How does the user obtain the partner's public key?

The user needs the public key of his partner in order to check the authenticity of his digital signature. This public key can be delivered by the partner himself but can also be retrieved from a database which is publicly accessible. Normally, the communication software of the user will automatically check the digital signature by retrieving previously stored public keys or accessing the relevant public database.

4.7   How can the user be sure this public key really belongs to his partner?

The authentication procedure is based on the presumption that the public key really belongs to the signer. This presumption is, however, not self-evident. The risk exists that somebody creates a key-pair, places the public key in a public directory under somebody else's name and thus signs electronic messages in the name of somebody else. Furthermore, a public/private key pair has no inherent association with any identity, it is simply a pair of numbers. Therefore, the assurance should exist that the public key really belongs to the claimed identity. The answer is to rely on third parties to certify public keys. A third party will guarantee the relationship between the identity and the public key. This association is achieved in a *digital certificate* that binds the public key to an identity. These third parties are known as Certification Authorities and must be accepted by all users as impartial and trustworthy, Trusted Third Party (or TTP).[42] In addition, the process of key certification must be foolproof and should be afforded the highest level of security. A Certification Authority will, by issuing a digital certificate, certify the identity of the user and guarantee that the public key really belongs to the claimed user. The act of using a registered digital signature to sign an electronic message becomes thus very similar to appearing in front of a notary public to manually sign a paper.

4.8   How does the certification authority check the identity of the user?

Some certificates are passed out after a simple E-mail address check. The assurance provided is minimal, and only good for establishing a consistent presence, not for guaranteeing that someone is a real person. Other certificates are issued after receiving third party proofing of name, address and other personal information provided in the on-line registration. Usually this will be a check of some consumer databases.

---

[42] ISO 9594-8-The Directory-Authentication Framework defines a certification authority as follows: *"An Authority trusted by one or more users to create and assign certificates. Optionally the CA may create the users' keys."*; For more details about the use of TTP and the legal issues involved, see the various reports on this topic: TEDIS, *Trusted Third Parties and similar services*, Final report, November 1991; The various INFOSEC studies (see INFOSEC 1994 Security Investigations, May 1994), LEGSEC, *Inca case study*, Final report, February 1995; TEDIS, EDITT Trusted Third Parties Workshop, February 1995; TEDIS II, *Report on Security in Open Environments*, Ver.7, February 1995; LEGSEC, *EBR Casestudy*, Final report, February 1995; LEGSEC, *ENS Legal and Security Issues*, Deliverable 2, May 1995.

The best identification check is, of course, personal appearance. Some certification authorities require someone to personally take their application to a notary, who will check identification before endorsing it. This adds an additional layer of credibility to the certificate (e.g., Verisign). It could also be possible to meet personally with a representative of the certification authority (e.g., Thawte). Most of the CAs offer a range of certificates, graded according to the level of investigation used to confirm the identity of the subject of the certificate.

4.9   What is the content of a digital certificate?

Digital certificates may contain every type of information necessary to identify the creator of the digital signature. Usually they contain the owner's public key, the owner's name, the expiration date of the certificate, the name of the Certification Authority that issued the digital certificate, a serial number, and perhaps some other information. The CA signs information and thereby adds credibility to the certificate. People who receive the certificate check the signature and will believe the attribute information / public key binding if they trust that certifying authority.

In order to allow an automated checking of the certificates it is important that certificates are built up in the same form. It is therefore necessary that standards be followed, describing the elements a certificate should contain. The emerging certificate standard is the X.509 certificate format, which has been around since 1988 and is part of the ITU-OSI group of standards. X.509 certificates are very clearly defined using a notation called ASN.1 (Abstract Syntax Notation 1) which specifies the precise kinds of binary data that make up the certificate. The X.509 certificate, version 3, is approved in 1997 and is currently being implemented in most applications. This version allows to insert additional information such as alternate naming, restricting the use of the key, identification data (E-mail address, ...), and information about a so called (cf. below) Certificate Revocation List (International Telecommunications Union, 1997).

4.10   What if the certificate is not valid any longer?

Many cases exist where an individual's certificate should not be used or trusted anymore, for instance when an employee leaves a company, or when someone's computer or smart card containing the secret key is stolen. When a certificate becomes compromised, there must be a way to call up the CA and request that the certificate be disavowed.[43] The most common way of making the revocation public is to put it in a database, called a **Certificate Revocation List** or CRL. The CRL can be accessed by the public to check if the certificate of a user is still valid. A Certification Authority thus must maintain two databases, a complete list of certificates and a list of revoked certificates.

---

[43] Furthermore, certificates based on the X.509 standard come with an expiry date to ensure that old, retired certificates can be removed from the network.

4.11   Why should the user trust the certification authority of the other party?

When one user, whose public key is certified by a CA, wants to communicate securely with his partner, certified by another CA, both users should trust each other's CA. One way to achieve this confidence is by *cross-certification*, this means that both CAs certify each other's public key.[44] Another solution could be that the two CAs are certified by a third CA, functioning as a top-level CA. In this *hierarchical CA structure* each CA only needs to be certified once in order to gain trust. At the moment, however, most CAs are certifying themselves by simply signing their own public key and posting this certificate on their own websites. This *self-certification* is possible because the CAs rely on trust gained from other activities, such as postal services or banking activities. In order to assess the level of trust that may be put into a CA, the CA should also provide a combination of *technology* (such as security protocols and standards, secure messaging, and cryptography), *infrastructure* (including secure facilities, customer support, and redundant systems), and *practices* – a defined model of trust and legally binding framework for subscriber activities and disputes. In short, a CA should be a trusted on-line service operating 24 hours a day, 7 days a week on a global basis.

Hierarchies are, however, not the only solution. There are cryptography solutions which are making use of a so-called *web of trust*. Your key might be signed by people who are trusting you, such as friends, family or colleagues. People who will want to verify the signature might know someone from this group and have a copy of his public key. It is self-evident, though, that existing webs of trust are too small to offer a practical solution for electronic commerce.

4.12   What is the difference between traditional and digital signatures?

The "signature" concept has a long tradition and is normally easy to describe. It gives basic mechanisms for secure traditional information management. A hand-written signature is physically tied to a carrier (the sheet of paper), which gives shape and structure to the information in an immediately readable format. This "lock" for the information, provided by the carrier and the signature representing the issuers unique patterns of handwriting, gives the reader reasons to believe that the object originates from the individual who is seen to be the originator and the identity attribute is inherent, not given to the signatory.

Digital signatures are not immediately readable and the "signature," the carrier and the signed object are not *physically* related to each other in the same "locked" and durable form. A manipulation of the data normally leaves no such traces as a manipulation in the traditional environment and portions of a signed information object may be stored on different locations, such as a hard disk. Visual inspection of a traditional example is replaced by technical verification of a signed information object, stored in a computer

---

[44] The X.509 structure did not allow the cross-certification structure until in its last version (v.3). The two first versions only acknowledged a strictly hierarchical model.

readable format and *logically* tied to the signature. As the digital attribute making the signature unique for the individual is assigned, not an inherent characteristic of the signatory, the signature process may be performed by anyone who has access to the secret and the procedures.

The hand-written signature furnishes the information with a physically unique sign of authenticity – it is an original example. Such signed objects may be in a person's possession, and can thus be the carrier of authority (e.g., power of attorney) or a certain right (e.g., bills of lading and other negotiable documents). However, the unique aspect of a digitally signed object has to be related to a pattern of data, which may easily be copied, and the duplicate will have exactly the same qualities as the "template." Consequently, the unique existence of IT material is built upon the storing and transmittal of original *contents* and certain IT applications such as shipping documents demands some form of registration; cf. the risk of double-spending of electronic money.

4.13   Can traditional signatures be replaced by digital substitutes?

The management of traditionally signed objects may in the main be replaced by digital equivalents. By making use of security techniques, such as digital signatures, the authenticity of the information can be maintained. The need for protection of such objects is already carefully considered in the traditional environment. An examination of electronic commerce, electronic handling of cases by administrative agencies and similar routines shows the same need for protection in the IT environment. However, the changes related to the transition from original examples to original contents have to be noticed where appropriate.

Consequently, current issues are in principle traditional matters of legal protection and security, which give basic mechanisms for the information management. Instead of creating a completely new legal framework, existing achievements should be utilized, as far as they are compatible with IT.

V   GENERAL OVERVIEW OF LEGAL ISSUES

This chapter shortly describes the different legal issues requiring further investigation if digital signatures and services are being introduced in the European Community and its main trading partners. The issues are subdivided into problems concerning products, services and signatures.

Currently, member states and trading partners are looking into the need to adjust or are already amending national law and regulation in order to provide for legal validity and enable businesses and citizens to use digital signatures without technical nor legal risk. The Commission Communication states that a wide range of regulations at national level could, however, inhibit the establishment of service providers across frontiers. These include differing professional requirements, differing prudential and supervisory systems, and notification or licensing requirements (for example for regulated professions or financial services) (EC, 1997). In order to ensure the proper functioning of the Internal Market the divergences between national regulatory frameworks for digital signatures and any resulting potential regulatory barriers should be analyzed.

5.1   Legal issues regarding the use of digital signatures

5.1.1   "Paper-Based" legislation in some member states may hinder a free flow of digitally signed electronic documents

Most member states have not adapted their national legislation to the new techniques of document management. Laws of evidence, as well as sectoral legislation, impose, explicitly or implicitly, the need for penned signatures on paper documents. Consequently, the uncertainty concerning the legal status of digitally signed electronic documents is slowing down the development of electronic commerce in Europe.

5.1.2   New "electronic-based" legislation in some member states may hinder a free flow of digitally signed electronic documents

This legal uncertainty concerning the acceptance of electronic documents and digital signatures has urged some member states to implement specific legislation explicitly accepting electronic documents and digital signatures. **Germany**, for example, recently approved new legislation, whilst Italy has adopted digital signature legislation in March 1997. The **United Kingdom** has launched a public consultation paper and **France** and **Belgium** are drafting legislation about digital signature services. Since there is no collaboration between the member states in drafting this new legislative rules, there is no Europe-wide consistency with respect to specific requirements regarding the legal acceptance of electronic documents. New national legislation would surely hinder the development of electronic commerce on the internal market: consumers having a national valid digital signature would not be able to use it in other member states, merchants would not be able to contract with consumers from other member states and digital signature services would not be able to deliver services in other member states. Moreover, the acceptance of national technical requirements could easily lead to national protectionism.

5.2   Legal issues regarding the introduction of digital signature services

The provision of trusted services is a completely new service sector. This sector is still in its infancy, but interested market players are positioning and preparing themselves. The sector is currently dominated by commercial undertakings based outside Europe, such as Verisign in **US**, Thawte CA in **South Africa** or the **Canadian** Keywitness. Some EU-based commercial companies have emerged, quite a lot of them are subsidized from EU R&D programs. It is expected that in the next years a significant number of new entrants will appear on the market. These new entrants seem to focus on their national market and do not, at least not initially, target markets in other EU member states. Legal uncertainties are certainly due to this hesitation.

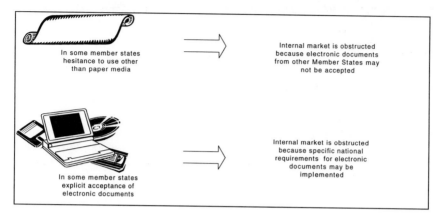

From the legal point of view it is important to distinguish clearly between on the one hand, the procedures and conditions governing the establishment of a Certification Authority, and, on the other hand, the conditions imposed on the different services provided by a Certification Authority. Different Treaty Articles (52, 59) apply to each of these situations.

5.2.1 National procedures and conditions on establishment may hinder the freedom of establishment of digital signature services

The establishment of a provider of certification services is subject to the law of the member state concerned. Some member states intend to impose specific establishment requirements and authorization procedures on Certification Authorities; others only require compliance with the general provisions in the law concerning the establishment of a company. Some member states may have voluntary authorization schemes, others may impose mandatory licensing. For example, the **UK** Public Consultation Paper envisages mandatory licensing, while the **German** law provides an optional legal framework for CA licensing. Restrictive practices with regard to the establishment of a Certification Authority should not undermine the freedom of establishment, for example by discriminating without justification on the basis of nationality or by restricting, again without justification, the number of service providers. Requirements for professional qualifications of Certification Authority staff and ownership requirements are also typical examples of establishment restrictions.

Some regulation may also impose that CA-activities can only be performed by the government. Exactly like this is the case for the issuance of identity cards in some countries (like in **Sweden**), the government would be solely responsible for the emission of digital certificates. This monopoly, together with an immunity for government CAs would certainly undermine the confidence in trusted services.

5.2.2 National conditions on providing services may hinder a free flow of CA services

Some member states intend to introduce regulation concerning the provision of cryptography related services. The definition of these services as well as the conditions imposed on each of them may be different from one member state to the other and therefore create Internal Market obstacles.

It is current practice that Certification Authorities define the rights and obligations of the parties involved in the certification services they provide in a so-called Certification Practice Statement. The provisions in such Statements should be compliant with the law of the country where the Certification has been legally established.

National rules on consumer protection
Member states may feel it necessary to include in their national law and/or in the license itself (if applicable), conditions with regard to the protection of the consumer, covering issues like transparent, non-discriminatory certificate delivery, pricing of services, an obligation to inform the consumers of best practice behaviour and certified products, limits on financial commitments, and liability and damage compensation. Especially the liability of CAs should be clarified and regulated on a European level.

National divergent scope of application
Non-harmonized delimitation of the scope of application may invoke refragmentation of the single market. For example, the **British** Public Consultation Paper envisages the mandatory licensing of all organizations offering or providing "encryption services." Encryption services encompass any service which involves any or all cryptographic functionalities like key management, key recovery, key certification, key storage, message integrity (through the use of digital signatures), key generation, time-stamping or key revocation services. Thus, a license will be required not only for certification services/Certification Authorities, but for all TTP Services. **France** will organize a TTP licensing regime, as well. However, a clear distinction is made in the new French Telecommunications Law between cryptography products or services, which, on the one hand, *cannot* have other objectives than authentication of a communication or the assurance of the integrity of the message and on the other hand, cryptography products or services which can also serve for confidentiality purposes. Only the provision of the latter services will be licensed. The use of cryptography for authentication/integrity functions only, as when using a digital signature, will not be regulated. Certification Authorities providing certification services only (identification, certificate issuance, certificate directory services) will not need a license to provide these services in France. On the contrary, the **German** digital signature Law precisely envisages the licensing and regulation of certification services.

National rules on certificate issuance

A Certificate links a name with a public key. Before issuing a certificate, the Certification Authority has to establish the identify of its client, assign a name, and verify the possession of the private key. The procedures followed by the Certification Authority determine the "strength" of a certificate. National legislation may determine how the Certification Authority has to proceed.

Some member states allow certificates related to digital signatures to be *issued to physical persons* only. For example, in the legal initiative announced by the **Belgian** Council of Ministers, natural persons only should have a digital signature. According to §2, 2 of the **German** Law, only natural persons can get a certificate. In the **Danish** proposal, Article 15 stipulates that authorized Certification Authorities may only certify key pairs for the purpose of digital signatures for natural persons. Certification of key pairs for legal persons is allowed for identification purposes only. Different authorities exercised by a physical person may be implemented by so-called attribute certificates. Digital signatures committing moral persons are either implemented via attribute certificates or by issuing a certificate to the moral person itself. In this second situation it is left to the internal procedures of the moral person to ensure that only duly authorized personnel can commit the moral person. The impact of these two different approaches requires further legal analysis.

Upon request a certificate could be issued to a person using a *pseudonym*. For privacy reasons such behaviour could be perfectly legitimate. Law enforcement or national security requirements could be met by setting out in the law the conditions under which the Certification Authority is obliged to provide the real identity. A complication may arise if the certificate has been issued abroad.

Rules concerning the identification of the applicant can vary from member state to member state and from CA to CA. This divergence in identification guarantees may cause different confidence capacities of the certificates. The lack of a common European approach may inhibit a free choice of certificates.

Many different certificates exist. For regulatory purposes it is important to identify clearly which types of certificates, and, implicitly, which kind of digital signatures are the subject of regulation.

National rules on the recognition of foreign certificates

Since certificates are the deliverables of certification service providers, which may operate across borders, provisions have to be made to recognize certificates issued by Certification Authorities established in either another EU/EEA member state or a third Country. Certificates issued in another jurisdiction could be recognized either directly (by recognizing certificates only) or indirectly (by recognizing digital signatures based on such certificates). Indirect recognition has the advantage that all elements constituting a digital signature (i.e., keys, certificate, signature product) have to be taken into account. Direct recognition of certificates only is easier.

The **Danish** proposal (art.19) stipulates that certificates issued by foreign certification authorities will have the same legal status, provided that a Danish certification authority guarantees that the foreign certification authority will comply with the Danish obligations. The **German** law (§15) only accepts foreign certificates if an equivalent level of security can be demonstrated.

The role and impact of cross certification practices, whereby a Certification Authority recognizes certain certificates issued by another Certification Authority, need to be studied further.

National licenses for CAs

Member states may charge a special body, or bodies, with the issuance and elaboration of, and the supervision of compliance with, authorizations concerning digital signature services. The **UK** Public Consultation Paper suggests a mandatory licensing system operated by the Department of Trade and Industry, whereas the **German** digital signature bill only stipulates a voluntary licensing system.

National licensing procedures and conditions could however, restrain the provision of services by foreign CAs. Therefore, some form of pan-European co-operation between national supervisory authorities might be useful, and could be facilitated by a Community instrument, if put in place.

National rules on the generation of the keys

Some member states may forbid the user to generate his keys himself. The CA or another organization may be imposed to produce the keys and even to keep them in escrow. Other member states may allow the user to generate his own key-pair. It is questionable whether a user of one member state could apply then for a certificate in another member state with different rulings.

5.3   Legal issues regarding digital signature products

In order to ensure reliable use and legal validity, and to combat fraud and misuse, digital signatures require adequate products for key generation, key storage, certificate storage and retrieval, signature generation and verification. National, as well as European Community rulings may however hinder a free circulation of these products.

5.3.1 National technical and operational requirements may inhibit a free circulation of digital signature products

Member states may establish at national level technical and operational requirements to be met by certain categories of digital signature products. Such requirements may differ from member state to member state and will continuously change due to the rapid technological developments. Different national technical requirements and unsynchronized adaptation to technological progress are well-known causes of Internal Market obstacles. **Germany**, for example, requires the fulfillment of certain technical and operational specifications in order to provide digital certificates and digital signatures with legal validity, if a foreign certificate meets its national technical requirements, it will only be valid if the same level of security can be guaranteed (§14 of the digital signature Law).

Member states have to communicate to the Commission, and through it, the other member states their intended technical rules, the observance of which is compulsory, *de jure* or *de facto*, in case of marketing, use, manufacturing or importation of a product, digital signature products including. [45] This procedure enables the Commission, and the member states, to identify those rules which, once adopted, will create Internal Market obstacles, and to take appropriate action, either issuing comments, a detailed opinion or by proposing Community measures. Community technical harmonization measures do not contain, in principle, detailed technical requirements, but limit themselves to establishing the essential safety requirements and leave technical details to international standardization.

5.3.2   National certification of products may inhibit a free circulation of goods

A plethora of digital signature products will become available. Some of them will be tested via well established certification procedures by recognized certification bodies against agreed evaluation criteria. Others may not be tested or fail to pass testing. Some manufacturers may even not want their products to be tested. The use of non-certified products may result in the legal validity of the related digital signature being uncertain and not recognized by the Courts.

The widespread use of digital signatures will inevitably lead to legal conflicts needing to be settled in court or by arbitration. Third party expert inspection of the products used and procedures applied would facilitate parties in providing proof that adequate products have been used and the necessary procedures have been executed. Adequate measures need to be identified in order to ensure that digital signature products are sufficiently open for such public inspection.

In order to enable citizens, business and government to decide what kind of product provides the necessary level of security, it is necessary that adequate security criteria are defined and an independent assessment of these products and services takes place, of which the results are made publicly available. Common evaluation criteria and procedures play a fundamental role in providing a basis for the international mutual recognition of digital signatures. Different schemes can be envisaged to implement the evaluation of digital signature products, and the related accreditation of recognized certification bodies.

---

[45] Council Directive 83/189/EEC of 28.03.1993 laying down a procedure for the provision of information in the field of technical standards and regulations; OJ L109 of 26.04.83.

The Council has recommended[46] the implementation of the Information Technology Security Evaluation Criteria (ITSEC). A number of member states have already established (or have indicated their intention to establish) ITSEC schemes. Some of these schemes could be used for digital signature purposes.

The need for harmonized certification criteria and procedures related to digital signatures has to be confirmed. If required, the EU could pursue the mandatory adoption of ITSEC for digital signature products until the Common Criteria are complete.

5.3.3   Current community legislation may hinder the free flow of digital signature products

The Dual Use Regulation[47] obliges member states to impose prior authorization procedures on cryptography products dispatched from one member state to another. Sometimes member states also impose authorization procedures before products can be distributed.

Since a digital signature does not, in principle, encrypt the contents of the underlying message/file, well-engineered "digital signature only products" should not impinge upon law enforcement or national security. Under these circumstances it is difficult to justify the restrictions on the free circulation and the use of this category of products for reasons of national security or law enforcement.

Maintaining intra-Community controls on digital signature products will also have a detrimental effect on the development of a European industrial capability in the field of digital signatures by denying industry the benefits of the size of the full Single Market. Intra-Community controls on digital signature products also have other negative circulation effects. Law abiding citizens will be required to remove digital signature tools, legitimate in their home country, from their lap-top computer, if they travel to another EU member state. This problem might be solved by establishing an exemption for the temporary, personal use of digital signatures products if the product remains in the possession of the citizen while traveling throughout the Union.[48]

5.3.4   National cryptography regulations may cause an internal market obstacle

In the case of digital signatures cryptography is not used to conceal information. It is widely recognised[49] that the use of cryptography for digital signature purposes is distinct from its use to ensure confidentiality and that each of these uses presents

---

[46] Council Recommendation N° 95/133/EC of 7.4.1995 on common information technology security evaluation criteria; OJ L93 of 26.04.97, p. 27.

[47] Council Regulation (EC) No. 3381/94 of 19.12.94 setting up a Community regime for the control of exports of dual-use goods, Article 19; OJ L367 of 31.12.94

[48] For a similar solution see US regulation ITAR, Section 123.25: http:/www.epic.org/crypto/export_controls/personal.htm

[49] OECD Cryptography Guidelines, recital clause 15, and principle VI on lawful access.

different issues. Therefore, digital signatures are of no concern to national security of EU members. However, since it is technically possible to use the same key pair (public and private key) for digital signatures as well as for confidentiality purposes,[50] this implies that regulatory provisions aimed at only one of these application areas could apply to the other as well, which may lead to unsatisfactory situations. National rules forbidding or limiting the use of cryptography could, indeed, inhibit the free use of digital signature products. In some countries the production, export (Dual Use Regulation, see above) as well as use of encryption techniques is restricted. Therefore, it might be worthwhile to consider the use of separate key sets for digital signature purposes and for confidentiality purposes. In the United States, for example, the NIST digital signature Standard (DSS) respects the distinction between cryptography for confidentiality purposes and for authentication purposes by providing a tool which only creates digital signatures.

VI   CONCLUSION

6.1   Digitally signed electronic documents

The legal value of digitally signed electronic documents is currently nonexistent, or at least doubtful throughout the European Union and beyond. A common European position in the form of a legal instrument could clarify the legal acceptance of electronic documents. Instead of creating a completely new legal framework, existing law should be utilized and adapted to new patterns of action in the IT environment. Consequently, there is a need for a definition of digital signatures and electronic documents. From a legal viewpoint technical descriptions should be avoided, since new security methods in accord with technical advances might arise. In the establishment of unified legal and technical concepts, more abstract formulations could be used where the conceptual functions are contained, while clarifying the demand for verification both for the originator and the contents.

6.2   Digital signature services

Governments have started to reflect on the need to regulate the new economic activity of delivering digital signature services, such as the issuance of digital certificates by Certification Authorities. Due to the inherently cross-border nature of these services, different national regulatory approaches and the lack of mutual recognition of each other's regulatory requirements may easily lead to a fragmentation of the Internal Market for electronic commerce and on-line services throughout the Union. (Potential) Internal Market obstacles, once identified, should be analyzed and the national regulations causing them should be scrutinized in the light of the free circulation provisions of the Treaty. Enforcement of the law of and control by the country of origin, complemented by the mutual recognition of each other's provisions, should be the preferred approach. Serious, but justified restrictions may require Community

---

[50] Although good security practice requires the use of different security mechanism for different purposes. A single key pair for all kinds of purposes is certainly not good practice.

harmonization of conditions and requirements. Although it may be licensed, the provision of certification services is, in principle, a commercial activity in a competitive environment. Individuals and businesses should be able to chose from the offerings of several Certification Authorities, established either in their home country or abroad. Digital signatures regulation, at national as well as at Community level, should not only pre-empt and avoid any distortion of competition but also actively facilitate cross-border competition in trusted services to the benefit of citizens and business.

Since different national conditions and procedures create obstacles to the proper functioning of the Internal Market, a harmonization of conditions and procedures must be envisaged. Country of origin control over Certification Authorities combined with mutual recognition should be the principle governing the establishment of Certification Authorities within the EU/EEA. A lot of thought should be devoted to the possibility and conditions of cross-certification by the diverse Certification Authorities, as well as the implementation of a hierarchical structure at the European level. Indeed, some commercial Certification Authorities are offering the provision of top-level Certification Authority as a special, highly priced service. The most prominent provider of this services is based outside Europe. National supervisory authorities do function as top-level Certification Authority on a country by country basis for licensed certification authorities. These national structures could be complemented by the EU authority which issues and publishes the certificates of the national level Certification Authorities. The concept of an EU top-level Certification Authority holds many promises and may encourage the development of certification services in Europe. Its implementation, operating conditions and potential impact still require further work.

6.3   Digital signature products

Further work has to be done in order to identify the need for pre-defined classes of digital signature products and the requirements applicable to each of them. If mutual recognition of each other's provisions concerning digital signature products does not result in a satisfactory functioning of the Internal Market, then common technical requirements for digital signature products will have to be established via a Community-wide legal instrument, supported by standardization.

Some form of consultation and co-operation at EU/EEA level on the scientific and technical evolution of the cryptographic technologies underlying digital signatures may be necessary. Regulation must keep pace with technology and stay abreast of the products available on the market. Common technical requirements and evaluation procedures and criteria play a fundamental role in providing a basis for the international mutual recognition of digital signatures.

Regarding the present regulated state of the use and export of encryption products, the Commission should not seek the immediate and unconditional abolition of the current controls. It should pursue, together with the member states, a policy allowing for the identification of the conditions (administrative co-operation, mutual assistance, other) which must be met in order to gradually abolish controls on intra-Community shipments of digital signature products.

Part Three:
Communities in Cyberspace

HOW COMFORTABLY DOES THE INTERNET SIT ON CANADA'S TUNDRA? REFLECTIONS ON PUBLIC ACCESS TO THE INFORMATION HIGHWAY IN THE NORTH

by Lorna ROTH

In 1974, Brenda Maddox introduced a book chapter titled "From CATV to Infinity" with the following passage (quoted in Streeter, 1987: 175):

> An almost religious faith in cable television has sprung up in the United States. It has been taken up by organizations of blacks, of consumers and of educational broadcasters, by the Rand Corporation, the Ford Foundation, the American Civil Liberties Union, the electronics industry, the Americans for Democratic Action, the government of New York City, and – a tentative convert – the Federal Communications Commission. The faith is religious in that it begins with something that was once despised – a crude makeshift way of bringing television to remote areas – and sees it transformed over the opposition of powerful enemies into the cure for the ills of modern urban American society.

In 1987, Thomas Streeter used this same passage to introduce his critical and insightful analysis of the cable industry entitled, "The Cable Fable Revisited: Discourse, Policy, and the Making of Cable Television," in which he argued that the democratic promise of a large body of discourse used in the early seventies to describe new technologies and, in particular, cable, created "a sense of expert consensus, of unity and coherence where there actually was a variety of conflicting motivations, attitudes, and opinions." (Streeter, 1987: 175) This shared feeling of awe and excitement "inspired a sense of urgency, of possibility, and of a need for action, for response" in relation to the technology (Streeter, 1987: 175). At the time, the Utopian strain in the discourse about cable technology could not be ignored. Cable was described as having the "potential to rehumanize a dehumanized society, to eliminate the existing bureaucratic restrictions of government regulation common to the industrial world, and to empower the currently powerless public" (Streeter, 1987: 181). Of course, as we are all aware, cable's performance did not live up to its discursive promise.

This retrospection is significant in that it gives us a critical context for rethinking current discourses about the information (super)highway and reminds us that the information highway debates are really only part of a longer historical trajectory of talk about new technologies and their impact on our lives.

In post-modern society, media have become central instruments and institutions of the public sphere – an arena where competing constituency groups strive for the right to be taken as representative of public opinion, of public interest (Raboy, 1990: xii). Access to the media, therefore, is crucial to the democratic promise of public life. Universal access to affordable technologies is at the heart of communication scholars' thinking about democracy and empowerment. It is what gives cultural communities the power to represent themselves to others. It is what enables the voices of minorities to be heard, after long and worthwhile struggle for the implementation of their communication rights. The many stories of the struggle for universal access make it clear that neither media technology nor policy makers are politically innocent.

As Nicholas Garnham so aptly notes, the developing relationships between the media and politics are often problematic "because they fail to start from the position that the institutions and processes of public communication are themselves a central part of the political structure and process." (Garnham, 1986: 37) Like Garnham, I want to argue that shifts in media discourse, structure, and policies, whether these stem from economic or technological developments or from public intervention, are properly political issues of deep significance and should be carefully debated in an informed manner. Central to this debate in Canadian society are competing economic and political views of technology as either a private commodity to be owned and used as a basis for profit, or as a public resource, to be shared as a universally accessible public service. Although Canadian governmental discourses promote public access in principle (Information Highway Advisory Council Reports), its decisions demonstrate a favouring of competitive practices and markets as means of expanding the information highway throughout the country. Although market forces can work to extend the information highway in densely populated urban areas, this is not so easy in Northern and remote communities, where government subsidies are required to equalize access to residents. This essay will draw on illustrative evidence from two cases in Northern Canada to argue that without public subsidization and cross-cultural adaptation, the Information Highway in the North will likely be subjected to repeated market failures. Small, culturally – and linguistically – diverse populations, prohibitive costs of telecommunications services, and lack of existing infrastructure, preclude the universal extension of an information infrastructure based exclusively on market forces.

I   HISTORICAL CONTEXT OF NORTHERN MEDIA

The Inuit of Nunavut and Nunavik Inuit[1] have a special place in Northern communications history. They have been television and radio pioneers in the past and are able to draw on their experience in planning initiatives with regard to current technology access. In some ways they are a model constituency group: they are

---

[1]Nunavut and Nunavik are vast areas. Nunavut consists of the portion of the former Northwest Territories that is occupied by the Inuit of Northern Canada. Together, Nunavut and Nunavik (the Inuit territory in Northern Québec), constitute approximately 1/3 of Canada and have a very small population. There are 96 communities in the NWT/Nunavut with a total population of 57,649; 17,500 are Inuit, according to the 1991 census. In Nunavik, there is a population of 7,500 Inuit. In 1999, both Nunavut and Nunavik will begin to exercise their right of self-government.

situated at a common distance from the institutions of power, have common interests in retaining their communication rights; have participated successfully in configuring Television Northern Canada, a pan-Northern television distribution service; and they have a common range of cultural and linguistic practices.

There were many initial barriers to overcome in bringing improved telecommunications facilities to the North. Geographically and atmospherically, these include: vast distances separated by huge expanses of water, mountains, permafrost (a condition that makes it impossible to set up a microwave system), atmospheric interference, tropospheric scatter, islands. Essentially, the western regions were able to establish communications systems sooner than the eastern areas because of road accessibility. They could be connected to the south via microwave towers. The eastern Arctic had to wait until the Anik satellite became operational in 1973 before it was able to receive adequate telephone and live broadcasting services.

Having the basic services of telephone and live broadcasting via satellite established a fair degree of "outside" accessibility for essential services. But there are still some people in the North who lack telephony – there is a 98.7 percent penetration of telephony in Canada, and many of those without access live in the North (Information Highway Advisory Council Final Report, 1997: 45). This problem is referred to as a network barrier. Northerners are experiencing a series of other barriers. These include "service barriers," which occur when a telephone network has already been established but there are only limited services available in the community. "Cost barriers" are evident in that many Northerners cannot afford to purchase individual connection, i.e., long distance charges to a variety of telecom services. There is the skill/knowledge question as well. How many Northern First Peoples are technology-literate enough to want to invest in computer packages and telecommunications services?

Despite and perhaps partly because of these telecom barriers, First Peoples have focused on broadcasting services and are internationally acknowledged as having the most advanced and fair Fourth World (indigenous peoples) broadcasting system. This distinction is based on the legislated recognition (1991) of their collective communications and cultural rights as Peoples with a special status. Aboriginal-initiated media in Northern Canada (North of the 55th parallel) have a relatively long history compared to Fourth World/indigenous communities elsewhere. The stages through which this broadcasting history have evolved were initiated by First Peoples themselves as they struggled for inclusion in the policy and practice decisions pertaining to broadcast services to their national communities. Partly as a result of pioneering activities by First Peoples to integrate their programming into the Canadian media infrastructure, they are now identified as a mediated model of cultural persistence.

II   BROADCASTING MEDIA

Radio entered the North in the late 1920s, at the same time that airplanes began to access the region. By the early thirties, trading posts, the Royal Canadian Mounted Police centres, and religious missions were equipped with high frequency radios to maintain contact with their headquarters in the South. Native peoples did not have direct access to these early radio services. In 1958, the Canadian Broadcasting Corporation's (CBC) Northern Service was established, taking over the infrastructure of short-wave transmitters established by the Canadian Armed Forces and the Department of Transport.

In 1960, the first Inuit-language broadcasts occurred and by 1972, 17 percent of the CBC short-wave service was in Inuktitut. The Canadian federal government's public subsidization of native-produced media began formally in 1974 with the development of its Native Communications Program (NCP) which granted funding to Native Communications Societies to operate community-based radio stations and newspapers in the North and South. Between 1974 and 1996, 117 First Peoples' community radio stations have become operational across Canada. With the exception of the Inuit service in the Northwest Territories, whose CBC regional radio programming has always fully represented their concerns, all other Northern regions have both a network of local radio stations and one publicly-subsidized regional service.

Both regional radio and television broadcasting evolved rapidly in response to the launching of the Anik satellite in 1972. When the North was hooked up to the South through live radio and television services for the first time in 1973, Inuit and First Nations had access to the images, voices, and messages that the United States and metropolitan-based Canadians produced with Southern audiences in mind. The parachuting in of Southern, culturally irrelevant television programming into Northern communities by the CBC Northern Service acted as a catalyst for indigenous constituencies to organize broadcasting in their own languages (or dialects), reflecting their own cultures, as they had already done with radio. After the initial mystique of TV dissipated, native peoples and their Southern supporters began to lobby for their own television programming and network services. They wanted participatory and language rights, as well as decision-making responsibilities about programming and Southern service expansion. By the mid-seventies, First Peoples across the country had secured funding, established 13 regional Native Communications Societies (NCS) responsible for administering their communications activities, and began operating local community television projects.

Beginning in 1976, and in response to articulate native demands, the federal government made available large grants for native organizations. Funding was to be used for technical experiments and demonstration projects with the Hermes (1976) and Anik B satellites (1978-81). Once these experiments proved successful, the federal government policy-makers were convinced of the economic and political viability of establishing permanent native broadcasting infrastructures throughout the North.

In 1981, the federal government undertook a one-year consultation and planning process, the outcome of which was the Northern Broadcasting Policy (1983), and an accompanying program vehicle, the Northern Native Broadcast Access Program (NNBAP). These policy and funding decisions were the foundation for the enshrinement of aboriginal control over broadcasting in the 1991 Broadcasting Act.

The Northern Broadcasting Policy set out the principle of "fair access" by native Northerners to the production and distribution of programming within their territories. It further established the principle of prior consultation with First Peoples before Southern-based decisions were made about Northern telecommunications services. NNBAP, managed by the Department of the Secretary of State (Native Citizens Directorate) was mandated to distribute Cdn\$40.3 million over an initial four-year period to the 13 NCSs. The money was to be used for the production of 20 hours of regional native radio and 5 hours of regional aboriginal television per week. Funding has eroded over the years but the Program is still operational.

As the NNBAP implementation process proceeded, it became apparent that the "fair" distribution of radio and television programming was a key problem. An implicit assumption within the Northern Broadcasting Policy was that this task would be taken care of by either CBC Northern Service or by CANCOM (Canadian Satellite Communications Inc.), the distributor of Northern broadcasting and programs since 1981. In both cases, negotiations between Native Communication Societies and broadcasters had become bogged down over prime time access hours and the pre-emption of national programming.

In 1988, the federal government responded to persistent lobbying by the National Aboriginal Communications Society (an interest group representing the NCS constituencies) for secure distribution services by providing a subsidy of Cdn\$10 million toward establishing a dedicated Northern satellite transponder (channel). By 1992, Television Northern Canada (TVNC) was on the air.

Operated and programmed by the 13 aboriginal broadcast groups along with government and education organizations located in the North, TVNC is a pan-Northern satellite service that distributes 100 hours of programming to 94 communities. It is considered to be a primary level service in the North. In 1995, TVNC applied for permission from the CRTC to be placed on the list of eligible channels to be picked up by cable operators in the South. In November 1995, approval was granted, making it possible for TVNC to become available in a variety of Southern Canadian markets, should cable operators decide to make it part of their discretionary packages. It is already accessible on an off-air basis to those owning satellite dishes because its signal is not scrambled. In 1996, however, it digitized its signal so that users had to upgrade their receiver dishes at their own cost.

In many ways, First Peoples have refashioned television broadcasting. They have indigenized it – transformed it into a tool for inter-community and national development. They have utilized television programming as a vehicle for mediation of their own historically ruptured past, and as a pathway into a more globally-integrated future.

III   TOO LITTLE, TOO LATE

Initial excitement about the dedicated Northern transponder service declined a year or so after TVNC's system was in place. This was partly due to the multiplicity of channels which had become available at the time and had effectively fragmented the Northern audience. What was also highly significant was that the symbolic level of representational access, access that mattered, had already been established and embodied in the TVNC. To some extent the federal government felt it had accomplished its duty to support the new delivery service. So, with TVNC well underway, the federal government subsidies began to dry up and bureaucrats began to demand that TVNC diversify its funding sources.

Thus by the early nineties, TVNC, along with all its individual NCS members, depended on shaky finances. Theirs was not an easy challenge. Services in the North cannot sustain the ongoing high costs of satellite linking through private market support, and new financial pressures sent TVNC scrambling for business opportunities.

Federal government cutbacks were not TVNC's only obstacle. As noted above, the dedicated Northern channel went on air just as cable services became available in half of the Northern communities. TVNC broadcasters had to compete like never before, with the disadvantage of having fewer resources to sustain their services. To make matters more complex, TVNC was placed in the sensitive position of having to compete with its own broadcasters for scarce funds from community-based businesses.

Budgetary constraints have forced Native Communications Societies and TVNC to downsize – to lay people off and be more frugal about resources. Most are managing to keep afloat but are unable to plan a secure future without a viable, lucrative funding source. This need distracts them from their prime objective of public service and takes up time and energy. TVNC has made several attempts to privatize, so has the Inuit Broadcasting Corporation and other NCSs. They have created businesses to sell production services, telecommunications equipment, and broadcasting skills. But Northern markets are less viable than those in the South because of low population density.

By 1993-4, public access to "ramps" leading to the Information Highway began to seem very attractive as a potential source of income. TVNC attempted to find a way in which it could become involved in configuring and controlling citizen access to appropriate routes to, from, and within the Northern communications environment.

IV   THE INFORMATION HIGHWAY DEBATES: CONNECTING THE NORTH

Meanwhile, in the fall of 1993, the Government of the Northwest Territories (GNWT) Department of Education, Culture and Employment commissioned the Inuit Broadcasting Corporation (a prominent Native Communications Society) to conduct seven separate audio teleconferences aimed at clarifying the communications needs of Northerners. During this process 62 people across the Arctic were consulted. The resulting report, entitled *Connecting the North: Defining Users' Needs*, confirmed Northern views on "the enormous potential of the emerging technologies to stimulate and promote economic, business and social development." (IBC, 1995: 5) The report identified two recurrent themes: "the lack of public awareness of communications issues, and the absence of a forum for joint discussion of these issues and formulation of coordinated plans and policies." (IBC, 1995: 6) On the basis of information derived from this consultation, IBC organized a three-day symposium in November 1994 to address these themes. The electronically-mediated public forum, called *Connecting the North*, enabled participants to talk about the information highway with all its aspects, issues and opportunities. Using TVNC's channel, this symposium was the only public debate on the information highway in Canada. Broadcast live, the debate lasted four hours per day over three days. It involved all of the First Peoples' leadership, thousands of home viewers, and received a great deal of coverage in the Northern press. Participants included stakeholders, users from various key Northern institutions, constituency group representatives, members of the general public. The symposium planners had to deal with a variety of Northern-unique challenges, among which were: a region of 4.3 million sq. km., reaching across 5 time zones; a sparse, widely distributed population of 100,000 Northerners; five stakeholder governments functioning in the consultation area (the federal government, and the governments of the NWT, Yukon, Québec, and Newfoundland (Labrador); 96 culturally and ethnically diverse communities; 17 languages.

The meeting included input from the Yuendumu Aboriginal community in Australia, and permitted various Canadian sector representatives to focus in on the uses of the Internet for the following services: education, health, social services and justice, public administration, self-government organizations, economic development, infrastructure providers, policy makers and strategists (IBC, 1995: 11). Some of the concerns raised are described in the report as follows:

> Public and private sector participants identified a similar range of service related concerns: the need to upgrade the infrastructure to enable access to Southern and global information systems; the need to develop a general awareness of the potential opportunities associated with new technologies; and the need for education and training in the use of new technologies. They also saw the use of new communications technologies as a means of reducing the high human and financial costs associated with the delivery of services and programs in the communities. They recognized the need for the pooling of

resources and the need to standardize and rationalize systems and equipment. They saw that the development of an infrastructure to meet the communication needs of the North would reduce a growing information systems disparity between the South and the North. (Nunavut Implementation Commission, 1996: 3)

Connecting the North was highly acclaimed as a tool for building constituency group consensus around complex and, in some cases, competing sets of project objectives. Although consumers, citizens, producers, and distributors of information and telecom hardware all had a variety of things to say about quality of services, rights, language, and use of the Internet for training, learning, telemedicine, among many other talking points, this paper only looks at issues of access. Because of the isolation of the North from the South, given its geographical vastness and its low level of business-profit potential (with the exception of resource extraction projects), it seemed clear from the meeting discussions that infrastructure would have to be put in place with some ongoing governmental financial assistance, particularly in relation to costs for long-distance services. In the words of the *Connecting the North* authors:

> Canada's telecommunication infrastructure development is market driven: services tend to develop in and between major centres, where density in population ensures maximum profitability. This principle, however, will not ensure that the residents of remote Northern communities who most need access to information highway services will in fact be able to use them. If infrastructure upgrading occurs in Iqaluit and Yellowknife, but not in Arctic Bay and Jean-Marie River, then the extension of the information highway to the North will favour people in large centres – centres which already have more resources than small communities. Communities both large and small require upgrading of the technology, based not on population, but on equality of access. (IBC, 1995: 25)

Two insightful comments follow which inform us of the user perspective in relation to the fear of being left out:

> Don't leave small communities behind! Don't forget us.[2] (Elisabeth Lyall, Talooyoak, June 1997)

---

[2]This statement is excerpted from notes for a report by Lorraine Thomas on Pauktuutit's Annual General Meeting in 1997. Not all communities have been forgotten, nor have all been left behind. There are several small communities on-line with large enough populations of users that the server is able to maintain its bottom line. These are Rankin Inlet, Cambridge Bay, Iqaluit, Yellowknife, and Whitehorse. Some schools are also hooked into SchoolNet; nursing stations and medical services have the finances to dial-up to servers down South; and the federal government's Community Access Program has assisted in getting two NWT and five Yukon communities launched onto the Information Highway.

There is a danger that such a system may be valued as a luxury service and be costed accordingly, rather than valued as a basic utility service in much the same way we currently value power/telephone services. (Inuvik – Community Discussion Group)

In 1995, a year after the *Connecting the North* teleconference, the question of public access resurfaced when the Nunavut Implementation Committee released two studies on Nunavut Telecommunication Needs in which they supported the establishment of Community Teleservice Centres in each community in the North. Known as "telecentres," "telecottages," "televillages," or "tele-offices," these are "multi-purpose centres" that provide telecommunications and computer facilities and support in small villages in rural and remote areas around the globe. They function as information gateways into communities; and out to the world. They have been described "as a 'virtual community' composed of people, firms, government agencies, schools, libraries, health care providers and others connected through a common vision or need linked through telecommunications, information resources and shared resources." (Nunavut Implementation Committee, 1995: 5) "They are a means of overcoming telecommunications service, infrastructure, financial, and skill associated barriers. Regardless of their size or the services that they provide, their primary purpose is the preservation of the quality of life through the resolution of economic problems associated with distance and remoteness." (Nunavut Implementation Committee, 1996: 1) The Telecentre is a model of public access that will likely be utilized extensively across the North, but it will require some public subsidy because of the high costs of telephone long-distance services for the local service providers, especially in communities where the population of users is too small to meet the servers' investment and operational costs, even before a profit is possible.

Connecting the North facilitated the formal beginnings of a Pan-Northern telecom dialogue. However, the North is divided into five distinct territorial jurisdictions: the Yukon, the NWT, Nunavut, Nunavik, and Labrador, over and above the northern parts of the individual provinces. Quite predictably, many regional demonstration projects and debates have been undertaken subsequently, and numerous constituency groups and consortia are in the process of putting together services for their specific regions. It is a time of technological pioneering in the North and competition over control of the information highway infrastructure construction is fierce. Over and above support for individual efforts on small projects, each of the regional governments is evaluating what it considers to be the best technical map for future developments. Important decisions are being made and the stakes are high for Northerners.

The last section of this paper focuses on two initiatives – the Nunavik demonstration project which took place between 1996 and 1997 and the Pauktuutit's (Inuit Women's Association) efforts to demand community access and control over the informatization process of the North. This will be followed by an overview of the decision-making process currently underway in the NWT concerning the information highway infrastructure. Due to the rapid daily changes in the decision-making processes, and for heuristic reasons, our discussion stops at the beginning of October 1997.

V   NUNAVIK.NET: A CASE OF MARKET FAILURE

In the fall of 1996, Nunavik.net went on-line. Designed as a pilot project for Northern Québec by the Inuit Native Communications Society (Taqramiut Nipingat Incorporated, or TNI), it used the idea of the Telecentre as its central organizing principle and set up CTSCs in three of the largest communities of Nunavik – Kuujuuaq, Salluit, and Puvirnituq, each having a population of roughly 1,000. TNI trained a resource person in each community to coordinate the public access venue and all seemed to be going well until the project lost momentum in August 1997 and was halted before its three-year term expired. With approximately 100 users in all three communities, and at a total monthly cost of Cdn$2,500 per community for the bandwidth access, TNI had gone into arrears with Bell Canada after 10 months. Why did the TNI project fail? There are a number of likely answers, including the following: the population was too small to support the payment structures – there is a need for cheaper bandwidth in the North; TNI might not have had the organizational and financial infrastructure to take on a project of this magnitude and sustain it over the three-year period; and private user support for the demonstration project was not wide enough, with only about a dozen paying customers per community participating in the project at a fee of Cdn$50 per month. Beyond institutional users, there is not yet that critical mass of people in Northern Québec Inuit communities who either own personal computers or desire access to Information Highway services on a public computer located at a Telecentre. To date, no evaluation of the pilots has been published or made available to the public and TNI's demonstration project has been closed down.

VI   PAUKTUUTIT (THE INUIT WOMEN'S ASSOCIATION):
REFLECTIONS ON COMMUNITY CONTROL AND ACCESS

The Inuit Women's Association is a model of action-oriented deliberative processes that ought to be taking place in the North in relation to citizen access extension. In 1996, the Inuit Women's Association, Pauktuutit, seriously contemplated the assets and liabilities of becoming involved in the information highway and, in particular, the one-stop kiosk idea of the Telecentre. In a series of meetings with feminist communications consultants, representatives from Pauktuutit articulated the point that Inuit women needed to be alerted to the complexities of access and participation if they were to get involved with the information highway. They discussed the importance of, and the values inherent in, the use of mediated communications and agreed to spend some time talking about telecommunications at their next Annual General Meeting in June 1997. The Pauktuutit women commented that they were positively disposed towards computers and other forms of media provided that their specified goals were met. But they insisted that their concerns be embedded in the debate about the Northern information highway right from the start. For example, if communities are to go ahead with building Telecentres, Pauktuutit women want to be sure that an appropriate building is used, one which is central, safe, and has a good atmosphere. They want to be involved in choosing that site as well. Of utmost concern is community-by-community control over access. This is a political issue to members of Pauktuutit – it is going public, being heard, and being counted in a technologically-driven debate which will, from now on, have multiple consequences on their lives.

Pauktuutit women are very aware that in joining the information highway's virtual communities, First Peoples will have to adapt to existing practices that have emerged from another culture. They may be able to change the language symbols and, in minor ways, the cultural images of life on the Net by additive means, but to a large extent, the infrastructural design is impregnated with the political roots, ideological constructs, and cultural biases of the designers of the technological apparatus and software applications.

To what extent will First Peoples be able to "indigenize" the Internet in the North? The answer to this question will depend on the degree to which they are able to use the net for purposes of cultural persistence, to be present on the net visually, socially, technically, locally, discursively – to make their presence felt. Women from the Pauktuutit organization are showing us a way of doing things with talk, contemplative practices, and action-oriented strategies. They are becoming involved in the community development process, focusing on the implications of the information infrastructure in their towns, and considering all of this in relation to their actual communications and media needs. In a culturally-thoughtful manner, they are pacing the changes about to enter their life-worlds. We, in Canada's South and elsewhere, could learn something important from their methods and values.

But, theirs is not the only Northern strategy. While Pauktuutit constituency members are thoughtfully configuring their position in the process of global integration, Northern entrepreneurs are in a rush to install the infrastructure and get on with building a clientele and making a profit.

VII   NEGOTIATING THE TECHNOLOGICAL INFRASTRUCTURE

In recent years the government has actively withdrawn from the mixed-model tradition. This can be seen in an amendment to the Telecommunications Act in 1994, shifting the initiative in communications from public service to market forces, and opening the doors to deregulation and privatization. It can also be seen in the Information Highway Advisory Council's report – in its general recommendation that the private sector should create and manage the infrastructure and operating systems of the information society free from public-interest interference. The retreat from the mixed model can also be seen in the cutbacks to cultural funding that we have witnessed since 1984, resulting in the loss of our collective memory – the "shadows on the wall" that anchor us to our particular place and time (Menzies, 1997: 3).

Since 1994, and in the context of the NAFTA agreement, GATT, and the World Trade Organization critiques of "protectionism," several complex issues have evolved and decisions about the Northern information highway configuration have been taken. It is hard to describe the events in a linear fashion because so many of them were entangled in the politics, practices, and interest-laden contexts of negotiation. What follows is one version of how things are unfolding.

In May 1996, the NWT government put out a call for proposals to establish a digital communications network throughout its region with the stipulation "that the winning consortium would preferably be northern-based and aboriginal-owned, committed to establishing nodes in the smallest communities, and prepared to finish the job by April 1999. It would have to guarantee initial access to government, education, and medical facilities in each community over a bandwidth of 384 Kbps." (Teitlebaum, 1997: 282) The NWT government's approach was this: it would purchase bandwidth to guarantee essential services in each community and then resell a portion of it (at a cheaper rate) to potential local consumers who could use it at their discretion. In other words, the NWT government would be subsidizing local users by enabling their purchase of cheaper access than is available elsewhere.

In response to the request for proposals, TVNC joined forces with CANCOM (the Canadian Satellite Telecommunications delivery system) to form a consortium and bid for the digital highway construction contract. In the meantime, Northwestel, the monopolistic telephone service company located in the Yukon, began a collaboration with Arctic Co-operatives Limited (the chief Northern cable operator) to compete with TVNC and CANCOM. The two groups planned highway infrastructures, each utilizing and expanding upon their existing Northern service delivery resources. TVNC and CANCOM intended to piggyback on their satellite receiver dishes, and Northwestel/Arctic Co-operatives Ltd. planned to amplify existing telephone and cable lines. As already noted, TVNC/CANCOM went digital in April 1996, and this meant that users required a new satellite receiver dish to downlink their digitally compressed video signals. With the exception of Iqaluit, where TVNC/CANCOM maintains its uplink (two-way [receiving/transmitting]) satellite dish, other communities' new dishes are only set to receive and not to transmit signals. Given the limitations of TVNC/CANCOM's existing technology, if it were to become the developer and guardian of information highway infrastructure, it would have to invest a large amount of new money into the expansion of bandwidth and into the additional purchase of two-way dishes, at a prohibitive cost. In other words, TVNC would not have been able to tap into existing satellite resources in each community without fairly large financial investment. It was prepared to do so, however. On the other hand, Northwestel's costs would be far less because their existing infrastructure is easier to modify. Furthermore, if the GNWT had any inclination toward public service, the fact that Northwestel joined forces with Arctic Co-operatives Ltd. (a community-accountable outfit) seemed to accommodate this principle.

In summary, the two consortia competed for the contract within a framework of private entrepreneurial principles. Pressure to do so in order to be considered credible and serious business players was "in the air," and was evident in the corporatized discourses circulating within the various levels of government involved in the decision-making process.

But TVNC is *not* a private business and is accountable to its Board of Directors and its constituency members in ways that private enterprises are not. In many ways, the TVNC/CANCOM joint model reflected the Canadian broadcasting system in that it was made up of weaker public and stronger private elements. The telephone and co-op contenders leaned more toward the private-based telecom model of private enterprise, but one with a slight socially-accountable twist. At least from a discursive perspective, their model included an element of a co-operative public consciousness although, in effect, it was grafted onto their proposal in a less significant way than if it had been a public-service prototype.

Partly because of politics, social relationships, cost, and the possibility of schmoozing in Yellowknife where the action was, Northwestel/Arctic Co-operatives Ltd. and NASCO (a third collaborator), won the tender for establishing information highway services in the North and is currently in the process of building them under a new company name, ARDICOM.[3]

> On April 24, 1997, the government of the Northwest Territories agreed to a Cdn$25 million (US$18 million) deal with a northern-based, aboriginally owned company called Ardicom, which runs off Canada's satellite system. Ardicom's task, now, is to establish this network, via satellite and terrestrial links, with nodes in all 58 of the Canadian Arctic's population centres. Installation of the new digital network began last fall, and Ardicom plans to connect the first 20 of the region's communities to its network by year's end. (Teitlebaum, 1997: 278)

VIII   CONCLUDING COMMENTS

The fact that the NWT awarded the contract to ARDICOM and not a First Peoples' public service organization is not a decision to be taken lightly. It is very revealing – as a sign that established public service models in the North, such as that of TVNC and of the NCSs, may no longer be perceived as viable economic options. The decision is a clear indication of the NWT's current position within the private/public service debate, as well as within that regarding ownership, control, and the need for public subsidy. Somewhat in the tradition of the "typical Canadian compromise," it is the NWT government's acknowledgment that it is, on the one hand, open to media

---

[3]This is not the only project infrastructure in the planning stage. Seven demonstration projects have been funded in the North by CANARIE (Canadian Network for the Advancement of Research, Industry and Education) for a total of Cdn$1.25 million, beginning in the fall of 1997. Things are moving quickly in the North.

privatization. On the other, it recognizes the need for minor public subsidies due to high telecom costs. In other words, it suggests the possibility of a parallel position developing in relation to broadcasting as well.

Will this trend toward privatization be restricted to information highway decisions in the future, or might it also apply to the broadcasting infrastructure of Native Communications Societies and Television Northern Canada? This is a question well worth asking given a recent proposal to the Department of Canadian Heritage. Submitted by two former Inuit Broadcasting producers, Zacharias Kunuk and Paul Apak, both located in Igloolik and both involved in Isuma Productions Inc., the proposal argued that the headquarters and control mechanisms of Inuit Broadcasting Corporation and TVNC should be relocated to Iqaluit from Ottawa and privatized. In moving the organizational infrastructure and control to the North and to independent contractees, they hope to develop a strong independent First Peoples production and distribution industry in the North. To date, there has been no official government response to their proposal.

The consequences of current technical and economic decisions are not felt solely in the technical and economic realms. As evident from their past media history, Northerners are not passive recipients of either media services or telecom bandwidth. Decisions about infrastructural development, and equitable, affordable access are deeply political, though they are often masked as economic and technical considerations. The NWT has demonstrated where it stands vis-à-vis the development of information infrastructures in the North. The federal, Yukon, Nunavut and provincial governments now have two emergent options in relation to Northern and remote communities, i.e., the mid-North, the Northern parts of the provinces, the Native Communications Societies and other Northern resources which they have, in the past two decades, publicly subsidized: either let market forces play themselves out without direct intervention, or show the good will necessary to recognize the universal access rights of the North as an economically-disadvantaged region with a small population by providing long-term, secure public service subsidies.

In the preliminary report of the Information Highway Advisory Council (1996), the national access strategy is clarified. Its guiding principles are: "universal, affordable and equitable access; consumer choice and diversity of information; competency and citizens' participation; open and interactive networks." (IHAC, 1997: 42) In its Final Report, IHAC restates these principles and adds:

> Consistent with the Council's philosophy, the government recognized that market forces would play an important role in putting these principles [of national, universal, affordable and equitable access] into action. However, the government also indicated: "Where market forces fail to provide this level of access, the government is prepared to step in to ensure affordable access to essential Information Highway services for all Canadians, regardless of their income or geographic location." (IHAC, 1997: 42)

Given the recent CANARIE (Canadian Network for the Advancement of Research, Industry and Education) funding of several Northern and/or native-based telecom demonstration projects, perhaps enough data will be generated over the next few years to pressure the federal and/or provincial/territorial/Nunavut governments involved to make evidence-based decisions in favour of public subsidization of the Northern Information Highway infrastructure.

The particularities of the Northern mediascape provide a benchmark of what basic service and special needs are in a region that visibly marks itself as an exemplary case for public subsidization and universal access. How the Northern access options are played out in the next few years will tell us a lot about the state of democratic communication rights for all Canadian citizens at the end of the twentieth century. Let us be watchful of the process.

POLICY-MAKING AND THE VALUE OF ELECTRONIC FORMS OF PUBLIC DEBATE: UNDERPINNING, ASSUMPTIONS AND FIRST EXPERIENCES

by Cees LEEUWIS

I   INTRODUCTION

One of the ways that new information and communication technologies are expected to contribute to the renewal of democratic processes is through an enhancement of societal debate within governmental policy processes (Van Dijk, 1991; Percy-Smith, 1996). This type of "teledemocracy" usually takes place in the form of electronic debates that are organized and operated by means of e-mail discussion lists or more advanced debating software on the World Wide Web. This article investigates the potential value of electronic forms of public debate in policy processes. Thereby, its scope is limited to those forms of debate which are purposefully initiated by governmental institutions in an effort to involve citizens in policy-making.

II   ELECTRONIC DEBATES FROM A COMMUNICATION SCIENCE PERSPECTIVE

A key question to be addressed is whether or not electronic media have specific properties which may lead to an improvement of the quality or effectiveness of public debate within policy processes. However, this question is hard to address in its present form. First, notions like "greater quality" and "effectiveness" have multiple dimensions (e.g., access, degree of participation, depth, relevance for policy-making, etc.), and can only be assessed on the basis of a normative framework. Second, the notion of "specific properties" is problematic. Even apart from the fact that different forms of electronic debate exist, various authors have stressed that the characteristics and specific properties of a particular electronic medium may depend on both the social context in which it is used (Fulk, Schmitz & Steinfield, 1990), and on the content of what is being communicated (Leeuwis, 1996). Rafaeli (1988: 119-20), for example, points out that "interactivity" should not be looked at as a medium-characteristic. In his view, the level of interactivity is constituted by the extent to which later communicative acts address the relation between two or more preceding statements (Rafaeli, 1988: 111). In this vision, media may pose preconditions and boundaries to interactivity, but they certainly do not determine the actual level of interactivity in a specific social setting. A face-to-face conversation offers ideal opportunities for interactivity but may in fact take place in a totally non-interactive manner (e.g., if people are not prepared to listen to each other), while the opposite may be true for an exchange which is mediated by a medium which is less optimal in this respect (e.g., a letter). A similar mode of reasoning can be applied to other so-called "media-characteristics" like speed, user-control, information richness (Trevino, Daft & Lengel, 1990), and the like. These "characteristics" must rather be looked at as features of communication processes that are shaped by active human agents in a specific setting.

The above discussion is relevant because it makes clear that the appropriateness of electronic media for "bridging the gap" between citizens and administrators will probably depend more on the attitude of the parties involved than on the medium itself. When governmental staff or citizens are not genuinely interested in a constructive debate, the use of ICT will certainly be useless. However, when there is a serious intent to communicate, the parties involved can make use of such a variety of media and discussion techniques that the added value of electronic debates is not immediately evident. The above discussion also teaches us that a study of the potential added value of electronic forms of debate should not start primarily from the "media characteristics" of electronic media, but first and foremost from the features (and problems) of specific communicative practices and settings: in this case, public debates in policy processes. This is why this chapter will first address the strong and weak points of *conventional* forms of (face-to-face) public debate, like the ones initiated by Dutch governmental institutions (see e.g., Rathenau Institute, 1994; Van de Poll & Glasmeier, 1997), and only then reflect on possible contributions of electronic forms of public debate in a similar setting. In this manner, we may get an idea of the potential added values and/or undesirable consequences of such electronic debates.

2.1   Characteristics of public debates in policy processes

As indicated above, an analysis of strengths and weaknesses of conventional or electronic forms of public debate in policy processes can only take place against the background of certain normative considerations. The following three normative criteria are used:

1. In a public debate all relevant and valid arguments must be raised, and considered, in the generation of conclusions.
2. A public debate must take place in an "open" fashion; participants must express a certain freedom of speaking, listening and thinking. In an "open" debate, arguments (rather than interests, power and positions) must be decisive (see Habermas' [1981] notion of "communicative action").
3. A "good" public debate has an influence on both the governmental policies generated and the public acceptance of these policies.

2.1.1   Selective participation due to place and time constraints

Because conventional forms of debate take place at specific places and times, a high degree of coordination and mobility is required from the participants, who are often representatives of societal interest groups and laypeople. This means that certain selection processes will take place. In a recent debate on nature development (Van de Poll & Glasmeier, 1997; Aarts & Te Molder, 1997), for example, it was difficult to find farmers who could spare the time to participate for several weekends during their busy season. Moreover, due to the physical presence of the participants, it is often considered impractical to accommodate more than 40 or 50 participants.

At first glance, time and place play a less dominant role in electronic forms of debate. During a debate over several months people can contribute at any time, and at any place where Internet facilities are available. Also, it seems easier with electronic debates to accommodate a higher number of participants. However, it is clear that other forms of participant selection will take place relating to computer access and skills, as well as to writing capacities.

Especially if one assumes that access to Internet facilities will increase significantly in the future, it seems that electronic forms of public debate can develop some advantages over conventional forms:

> Assumption 1:
> For those policy issues where a relatively large number of interested people and/or stakeholders have access to Internet, electronic forms of public debate can accommodate a larger number and wider variety of participants than conventional debates (given a certain amount of organizational input).

> Assumption 2:
> The larger the number and wider the variety of participants in a public debate (to a certain degree of saturation), the greater the chance that (a) relevant arguments and perspectives are raised; (b) policy makers will incorporate some of the conclusions in their policies; and (c) citizens' acceptance of policies is increased.

2.1.2 The "peak" rhythm: Concentration of the debate in time

Conventional debates tend to be concentrated in time; that is, they take place at a series of well defined meetings of variable length (ranging from hours to days). During these periods the intensity of the debate is high, while communication tends to very limited in the long intervals between meetings. During the meetings, the verbal mode of communication generally results in many short statements being generated at a high speed. Although this "peak" rhythm provides participants with a clear sense of the amount of time to be invested in debate, we have seen that it may also result in excluding particular categories of people. Moreover, the peak rhythm tends to go along with a lot of time pressure during the meetings, thus limiting the number of issues that can be thoroughly discussed. Also, the rapid pace of exchange tends to allow fast thinkers and verbally strong participants to dominate the debate.

Electronic "meetings" can be much longer in duration than conventional ones. The rhythm of electronic debates is not only more even (i.e., less concentrated), but also slower. In a lively electronic debate one can expect some 10 or 20 contributions per day, instead of some 100 speech-acts per hour in a conventional debate (with fewer participants). The nature of these contributions tends to be different as well. In addition to short reactions, some participants tend to write long and well prepared analyses, based on careful study and editing. A disadvantage of all this may be that participants have to spend more – if fragmented – time in order to follow and participate in the electronic debate. At the same time, such debate puts the easy writers in an advantageous position, even if less capable writers have more time for editing. A possibly relevant research finding in this respect is that participation in electronic debates tends to be more equally distributed than in conventional debates (Dubrovsky, Kiesler & Sethna, 1991; Kiesler & Sproull, 1992). While these authors attribute this phenomenon to a reduced influence of power and status (see below), others have suggested that (time-)technical dimensions play a role (Spears & Lea, 1994).

These considerations lead to the conclusion that electronic debates may have a couple of additional advantages over conventional debate:

> Assumption 3:
> Because of the "(time-)technical" conditions that go along with electronic forms of debate, time pressure will play a less significant role than in conventional debates.

> Assumption 4:
> A reduction of time pressure during debate will result in (a) a more egalitarian use of participation opportunities; and (b) better prepared and more thoughtful contributions by the participants. Hence, the reduction of time pressure will lead to an increase in the number of active participants and to a more extensive articulation of relevant arguments, both of which may in turn result in increased policy influence and policy acceptance (see assumption 2).

2.1.3   The timing of collective memory and information provision

For purposes of preparation, participants in conventional public debates are usually provided with a selection of articles, reports and/or presentations by experts before the actual debate starts. During debate, it frequently happens that lines of argument develop which had not been anticipated in the preparatory information provision. Due to the peak rhythm of conventional debates, it is often impossible to correct this. At such points the debate is either interrupted or continues on the basis of sub-optimal information. The information provision about the debate itself usually takes place through note-taking by individual participants (a somewhat distracting exercise), and/or through summaries by a discussion leader, or minutes.

In many ways information provisions preceding electronic debate resemble that in conventional debates. If written sources are supplied in electronic form, it may be easier to provide a somewhat greater selection of preparatory material from which participants can choose. During the debate itself, however, information provision may differ significantly. Moderators or participants can at any time bring in new documents or resources, and these can be immediately incorporated into the electronic debate. Also, the debate itself is completely documented; all original contributions are available to everybody.

Again, we can assume a potential added value of electronic debates:

> Assumption 5:
> The relatively slow rhythm of electronic debates – when compared with conventional ones – makes it possible for the provision of information into the debate to be adapted and extended while the debate unfolds.

> Assumption 6:
> As the flexibility of the information provision during a debate increases, participants feel better-equipped to arrive at a well-considered conclusion.

2.1.4 Sequential organization and the role of the discussion leader

Plenary meetings and parallel sessions are discussion methods used in conventional debates, and the latter make it possible to discuss different topics simultaneously. An important limitation, however, is that each participant can participate in only one line of debate at the same time. In that sense conventional debates are sequential in nature. Even if there is some space to maneuvre for participants hoping to influence the agenda in a meeting, we often see that in order to reach a conclusion within a certain time-frame, discussion leaders tend to be rather strict in ensuring that the discussion does not deviate into "side-lines" which are deemed "irrelevant." In doing so, however, potentially relevant topics may not be sufficiently dealt with. A bad chairperson can do a lot of damage in this respect.

Existing debating software allows participants to participate in several discussion lines (or "meetings") at the same time. Moreover, it is relatively easy to open a large number of new discussion lines if desired. In order to arrive at a conclusion, discussion leaders (moderators) can provide summaries and proposals to which the participants can react. In order to prevent a debate from spreading like an oil slick, a certain amount of control remains necessary. Given the fact that going into separate "side-lines" does not necessarily prevent progress within "main-lines," such control can be less stringent than in a conventional debate. Here too, bad moderators can be detrimental. However, the rhythm of electronic debates probably makes it easier to correct discussion leaders if necessary.

In all, it seems that electronic debates can be structured more flexibly than conventional debates. This leads to the following potential advantages:

> Assumption 7:
> The opportunities for structuring a debate more flexibly make it possible for in-depth discussion to take place along a larger number of discussion lines, and with a greater number of participants per line than in conventional debates. This increases the chances that participants "have their say," which in turn contributes to the identification and evaluation of relevant arguments.

Assumption 8:
In electronic debates, ineffectual discussion leaders are more likely to be corrected than in conventional debates.

2.1.5 Social presence and convergence

In conventional debates participants not only use written or verbal language, but also non-verbal forms of communication. Moreover, the exchange of ideas can be supplemented with social events like eating, walking, drinking, etc. Thus, there is a high degree of "social presence" (Short, Williams & Christie, 1976). Social psychological studies point out that in such conditions less polarization may take place (Kiesler, Siegel & McGuire, 1984; Siegel, Dubrovsky, Kiesler & McGuire, 1986; Spears, Lea & Lee, 1990) and that there may be a greater willingness to compromise (Morley & Stephenson, 1970; Spears & Lea, 1992) than in more "anonymous" computer-mediated conditions. This phenomenon is not only attributed to a greater degree of group identification, but also to differential power and status processes. As mentioned earlier, the finding that electronic communication often goes along with more equal levels of participation has been connected by some to a supposedly reduced influence of power and status (Dubrovsky et al., 1991; Kiesler & Sproull, 1992). In this view, participants in electronic forms of communication tend to speak out more freely as they are less constrained by the social influence of others, as the latter's social presence is reduced. This, then, goes along with phenomena like "flaming" (Siegel et al., 1986). In contrast, power and status processes would play a more significant role in conventional debates, and provide the necessary social pressure for participants to accept compromises. However, research findings on the willingness to compromise are not consistent (see Spears & Lea, 1992), and the thesis of reduced status and power influences has been contested. Spears and Lea (1994) argue that more equal participation in electronic forms of communication has more to do with time-technical issues (see 2.1.2). According to them, participants can take on a variety of identities in a discussion (see also Aarts & Te Molder, 1997), which implies that the question of whether or not an agent conforms to others can only be answered against the background of the specific identity that a participant takes on. They show that social influence always plays a role if one takes into account the "active identity."

Although we can conclude that power and status are influential in both conventional and electronic forms of debate, it remains likely that a group identity is formed more easily in conventional debates. Hence, it is plausible that in the latter it is more easy to reach compromise on eventual conclusions. Assuming that some degree of compromise and consensus about conclusions is a precondition if one wishes to influence and/or direct policy, we can formulate the following assumptions:

Assumption 9:
The reduced social presence in electronic debates (when compared with conventional debates) hampers the formation of group identity, and reduces the chances that the participants reach agreement.

Assumption 10:
The larger the degree of agreement in the outcomes of a public debate, the greater the chance that the debate has an influence on policy formation and policy acceptance.

2.1.6 Negotiation, openness and flexible identities

The fact that power plays a role in all communication implies that in many ways we are dealing with a negotiation process (see Leeuwis, 1996). The negotiation metaphor is even more appropriate for public debates since stakeholders and their representatives often participate. At the same time such debates imply a learning process. During the debate participants gain insight into diverging views, perspectives and interests. This merging of communication, learning, and negotiation goes along with several complications. Participants tend to forward those arguments which are in line with their position, role and interest (see Aarts & Te Molder, 1997), and find it threatening to give up an argument, adopt another, or engage in a new line of thinking for which the consequences cannot be overseen. Moreover, putting forward particular views and arguments may damage or disturb social relations. A discourse analytical study of a public debate (Aarts & Te Molder, 1997) suggests that participants make use of a repertoire of identities (e.g., group member, stakeholder, layperson, expert) in forwarding and/or combating particular views and arguments. Thus, different identities are not used to present *diverging* views and arguments, but rather to construct a coherent story. Of course, the repertoire of identities that participants may take on sensibly is limited, even if it can be expanded by speaking on behalf of others (i.e., on enrollment or recruitment, see Latour, 1996).

In all, stakeholders often hold back and stick to their views, even if – from yet another identity – they may feel sympathetic to other positions. We frequently see that such *risk-avoiding* behavior reduces the openness within conventional debates, and thereby hampers learning and progress on joint policy recommendations. Both the limitations in the repertoire of identities, and the tendency to stick to particular arguments and views (i.e., the lack of openness in the debate) are connected to the fact that in a conventional debate all statements can be *traced* to particular individuals whom other participants expect to show a certain degree of consistency. In other words, participants can suffer negative consequences from daring statements and identity shifts *because* they can be identified as individuals.

In principle, similar processes to those described above are likely to take place in electronic debates. An important difference may be (depending on the set-up of the debate) that the participants get to know each other less well, and may be less aware of one another's societal positions. This may make it less clear why people put forward particular views and arguments. Despite this relative "anonymity," it is quite common in electronic debates (at least those in policy processes) that contributions can be traced to specific individuals. Participants usually have a recognizable electronic address, and often sign contributions with their own names; both in principle create risks comparable to conventional debate. However, in other types of debate on the Internet (e.g., chat-boxes and newsgroups) we see that people have a greeter freedom to play around with their identities (e.g., in terms of their sex, race, and location, see Turkle, 1995), precisely because they are anonymous and non-traceable. From a technical point of view, it is quite possible (at times) to give participants in electronic public debates the opportunity to communicate in a non-traceable fashion. In such conditions, the risk of suffering negative consequences from one's statements is reduced, so that participants may be more prepared to engage in an "open" debate. That is, they may speak out more freely and explore new modes of thinking. A potential disadvantage is that this may lead to more polarization, flaming, and bending of facts. Nevertheless, non-traceable communication may be an attractive option for individuals who find themselves in a sensitive position due to media attention, the interests that are at stake and/or their function (e.g., government administrators).

The above considerations lead to the formulation of the following assumptions:

> Assumption 11:
> Participants (and especially those in sensitive positions) tend to be more prepared to engage in an "open" debate when they have (at times) the opportunity to contribute to the debate in a non-traceable fashion.

> Assumption 12:
> Within electronic debates it is much easier to build in facilities for non-traceable communication than in conventional debates.

2.1.7 Participation of decision makers and the influence of the debate

Active participation in a public debate requires that the participants have confidence that the results will be taken seriously by policy makers. Experiences with conventional (and electronic) public debates suggest that the involvement of decision makers may be important for generating a commitment to use the results of the debate, and also for ensuring that decision makers can apply the debate results. However, it is often practically impossible for decision makers to play a role in a public debate.

In electronic debates it is – from a logistical point of view – much easier to involve decision makers in one way or another. Decision makers can follow the debate behind the scenes, and contribute if necessary, with or without making use of facilities for non-traceable communication. In the first instance, it is important that the participants know that decision makers are taking part; rather than being "anonymous" the latter may at times be untraceable.

The above can be summarized in the following two assumptions:

Assumption 13:
Actual involvement of decision makers in a public debate enhances: (a) the motivation of participants to participate actively; (b) the chance that conclusions emerge which decision makers can use; and (c) the commitment on the side of decision makers to use the results.

Assumption 14:
For logistical reasons, it is easier for decision makers to be involved in electronic debates than in conventional debates. This involvement will be even easier if opportunities for non-traceable communication are provided (see assumption 12).

2.2   Conclusion on advantages and disadvantages of electronic forms of public debate

The foregoing shows that it is plausible that electronic forms of public debate may have several advantages over conventional forms, given a number of normative criteria and conditions. The most significant disadvantage is that it may be relatively difficult to reach agreement on conclusions among participants in an electronic debate. The most fascinating potential added value is that electronic debates may contribute to creating conditions for what Habermas (1981) calls "communicative action" in an "ideal speech situation." Even if power undoubtedly plays a role in electronic debates (so that a real "ideal speech situation" will never exist, see also Leeuwis 1993: 98) it is significant that the chances for more egalitarian participation seem to be higher in electronic debates. Moreover, the greater openness that is likely to emerge in electronic debates is an important advantage from a Habermasian perspective. Another interesting added value seems to be that electronic debates provide an environment where people in sensitive positions (e.g., administrators and politicians) can communicate safely and easily with citizens. This would indeed imply a reduction in the gap between government and citizens.

III   THE ASSUMPTIONS IN PRACTICE: A PRELIMINARY EXPLORATION

As electronic forms of debate in policy processes are a relatively new phenomenon, few research results are available. Moreover, existing studies are neither designed to make a comparison with conventional debates, nor to test systematically the assumptions generated in this chapter. Nevertheless, it seems possible to draw some provisional conclusions in relation to some assumptions, and give some impressions with respect to others.

First, it seems possible indeed – provided that debating software is already available – to involve more participants in an electronic debate with comparatively little effort (see assumption 1) (Leeuwis et al., 1997; Van Beelen, 1997; Crasborn, 1997; Hamers, 1997).

It must be noted, however, that the moderation of debate appears to require a considerable amount of time, so that there may be limitations of scale in which a debate can take place sensibly (Leeuwis et al., 1997; Hamers, 1997). Thus, the significance of this added value must be nuanced. A second limitation seems to be that so far, participants in electronic debates tend to be mainly highly educated and middle-aged males with a job (Leeuwis et al., 1997; Hamers, 1997; Jankowski et al., this volume). Hence, it is misplaced to speak of a "larger variety of participants" (see assumption 2), unless one combines electronic forms of debate with conventional forms. In line with assumption 14, however, we do see that very busy administrators (Leeuwis et al., 1997) and civil servants (Boussen, 1997; Crasborn, 1997) find it possible to participate more actively in electronic forms of public debate than in conventional forms.

As electronic debates also appear to be dominated by a relatively small number of participants (Leeuwis et al., 1997; Hamers, 1997; Jankowski et al., this volume) there seems little reason to speak of more egalitarian participation due to reduced time pressure (see assumption 4). More generally, it seems incorrect to speak of "reduced time constraints" and "less time pressure" (see assumptions 1 and 3). It emerges that in electronic debates, too, a number of time-related factors have a significant impact on the way in which the debate unfolds (e.g., slowness of the computer system; reading time; response time). Time pressure plays a role as well, as many participants find it difficult to find time to participate in their everyday routine as work and other duties continue as usual (Leeuwis et al., 1997).

Given the reservations with regard to assumptions 1, 3 and 4, it seems unlikely that a wider variety of relevant arguments and perspectives have been raised in the electronic debates studied (although this issue has not been systematically explored). Nevertheless, government administrators and civil servants point out that they have been confronted with new and surprising insights and arguments which they would not have encountered otherwise (Leeuwis et al., 1997; Boussen, 1997; Crasborn, 1997). It seems that through the direct involvement of administrators and civil servants in electronic debates, a number of organizational "filters" are bypassed; filters that tend to remain intact in cases of conventional debate. Although it is too early to draw conclusions, it may be that such direct involvement of senior government staff will indeed go along with a greater impact from the outcomes of debates on policy development (see assumptions 2 and 4).

A striking feature of recent electronic debates is that a number of specific opportunities have hardly been used at all. This holds in particular for the indicated potential for a flexible information provision and structuring of the debate, and for the opportunities concerning non-traceable communication. This makes it impossible to make concluding statements with respect to quite a few assumptions (5, 6, 7, 11 and 12). However, participants in some electronic debates indicate the need for a more active and creative moderation and structuring of the debate (Leeuwis et al., 1997). At the same time, observations in other electronic debates show that the active interventions of moderators often meet resistance or are simply ignored. Thus, the potential of various opportunities for structuring the debate may in actual practice be more limited than suggested (see assumption 7).

With respect to assumptions 11 and 14, the impression remains that it is not so much the government administrators who tend to hold back under conditions of traceable communication, but rather those participants who somehow represent others (e.g., representatives of societal organizations and pressure groups, see Leeuwis et al., 1997). In addition, there are indications that it is tricky for civil servants to participate in traceable electronic debate, as others can be held responsible for their ("semi-black-and-white") statements. Hence, there indeed seem to be particular categories of actors who might benefit from facilities for non-traceable communication.

Finally, it emerges (in line with assumptions 9 and 10) that little convergence is achieved in electronic debate. Participants seem eager to put forward their own particular points of view but show little interest in the standpoints of others and are not inclined to adapt their views.

IV   FINAL CONCLUSION

On the basis of insights derived from communication science, it seems plausible that electronic forms of public debate have – under certain conditions – an added value vis-à-vis conventional forms of public debate. A provisional exploration of current practice indicates that some of the postulated advantages are indeed realized. This holds, for example, for the larger number of participants and the involvement of government administrators. The latter implies a more direct form of communication between government and citizens. For other suggested added values – such as greater variation among participants and more egalitarian participation – there is little empirical evidence. The most significant disadvantage – the assumed lack of convergence in electronic debates – seems to be confirmed in actual practice. Furthermore, it is striking that several specific opportunities within electronic debates have hardly been used so far. Among these under-utilized opportunities are the most fascinating and challenging aspects of electronic forms of public debate, such as the assumed potential for information provision, structuring and moderation of the debate, and facilities for non-traceable communication. Actual utilization of these opportunities may lead to a greater added value of electronic forms of public debate in the future. However, an overall added value is most likely to occur in debates that are directed solely towards making an inventory of arguments and perspectives. If the goal is that participants reach agreement on a joint statement or a future policy, it is unlikely – given the problems that can be expected in creating convergence – that an electronic debate will suffice. In such cases, conventional forms of public debate seem more appropriate, possibly in combination with an electronic counterpart.

TWO CANADIAN MODELS OF COMMUNITIES ON THE NET: SCHOOLNET AND COMMUNITY ACCESS
(www.schoolnet.ca)

by Alan L. COBB

In this paper I will outline recent experience in Canada with two national initiatives, SchoolNet and the Community Access programs. These two programs are helping Canadians, especially our youth, to live, learn and earn a living in an increasingly knowledge-based society and economy.

I   RELEVANT FACTS ON CANADA

Before dealing with the specifics of the two programs and some of their underlying principles and approaches, it might be helpful to give some understanding of the Canadian reality:

• Canada is a constitutional monarchy and a federal state with a bicameral parliament, ten provinces and two territories – one of the world's most highly decentralized federations;

• Canada is a geographically immense and diverse country, a relatively small population, blessed with a vast storehouse of natural resources, a strong and developing manufacturing sector, and a highly competitive service sector. Canada is a leader in communications technology and launched the world's first commercial communications satellite in 1972;

• Canada is the eighth-largest trading nation among the industrialized market economies: some 30 percent of our total output of goods and services is exported, mainly to the United States of America. Interestingly, natural resources account for only 20 percent of exports now, compared to 40 percent in 1963. Less than 6 percent of the workforce is employed in the primary resource industries, compared with 13 percent in 1963;

• the European Union countries taken together constitute Canada's second-largest trading and investment partner. Only 17 percent of Canadian exports to the EU in 1993 were raw materials;

• Canada has one of the world's highest living standards. Canada ranks first among 175 nations on the 1997 UN Human Development Index. In terms of the first measure, 83 percent of households have at least one car, over 98 percent have a phone, with cellular services available to 90 percent of Canadians. Almost 98 percent have colour television, with 95 percent having access to cable TV, and almost 29 percent of Canadian households had personal home computers in 1995, with some 42 percent of those computers being equipped with modems.

- much of the population is stretched along the Canada-US border, and all Canadians are within easy broadcasting distance of American television and radio stations;

- over 76 percent of Canadians live in cities and towns while 23.4 percent live in rural areas (31 percent of the 30 million total population live in the three largest cities of Toronto, Montreal and Vancouver);

- English, the mother tongue of over 16 million Canadians, and French, the language of about 7 million, are Canada's two official languages. The balance speak a mother tongue other than English or French;

- some 42 percent of Canadians claim something other than English or French as their ethnic origin. Over one million of these claim to be of native descent, including North American Indian, Metis, and Inuit;

- education falls within the jurisdiction of the provinces and territories. Of Canadians aged 15 years and older, 57 percent have attended secondary school, 32 percent have gone to a trade school or other type of post-secondary institution, and 11 percent of the population have a university degree;

- about five million children are enrolled in elementary and secondary schools, with over 550,000 students at the community and technical college level, and almost 900,000 enrolled in universities;

- there are over 300,000 teachers in Canada; significantly, some 20 percent of Canadians are enrolled in part-time adult education courses;

- Canada has 4,796 networks linked to the Internet compared to 28,470 in the US. This translates into 114 networks per one million in population in the US compared to Canada's 192. The seven most-wired countries based on networks per million of population are:[1]

Canada (192)	Britain (24)
United States (114)	Germany (22)
Australia (110)	Japan (15)
France (37)	

---

[1] Toronto *Globe & Mail*, 23 May 1997, based on a Morgan Stanley study.

II   THE POLITICAL AND POLICY CONTEXT

To appreciate the Canadian experience, it is important to also understand some aspects of the political and policy environment at the federal level. There are five political and policy factors that may be viewed as giving stimulus to the acceleration of Canada's advances on the Information Highway:

1.   The current federal government, since it came to power in 1993, has a micro-economic policy with a central objective to respond to increasing globalization and its impact on trading patterns and practices, investment flows and competitiveness pressures, including the challenge of adjustment from mass-production to knowledge-based growth; Agenda: Jobs and Growth and Building a More Innovative Economy;

2.   The innovative economy component has four policy pillars – market place climate, trade, infrastructure, and technology with priority assigned to three areas for strategic government intervention: jobs and growth, science and technology, trade and youth;

3.   As part of deficit reduction, largely through cuts in government spending, the government launched a major downsizing of the federal public service (about 50,000 jobs were to be eliminated out of some 220,000, excluding the armed forces, which were subject to proportionately greater reductions);

4.   An unprecedented Program Review is redefining the role of government and the nature of the programs and services it offers to its citizens. One of the major results of Program Review is a drive to develop innovative ways to deliver services, including the greater use of information and communication technologies;

5.   There has been an increased focus on education as a key to better prepare young Canadians for future success in a knowledge-based economy. Clearly, the federal government has given voice and facilitating support in education, but the constitutional responsibility rests with the provinces and territories who are making good progress in reforming their education systems.

In summary, geographic, political, social, economic and trade, culture, and linguistic circumstances created an environment in Canada in the 1990s that is demanding and supporting innovation and change. The proximity and influence of American culture and values make us concerned about ensuring that we have an adequate amount of Canadian content on the Net, especially for use in our schools. Our constitutional difficulties, especially, have made Canadians more aware of the need to share, improve understanding, and expand dialogue at all levels of society. This national need for cohesion-building mechanisms, combined with Canada's long-standing international orientation, gives further impetus to the types of models of community-building and networking represented by the SchoolNet and Community Access initiatives.

III   CANADIAN NETWORK FOR THE ADVANCEMENT OF RESEARCH, INDUSTRY AND EDUCATION (CANARIE)

At this point one important player on the Canadian scene should be introduced: CANARIE. This is an industry-led and managed not-for-profit consortium of 140 fee-paying members. It was created as an innovative way for the federal government, the research community, and the private sector to collaboratively stimulate the development of the Information Highway in Canada. CANARIE's mission is to facilitate the development of Canada's communications infrastructure, foster the development of next generation products, applications and services, and communicate the benefits of an information-based society.

Examples of CANARIE activities are:
- between 1993 and 1997 the capacity of Canada's research and education Internet backbone, the CA*net, was increased 13-fold;
- a National Test Network was established in 1994 to explore new technologies, test hardware and software, and develop new service capabilities. It is one of the world's largest high-speed, broadband networks, spanning 6,000 kilometers and linking the nation's regional research, industry, and education networks while providing high-speed connectivity to Europe as well as Asynchronous Transfer Mode (ATM) satellite connectivity;
- a new advanced networking initiative called CA*net 11 has been launched, involving deployment of a *Next Generation Internet Network.*

It is also significant that in 1994 the federal government adopted a Canadian Information Highway Strategy, created an Advisory Council, and established three overall objectives:
- to create jobs through innovation and investment;
- to reinforce Canadian sovereignty and cultural identity;
- to ensure universal access at a reasonable cost.

To achieve these objectives the government is:
- overhauling Canada's telecommunications policies;
- moving towards having four competitive lanes serving Canadians on the Information Highway: telephone, cable, wireless, and satellite.

CANARIE, SchoolNet and Community Access are part of a clear strategy, led by the Industry department, to use the information highway as one of the primary tools for developing Canada and its international competitiveness over the next decades. The three programs are intended to bring large volumes of additional users on to the Net much sooner than might otherwise occur and, in the process, stimulate the creation of a domestic market for various electronic services and systems which can then be exported.

IV   SCHOOLNET

Launched in 1993, SchoolNet is surpassing all expectations and is considered to have been an outstanding success. "It's very exciting to see what's going on here in Canada in a number of areas; SchoolNet is the leading program in the world in terms of letting kids get out and use computers." (Bill Gates, 1995)

SchoolNet connected 300 schools by 1994. Over 9,500 (60 percent) are now connected. All 16,000 schools will be connected by 1998. In addition, 400 of the 450 First Nations schools and 2,100 of the 3,400 libraries will be connected by the end of 1997. By the end of 1998 it is anticipated that all libraries and First Nations schools will be connected. Each month SchoolNet receives 2.5 million "hits." Every day, on average, someone signs on to SchoolNet over 83,000 times.

But beyond getting kids to use computers, what is SchoolNet?
- a set of over 1,000 Internet-based educational services and resources that stimulate learning and put creativity directly into the hands of the users, especially teachers and students in the elementary and high schools;
- a recognizably Canadian and quality place for learning, with content created, in large measure, by the students and teachers;
- a national facility for collaboration and networking by the partner and stakeholder communities of interest;
- a Network of networks, encompassing such special groups as native Canadians, special needs interests, and the education networks of the provincial ministries of education;
- a place where the many communities can begin to address some of the important national policy issues in education, e.g., telecom access rates and other regulatory issues;
- a partnership of federal, provincial, and territorial governments with the education and industry communities;
- a springboard for the further development of the education services, communications, and information technology industries.

In addition to the core SchoolNet site-specific facilities, there are several associated programs that play an important role in creating a fully integrated and robust national service: Computers for Schools, Grassroots, and the Digital Collections.

Computers for Schools
Started in late 1993, this programs brings educational institutions, communities, business, and provincial and territorial governments together with the federal government to channel surplus computer equipment to Canadian elementary and secondary schools and to libraries. All usable donated equipment is tested, refurbished and then delivered to recipients free of cost. Some 38,000 computers have been delivered to date, well on the way to meeting the target of 100,000 by year 2000.

Grassroots
This is a support program to help Canada's teachers create and run small, curriculum-specific, Internet-based classroom projects. It is creating the world's largest and most comprehensive, pedagogically sound, on-going collections of Internet resources researched, designed, and implemented by teachers and their students (all for the low program cost of Cdn$300 per project). To date some 50,000 students have participated in developing Grassroots projects.

Digital Collections
This is a unique website displaying over 100 heritage collections from the holdings of Canadian archives, libraries, museums, businesses, labour unions and other organizations. Young people, with financial support from SchoolNet, are producing this multimedia portrait of Canada. In the process other important goals are being pursued:

- to develop knowledge-based-economy skills for unemployed or under-employed youth;
- to develop an economical Canadian digitization cottage industry, especially in remote, rural, or economically-disadvantaged communities.

V   COMMUNITY ACCESS

Launched in 1995 as an offshoot of SchoolNet, the Community Access Program is an equally outstanding success to date. Beyond the use of computers, the purpose of Community Access is to provide Canada's rural communities with affordable public access to the Information Highway and to familiarize rural Canadians with how the Information Highway can be used for economic and community development, particularly the creation of jobs and growth. Community Access has four primary objectives:

1.   to raise awareness within Canada's rural communities (defined as having a population of less than 50,000) of the benefits and opportunities of using information technologies and services;
2.   to accelerate access to, and use of, Information Highway learning tools and services that help sustain jobs and growth in rural communities, and to foster the electronic exchange of ideas and information;
3.   to promote opportunities for local entrepreneurs, employees, educators, students, and others to improve their computer, information management, and networking skills;
4.   to foster the conversion of existing government and other services to electronic delivery with a view to providing better and more economical services to all Canadians regardless of where they live.

The Program provides assistance of up to Cdn$30,000 to help cover the start-up costs of establishing a community site, including equipment, Internet connections, staff, training, and technical support. A site is usually situated in a community center, library, school or other public facility. Average program costs to date (i.e., the 50 percent share) is some Cdn$20,000.

Starting with 20 sites in 1994, there are now over 1,200. While the current target is to establish sites in 5,000 remote communities by year 2000, there is a proposal to increase the target to 10,000 communities in the same timeframe. An example of the training and job component of Community Access is the 1,000 local young people hired this past summer to help sites and organizers. Funding for this initiative came from an existing student summer employment program of the federal government.

VI   CRITICAL SUCCESS FACTORS

Experience with SchoolNet and Community Access over the past four years suggests the following as critical success factors:
- think big, start small, leverage your assets;
- provide strong facilitating leadership, and build strong and broadly based partnerships, including with industry;
- bring public information providers on board early;
- use accessible technologies, but showcase more advanced technology;
- seek public input and support by conducting needs assessments and developing responsive action plans;
- include learning about community cooperation and development, and about the technology of networking and the Internet, as part of everyone's experience;
- use the project to build the community's capacity to manage its economic growth and development locally;
- provide a way for members of the community to internalize technology. Build into your training plan a way for people to see how they can transfer computer and information technology into fields where they had not thought of using it before;
- plan carefully for financial self-sustainability, since only 50 percent of start-up costs are provided by the government;
- personal enthusiasm and commitment are essential; recognize and reward champions;
- a visionary approach to finding new sources of employment and economic growth;
- create publicity, generate lots of excitement, and do some good PR work;
- use students to help with the site set-up, technical support, training, and home page development, and use volunteers as well;
- enable and support education content by teachers, students, local groups and businesses;
- maintain clear focus, but create ancillary products and services, especially to generate self-sustaining revenues;
- go international.

VII   THE VOLUNTARY SECTOR – A NEW CHALLENGE

The success of SchoolNet and Community Access led the recently re-elected federal government to commit itself to establishing a program to enhance the capacity of voluntary organizations by providing access to computer equipment, the Internet, new information technologies, and training. This challenge is great, as is the need. The almost 180,000 voluntary organizations in Canada employ 1.3 million people (9 percent of the labour force). In addition, over six million volunteers contribute one billion hours in labour each year.

7.1   Common vision

Beyond infrastructure, networking, and industrial development, and beyond accessing education resources, the common vision underlying SchoolNet, Community Access, and the new Voluntary Sector network initiative is more fundamental and far-reaching. It is to:
- create communities of learners;
- build smart communities;
- stimulate social and economic development;
- facilitate the emergence of sets of values as the "glue" to hold everything together.

More specifically, SchoolNet and Community Access (along with the new Voluntary Sector network) strive to be **the** national facilities helping every Canadian to acquire the skills, learning tools, information and affordable/equitable access to the best Canadian and world-wide resources, and to succeed in a global economy that is increasingly knowledge-based. At the level of the education system, these goals imply that:

1.   knowledge for some could be transformed into knowledge-building for all;
2.   the hierarchy of education will become increasingly open, distributed, and less structured;
3.   the role of the school in the community could be enhanced;
4.   education will be further moved from teacher-based to learner-based.

In social terms, SchoolNet and Community Access can be key nation-building instruments because Canadians, especially our youth, from the remotest corners of the country will collaborate, communicate, and better understand each other.

VIII   CONCLUSION

In Canada, most policy makers understand that expanding public access to the Internet and its effective use makes for good economics, good social policy, as well as good politics. It is an example of that prevalent belief held by government mandarins of days past that: *good public policy also makes good politics.*

However, there is a great need for research into this whole area, not only to assess end results but to help policy makers, educators, industry, and the general public make better informed decisions. Certainly such guidance, particularly from the academic and research communities, needs to be timely, accessible, and understandable to the public at large. The issues and debates should not be restricted to the halls of academe or government or the boardrooms of industry and commerce.

In Canada, at least, the doors into cyberspace are swinging wide open for Canadians no matter where they live and no matter what their socio-economic status. The many initiatives in Canada, represented by the SchoolNet and Community Access models, are dedicated to accelerating the pace of pervasive public access and effective usage of the Internet.

We feel that the benefits of being "first" are great, as is the need in our country to:
- communicate, collaborate, and share;
- become more efficient, productive, and competitive in all sectors, including industry, our public institutions, and the voluntary sector;
- develop learning skills for a knowledge-based economy and society;
- expand business activities and create jobs;
- improve our export performance.

SchoolNet, Community Access, and the other programs are integral parts of Canada's overall strategy to succeed into the next millennium as a modernized nation providing the best quality of life on the planet for its citizens.

TELEDEMOCRACY IN THE PROVINCE:
AN EXPERIMENT WITH INTERNET-BASED SOFTWARE
AND PUBLIC DEBATE

by

Nicholas JANKOWSKI, Cees LEEUWIS, Peter MARTIN,
Margreet NOORDHOF, and Jeffrey van ROSSUM

I   INTRODUCTION

With the popularization of the Internet, concern for forms of teledemocracy has been rekindled and discussions intensified.[1] An explosion of conferences, some accompanied by publications, has taken place recently with reference to virtual democracy, electronic democracy and similar expressions.[2] Only a small number of the initiatives reported, however, have been monitored by systematic research. And none of these initiatives has included specially designed software to support public debate, opinion polling and voting activities.

Such an experiment with supportive software took place in November 1996 in the Dutch province of North Brabant, where residents and interest groups were invited to participate in a public debate conducted on an Internet site established for the event. The central issue of the debate was formulated with the question: "Is space running out in North Brabant?"

The final report of the investigation (Leeuwis et al., 1997) which monitored this experiment served as the basis for this chapter.[3] Here, a portion of the data gathered during the investigation of the experiment is presented. First, though, the model for teledemocracy employed in the experiment, called *Besliswijzer* ("decision assistant"), is outlined. The following section of the paper notes the main research questions and theoretical perspectives which guided the work. The research design is briefly presented thereafter. Next, a profile is given of the participants in the experiment. The major section of the chapter, "participation in the debate," follows. Involvement in the debate by organizations and the provincial government is subsequently considered. The paper ends with a summary of the main conclusions from the final report on the *Besliswijzer* experiment and a series of suggestions for further research regarding this and other models for teledemocracy.

---

[1] Rekindled in the sense that there has been interest in teledemocracy at least since the 1960s, when public discussion emerged around functions and services for cable television systems. More broadly, there has almost always been discussion about the democratic value of whatever communication technology happened to emerge at a particular point in time; see Jankowski & Malina (1996).
[2] An extensive annotated bibliography has been compiled by London (1994); another more recent annotated bibliography has been prepared by Flos (1996). Two journals – *Media, Culture and Society* and *Javnost/The Public* published theme issues on virtual and electronic democracy in 1996.
[3] Previous conference papers and presentations (e.g., Jankowski, 1997; Jankowski et al., 1997) about *Besliswijzer* were also valuable in the preparation of this chapter.

II   *BESLISWIJZER* – MODEL FOR TELEDEMOCRACY

The conceptual model and related computer software employed for this experiment with teledemocracy, known as *Besliswijzer*, is Internet-based and provides various components of real-life political debates: platform statements by interest groups and political parties, information from media sources (in this case, access to current and archived editions of the regional newspapers), opportunity for contributions to discussions on topics related to the general theme, opinion polling during the course of the debate, and finally, a secret ballot at the end of the experiment related to the central theme of the debate.

The developers of *Besliswijzer* made arrangements with the regional government in the province of North Brabant and with a consortium of social and cultural organizations to hold an experiment with the *Besliswijzer* model and software. One of the salient issues in that province is the increasing scarcity of space, and that topic was selected as the focus for a month-long public debate.

It was decided to invite 100 persons to participate in the debate. Both private individuals as well as representatives from organizations active in the province were welcome to participate. The debate was divided into phases, each with a main activity. The first week, for example, was intended for general discussion related to land use in the province of North Brabant. During the second and third weeks, discussion focused on various subtopics. In the fourth and final week, concluding statements and proposals for solutions were to be assessed and – in the form of a general secret ballot – participants could vote for their preferred spokespeople. At various moments during the debate, voting options were provided, including a so-called voting advice and a "passion option," a provision for attaching extra emphasis or weight to a vote.

III   RESEARCH QUESTIONS AND THEORETICAL PERSPECTIVES

The organization which initiated *Besliswijzer* and funded the research was interested primarily in a series of concerns related to how the software performed, the quality of information provided for participants, the degree to which the editorial group was able to function as an independent organ, whether the moderation of the debate was adequate, the value of the opinion polls and the electronic voting opportunity at the end of the debate, and the degree to which the debate provided added value to political discussion in the province on issues regarding land use.

The following research questions were formulated to guide the research activities:
- What were the main characteristics and levels of involvement of the various actors involved in the experiment?
- What was the nature and quality of the discussion during the experiment?
- What was the experience and assessment of the various actors regarding *Besliswijzer*?

Although the interests of the funding agency were decisive in the formulation of research questions and project design, a number of theoretical perspectives also played an important role for members of the research team, all of whom were trained or employed in fields of communication studies. The main perspectives of interest to the research team are briefly noted below.

3.1   Communication between citizen and government

The *Besliswijzer* experiment should be placed within the context of a growing degree of dissatisfaction with the gap between government action and citizen involvement. There is a general feeling that introduction of new forms of communication could improve this situation, but different visions and ideas exist as to what forms of communication are most suitable. Three different visions can be identified. The first emerges from the idea of network management whereby government plays the role of facilitator, allowing diverse interest groups to present their opinions (Koppenjan et al., 1993). The second vision is known as "interactive policy development" (Van Woerkum, 1997). Here, the government retains a central role, but is required to develop better awareness of the context and impact of a particular policy through exchange with those immediately affected. The third vision relates to the ideal of the Athenian agora and the libertarian notions of Thomas Jefferson (1969). Proponents of this last vision are in favor of more direct forms of democracy whereby citizens attain greater possibilities for involvement in political decision making through, for example, referendums.

The *Besliswijzer* experiment is particularly interesting with regard to the specific conditions imposed, and how it may relate to the above three visions. The design of this Internet-based software makes it possible for individuals to discuss issues among themselves, but also directly with representatives of government. Also, the planned opinion polling and voting provide opportunity to assess how these options are experienced by those involved in the experiment.

3.2   Impact of technology

The introduction of new technologies is often accompanied by widespread speculation about the societal consequences of the innovations. On the one hand, these speculations express optimism about the positive transformation of society; on the other hand, doomsday scenarios abound. The relation between the introduction of Internet services and democracy reflects both of these perceptions: a utopia of direct democracy (Becker, 1991; Bullinga, 1995) along with a dictatorship controlled by a new elite (Laudon, 1986). Both visions have a technologically deterministic perception in common. Others (e.g., Van de Donk & Tops, 1992) suggest that the contextual situation of a specific technological innovation may be of importance as to whether an Orwellian or an Athenian development emerges.

3.3   Electronically-mediated versus conventional forms of public debate

The organization of public debate on a variety of social and political issues has been a relatively common practice in the Netherlands for some time. With the emergence of various network-based media, questions arise regarding the possibilities and limitations of this type of debate as compared to conventional public debates. A number of important differences can be identified, based on social-psychological and communicative insights:

- the nature and perception of aspects of time (e.g., moment and duration of debate, sense of urgency, nature of exchanges, use of available time for debate);
- the nature of place and "location";
- the nature of the structure of the communication process;
- group identity processes;
- the identity of individuals in debate and their contributions to debate.

On the basis of such general differences, Leeuwis & Voorburg (1997) constructed a number of hypotheses regarding the specific possibilities and limitations of network-based and conventional, media-supported public debates. The most important differences between the two forms of debate seem related to:

- level of participation;
- intensity of involvement;
- quality of information;
- involvement of particular actors (e.g., government officials);
- influence of debate on political decision-making.

3.4   Interactivity

One of the frequently mentioned characteristics of new media is "interactivity." Many definitions of the term are in vogue (see, e.g., Hanssen et al., 1996), but generally speaking, interactivity is related to the degree of exchange between persons engaged in communicative action. Interactivity is not, in other words, related to the medium of exchange; nor is it the case that interactivity necessarily leads to increased awareness or understanding. Even with these restrictions, it remains valuable to examine the degree of interactive communication which transpires in a system such as *Besliswijzer*.

IV   RESEARCH DESIGN

A wide array of data collection and analysis methods was employed to attend to the noted research questions. An Internet-administered questionnaire was distributed among all 87 registered participants at the very beginning of the experimental period. Some 36 persons completed this questionnaire, a response rate of 41 percent. A second Internet-administered questionnaire was distributed at the end of the experimental period. Due to technical problems the response rate was low. It was decided to redistribute the same instrument by conventional post which resulted in 49 usable questionnaires, a response rate of 56 percent. Basic data were extracted from a short registration form all participants were required to complete. This data was also made available to the research team. A similar arrangement was to be made for the so-called Internet site log data recorded during the course of the experiment. Due to technical problems, however, this data proved unreliable.

Open-ended personal telephone interviews were conducted with individual participants and representatives of organizations. Initial interviews were held with 18 persons; with 10 members of this group, follow-up interviews were conducted. Regarding representatives of organizations, 7 usable interviews – from half of the organizations invited to take part in the experiment – were completed. For an analysis of the contributions to the debate, a selection was made of the discussion lines representing both short and long series of contributions made during the three phases of the debate. Finally, a member of the research team was permitted to listen in on the editorial board meetings held on a weekly basis by telephone. These observations provided insight into the functioning of the board and the periodic assessment of the debate by board members. Detailed information on this and the other research methods may be found in the final report of the project (Leeuwis et al., 1997).

V   PROFILE OF PARTICIPANTS

Given the self-selective manner in which persons chose to participate in the *Besliswijzer* experiment, the group cannot be considered representative of the general population of the province. Interest in Internet-based discussions undoubtedly played some role in the decision to participate, and it would be expected that at least some of the characteristics of Internet users would be reflected in a profile of *Besliswijzer* participants. Also, the special nature of the topic of this experiment with teledemocracy – land use within the province – would influence which persons volunteered to take part in the experiment.

Upon registering to participate, persons were required to complete a brief form requesting contact information and basic demographic data. This source of information provides the most complete overview on all 87 persons who registered to participate. These persons were also requested to complete a short, electronically-delivered questionnaire at the beginning of the month-long experiment. This questionnaire was designed to supplement the information on the registration form.

No data were available to compare the pattern of responses to the questionnaire with characteristics of the total group of registrants. Consequently, it is not possible to assess the degree to which this data is representative of the entire group. This uncertainty must be taken into account during any extrapolation of findings to the group as whole. From these two sources of information, the registration form and the electronically-delivered questionnaire, the following profile of the *Besliswijzer* participants has been constructed.

The age of the participants ranged from 15 to 74 years, with age 40 being the average for the group. Only two of the 87 registrants were female. As for level of education, more than three-quarters had completed a professional training program or university degree. Considering these and other demographic data, the profile of respondents suggests that those who registered to participate in the teledemocracy experiment were well-educated males, employed, who had lived for a long time within the province. The group as a whole had already reached middle age, lived with a partner, had one or more children, and owned their own homes. Apart from the gender bias, this group could be considered a reflection of the established and settled sector of the population with long-term "roots" in the province.

Most respondents had less than a year's experience with Internet services. Half spent less than four hours per week logged onto the Internet; almost a quarter of the respondents said they were logged on more than seven hours per week. E-mail facilities were the primary Internet service respondents made use of; half indicated that they used this service "much" or "very much." The World Wide Web is used to a similar degree; only a few respondents had made use of Internet services like Internet Relay Chat and File Transfer Protocol.

The interest and involvement of participants in political topics was generally high. Almost 40 percent indicated that they were very interested in political topics, and almost 60 percent indicated interest in land use politics. A majority of the respondents (58 percent) had taken part in discussions and hearings organized by either the regional or municipal government. Some two-thirds had contact with regional or municipal government officials on various matters.

The expectations of participants in this experiment were generally high. Three-quarters said they expected to make between an "average" to "large" number of contributions during the debate. Not only was a substantial quantity of contributions anticipated, respondents also expected the material to be of high quality. There were, however, differences of opinion regarding how easily the debate would proceed via computer-mediated communication. One third felt the debate would proceed without problems, while another third expected considerable difficulties and cost. Half of the respondents believed that contacts with other participants would remain distant. In summary, the participants seemed quite interested and active in political matters. They were, taken as a whole, optimistic about the value of this experiment with teledemocracy.

VI   PARTICIPATION IN THE DEBATE

The debate was organized in three phases: discussion of the problem, discussion of solutions, and the voting phase. Individuals and representatives of organizations were able to contribute statements during all three phases. Of the 87 persons who registered to participate in the experiment, 45 were responsible for the 335 contributions to the debate.[4] Table 1 indicates the number of participants, contributions, and discussion lines or subtopics for each of the three phases. Clearly, most activity took place during the second phase of the debate, the solution phase, when almost two-thirds of all contributions were placed in more than half of all the discussion subtopics. The second phase also lasted the longest in terms of time – 15 days, as opposed to 10 days for the problem phase, and 5 days for the final phase when voting took place.

Table 1: *Number of participants, contributions and discussion threads during debate*

	participants	contributions	threads
problem phase	37	123	27
solution phase	33	197	41
voting phase	7	15	4
total	45	335*	72

Note: * total includes 37 contributions which were made mainly as preliminary tests during first weeks of debate.

Upon examination of the largest discussion lines during the problem phase, reflected in Table 2, it can be seen that one line far surpasses all others: the line initiated by Van Geel, political representative within the provincial government responsible for land use policy. Nearly three times as many contributions were made to this discussion line as the runner up, and twice as many people participated in that discussion than the following two lines.

Table 2: *Five largest discussion threads during problem phase*

	initiator contributions	participants	longest chain
Van Geel*	28	15	7
Damen**	10	7	5
Meeuwis**	9	7	5
Van Putten**	9	2	5
Matthijs**	6	5	4

Note: * representative of regional government, ** individual participant

Another way to examine participation is the total number of contributions from individuals and the number of reactions each of these individuals received to his or her

---

[4]Although 335 contributions were recorded, 37 were rejected by the monitoring group for the debate because of irrelevancy. Most of these 37 contributions were tests submitted by participants during the first weeks of the debate. Further, contributions submitted by the editorial group serving as moderator for the debate have been deducted, to arrive at a total of 278 contributions.

contributions; see Table 3. The largest number of contributions (28) to the debate across all three phases was made by an individual participant (Bruggink). The participant from the regional government, Van Geel, contributed half that number (15), but received more reactions – an average of 2.4 – for his efforts than any other participant.

Table 3: *Average number of reactions for active participants*

participant	contributions	reactions	average
Bruggink	28	17	0.61
Van Putten	25	13	0.52
Van Diepen	19	5	0.26
Smit-Zevenhek	17	5	0.29
Van Wijk	16	8	0.50
..	..	..	..
Van Geel *	15	36	2.40
Verkuylen **	13	13	1.00
Baeten **	11	11	1.00

Note: * participant from regional government
          ** participant from organization in province

The data in the above tables suggest that the discussion seemed to revolve around contributions made by the representative from the regional government. The debate was, in fact, an unusual opportunity for citizens to engage in discussion with the representative from government directly responsible for the policy question under discussion. There was a clustering of debate activity around the participant most representative of political power. Much less clustering was evident regarding the average number of reactions the representatives of organizations received. The two organizational representatives noted in Table 4 each received an average of one reaction per contribution. There was also a concentration of contributions among a small group of participants. As reflected in Table 1, 45 persons were responsible for all of the contributions during the course of the debate. Most of these persons, however, made only a single contribution during the debate. In fact, 15 persons were responsible for three-quarters of all the contributions to the debate.

This situation – a small minority being responsible for the bulk of contributions to a debate – is not entirely unusual for public debates, generally speaking, and for electronically-mediated debates specifically. Schneider (1996), for example, investigated a newsgroup for a one-year period and concluded that 10 persons were responsible for 40 percent of the more than 46,000 contributions. Further, often the same persons were found to be reacting to each other during different time periods during the year under investigation – suggesting a limited amount of interaction among different groups of the more than 3,000 persons who were involved in that newsgroup.

VII   INVOLVEMENT OF ORGANIZATIONS AND PROVINCIAL GOVERNMENT

An original intention of the organizers of the debate was to involve organizations in the province in the experiment so as to increase the diversity of opinions presented during the experimental period. A total of 22 organizations directly or indirectly involved with land use activities were invited at the beginning of the debate to submit statements of their perspectives on the central issue of the debate: the scarcity of space in the province. Of those invited, 14 submitted statements but less than half made contributions during the course of the debate. Four organizations made single contributions, and one exceptionally active organization made 11 contributions during the period of the debate.

The expectation that representatives of interest groups would play a pro-active role in the debate turned out to be highly mistaken. The reason, it turned out, had little to do with lack of motivation; most representatives of organizations interviewed were actually enthusiastic about the experiment. The main problem was, in fact, technical in nature: many organizations either did not have an Internet connection or were insufficiently familiar with the protocols to consult Web pages. Those organizations which were equipped and trained to use Internet complained about the slowness of the network connection or other technical difficulties. And, to complete the list of problems, there was a lack of clarity within some organizations regarding the authority to make contributions to the debate reflective of internal organization policy.

This last point was also prominent among representatives of the provincial government as an explanation as to why they did not become involved to a greater degree. Governmental bureaucracy is not accustomed to taking part in public debates or issuing public statements without extensive internal considerations of formulation and consequence. Further, there was division between the politically elected figure (Van Geel) who saw value in the debate and less enthusiastic government employees, who were reluctant to have such a public debate interfere with existing policy. The debate, consequently, never achieved much support within the division of regional government concerned with land use. The experiment displayed a rather ad hoc character and ran well outside the conventional channels for policy formulation.

Most striking was that one of the initial agreements, that a meeting would take place after the debate, with all involved, in order to assess what points had made their way into government policy and thinking generally, proved almost futile. That meeting was postponed twice and finally held in late May, six months after the experiment. Then, at the meeting, reference was made to various statements and ideas generated during the debate, but no indication was made that the experiment would be repeated. *Besliswijzer* was, as far as the province North Brabant was concerned, a one-time experience with limited impact and value for policy development.

VIII CONCLUSIONS

The experiment with *Besliswijzer* provided an opportunity to explore the possible contribution that a new communication technology could have on citizen involvement in political debate. The number of participants in the experiment was limited, because of practical considerations, to 100 persons living or working within the province North Brabant. Ultimately, 87 persons registered to take part in the experiment. Of these registrants, only 45 actually made one or more contributions to the debate during the month-long experiment. And of these 45 persons, a relatively small number – 15 percent – were responsible for nearly three-quarters of the 298 contributions made to the public debate.

The involvement of organizations in the debate was problematic from the very start. A total of 14 organizations were approached to submit initial standpoints on the theme of the debate, and to participate during the course of the experiment. Nearly all of these organizations contributed initial statements but less than half of this group intervened during, or contributed to, the debate itself.

There were considerable differences in intention between the various actors. Some representatives of the provincial government saw the debate mainly as opportunity for communication between citizens and organizations active within the province. Citizens and organizations, however, expected the provincial government to take an active role in the debate.

One of the most important intentions of the experiment was that the results of the *Besliswijzer* debate would contribute in some manner to formulation of regional land use policy. This aspect was one of the most problematic. One reason for this was that the debate was initiated outside the division of the provincial government responsible for land use; the government officials from this department consequently played a very limited role during the debate. Moreover, there was from the very beginning a lack of clarity as to how the debate might enhance policy formation. In fact, land use policy had already reached an advanced stage of completion and it was consequently uncertain what role there might even be for "interesting ideas" emerging from the public debate.

Most participants had expected a greater level of participation from the provincial government in the debate. Despite their disappointment, the political representative for regional land use was indeed one of the most prominent participants in the debate. However, one of the most important intentions of the experiment was that the results of the debate would find some form of reflection in further policy development. The lack of such reflection was a frequent criticism made by participants at the end of the experimental period.

8.1   Further research

This experiment, albeit small in scale, suggests a framework of six areas for further study of teledemocracy initiatives. First, the possibilities for acquiring *access* to the forums of electronically-mediated public debate remain of foremost concern. Access as a concept is complex (see Jankowski, 1995), but two basic areas requiring attention are access to the technology required for involvement (the hard- and software on which teledemocracy depends), and the skills (both technical and communicative) necessary to make use of the technology, once citizens have it at their disposal.

Second, the *control* and procedural mechanisms imposed on the debate may be of central importance in how such an event develops and in the degree of citizen involvement. In the case of *Besliswijzer*, the more or less artificial stages imposed on the discussion may have been determinant. In other situations, the role of a moderator or (as in *Besliswijzer*) an editorial organ responsible for summarizing and assessing the relevance of contributions, may be critical for the further development and direction of discussion.

Third, the range and degree of *participation* in an electronically-mediated public debate is of paramount importance in assessing its value for the democratic process. By design, and because of structural restraints, the *Besliswijzer* experiment was limited to a small, self-selected minority. It cannot be considered reflective of how such an instrument for teledemocracy would function on a larger scale. It remains a fundamental – as yet unanswered – question whether instruments of teledemocracy such as *Besliswijzer* can possibly contribute to increasing citizen involvement and improving the nature of the democratic process. This experiment was much too small in scale and narrow in design to suggest a possible answer. The many restrictions of the technology, along with its limited penetration, are formidable obstacles. But even in the best of technological worlds, where all worked perfectly and everyone was "wired," there would remain serious, nearly insurmountable difficulties, e.g., lack of varied sense data and dependency on text-based communication.

Fourth, characteristics of *contributions* to electronically-mediated debates – and how they are similar or different from real-life variants – remain an area full of unknowns. Much effort is ongoing to isolate and study the various facets of real-life versus virtual communication, often with a view towards formulation of prescriptive statements on how the virtual variety can be organized and structured so as to improve "performance." Leeuwis & Voorburg (1997), for example, have formulated a series of hypotheses based on a review of the literature on computer-mediated communication, regarding the differences between face-to-face and electronic debates, which deserve empirical examination.

Fifth, the *assessment* of debate by participants and other involved actors is of central importance in any overall research agenda. Comparing experiences between real-life and virtual debates, along a range of features, is of paramount importance. And sixth, the *relation* of virtual debates to real-life debates and further political action is uncertain (see Fernback & Thompson, 1995). The same reservation remains for the potential of teledemocracy initiatives: in what manner and to what extent can they influence the real-life political process?

Part Four:
(Business) Opportunities on the Net

WORK AND COMMUNITY IN NETWORKED ORGANIZATIONS

by Caroline HAYTHORNTHWAITE

I COMPUTER-MEDIATED COMMUNICATION IN ORGANIZATIONS

The many new types of computer-mediated communication (CMC) technologies provide co-workers with an increasing number of ways to exchange information. The traditional face-to-face meeting and office memo are now supplemented by electronic mail (email), listservers, bulletin boards, the Web, the telephone, voice-mail, videoconferencing and group decision support systems. As organizations make greater use of CMC, there has been a corresponding interest in understanding how the use of computer media fits with and serves the work of the group, team, or organization. Organizational and institutional decision makers want to know how computer media can aid the information exchange process, what types of information are best delivered through which media, and why people choose to use one medium over another.

Research on CMC and other forms of "groupware" is often technology-driven, focusing "on solving the technical problems of providing multiple-user facilities for any application program." (Bannon & Schmidt, 1991: 7) Studies are directed at improving features of the medium, such as screen displays and functional capabilities. Studies of the use of such technologies have also tended to take a technological approach, focusing on the attributes of computer media, such as what visual, auditory or vocal cues can be transmitted. The lack of cues has been associated with a lack of "social presence" (Short, Williams & Christie, 1976) or a lack of "richness" in the capacity of the medium (Daft & Lengel, 1986). Analysts suggest that rich media (e.g., face-to-face contact), that convey the full array of verbal and non-verbal cues, are best suited for messages, including rich information, e.g., communications that involve negotiation or consensus building, or which include intellectually difficult or socially sensitive content (Fish, Kraut, Root & Rice, 1992; Sproull & Kiesler, 1991; Daft, Lengel & Trevino, 1987).

In contrast, studies from a Computer-Supported Cooperative Work (CSCW) or "social informatics"[1] perspective consider social and organizational aspects of media use. CSCW studies strive to understand the work and information exchange needs of an organization and to adapt the technology to the organization or vice versa (Bannon & Schmidt, 1991). The social informatics perspective expands the social aspects of information technologies to include "the roles of information technology in social and organizational change and the ways that the social organization of information technologies are influenced by social forces and social practices."(*Social Informatics* home page)

---

[1] See the *social informatics* home page at http://www-slis.lib.indiana.edu/SI/
See also the forthcoming issue of *Journal of the American Society for Information Science* (JASIS); details on this issue are available at http://www.asis.org/Publications/JASIS/socialinformatics.html

Studies on computer technology that take a CSCW or social informatics perspective include examination of: the ways in which the adoption of information technologies either change social structures in organizations (e.g., Burkhardt & Brass, 1990), or compete with the existing organizational structures (Markus 1983; Noble & Newman, 1993); how organizational mandate can affect media use (e.g., Markus, 1994); and how social interaction defines and redefines the meaning and appropriate use of media (e.g., Contractor & Eisenberg, 1990; Markus, 1990; Rice, Grant, Schmitz & Torobin, 1990; see also the collected papers in Fulk & Steinfield, 1990). These studies show that the use of computer technologies (including CMC) affects and is affected by the norms and social structures of the environment in which the technology is situated.

Moreover, the use of CMC is not an individual decision. Its usefulness and manifestation in any environment depends on complex interactions between who is talking to whom and about what, the array of available media, the group norms associated with media use, and the norms associated with communicating with different types of people. When a computer network links people as well as machines, it creates and sustains a social network (Wellman, 1997; Wellman et al., 1996). It supports strong, intermediate and weak ties between people – allowing friends to exchange social support, arrange meetings and coordinate activities, and allowing those who have never met to exchange support about a specific problem in on-line chat rooms, or to find technical know-how among members of an organization (Constant, Kiesler & Sproull, 1996; Feldman, 1987). Such networks can support specialized relationships, such as those based on single interests such as a particular type of car, health issue, or hobby (e.g., Baym, 1997; Mickelson, 1997). They can also support more broadly-based relationships such as those between work friends whose collaboration on projects also includes a measure of "socializing."

For the past seven years, members of our Virtually Social Research Group have been studying *computer-supported social networks* (Wellman, Salaff, Dimitrova, Garton, Gulia & Haythornthwaite, 1996). Research by members of the group includes studies of: the *role of CMC* in social networks within organizations (Garton, 1995; Garton & Wellman, 1995; Haythornthwaite, 1996a; Haythornthwaite, Wellman & Mantei, 1995; Haythornthwaite & Wellman, in press); *telework* (Dimitrova & Salaff, in press; Salaff, Dimitrova & Hardwick, 1996); and the *invisible colleges* of scholars (see Table 1). In keeping with CSCW and social informatics researchers, the context in which computer networks are placed is considered an important factor in the ways that computer networks support social relations. Thus, rather than conducting laboratory studies, research by our group members includes fieldwork, in-depth interviews, and social network surveys studying communication in actual organizations.

The principles and techniques of *social network analysis* guide the studies of computer-mediated communication conducted by this group. Social network analysis is the study of social structure and its effects. Analysts focus on *patterns of relations between actors* and examine the availability of resources and the exchange of resources between these actors (Haythornthwaite, 1996b; Monge & Contractor, in press; Wasserman & Faust,

1994; Wellman & Berkowitz, 1988). This focus on patterns of relationships, such as who works with whom, or who exchanges information with whom, distinguishes social network analysis from other analysis techniques. Regular patterns of relations reveal themselves as *social networks*, with actors as *nodes* in the network and relations between actors as *connectors* between nodes. When visualized in graphic form, network structures can be compared to physical networks such as roads: just as roads structure the flow of resources between cities and towns, relationships structure the flow of resources among major and minor actors in a social environment.

The resources that are exchanged can be of many types, including tangibles such as goods or services, and intangibles such as information, social support or influence. Each particular type of resource exchange represents one social network relation. Network relations can be differentiated by their content (work directions, socializing), direction (from a supervisor to a supervisee), and strength (how often are work directions given, how much of a resource is exchanged). Thus, researchers ask questions such as, "How often do you give advice to... [each member of their group]?" The patterns of relations between actors revealed by such questions indicate the likelihood that individuals will be exposed to particular kinds of information. Patterns of forwarding and receipt describe networks that show how resources move around an environment, and how actors are positioned to facilitate or control the resource flow.

The social network approach, with its identification of relations and ties, provides a useful means of viewing Internet and intranet relationships. In a CMC context, the types of resources that can be exchanged are those communicated to others via text (e.g., via email), visual images, and/or audio (e.g., video-mail, voice-mail). For example, actors can share information (news or data), discuss work, give emotional support, or provide companionship via CMC. In organizations, CMC networks can be internally-oriented, supporting intra-organizational activities via organizational intranets, proprietary email networks, and bulletin boards. They can be externally-oriented, facilitating cooperation across organizations or groups. CMC networks also support individuals outside the organizational context, as seen by the vast array of Usenet interest groups. Organizational networks may support multi-stranded ties when co-workers mix work and social exchanges (McGrath, 1984, 1991; Haythornthwaite, Wellman & Mantei, 1995; Wellman, Carrington & Hall, 1988), and they can support single-stranded ties when co-workers solicit help across the internal network (Constant, Kiesler & Sproull, 1996; Feldman, 1987). Extra-organizational networks also support multi-stranded relationships, for example, when family members communicate via CMC. They also allow individuals to maintain single-stranded ties, for example, when individuals join an interest group that focuses on one topic. (For further details on using a social network approach for the study of CMC, see Garton, Haythornthwaite & Wellman, 1997.)

In the research conducted by our group, we use a social network approach to address such questions as: Are the norms and practices of computer-supported social networks different from face-to-face networks? How do gender, organizational position, friendship, work relations, and geographical proximity affect the use of different media for different sorts of interaction? Are computer-mediated ties more stable or unstable than those developed by more traditional means? Do computer-supported social networks flatten differences in status or physical proximity?

Across the studies, we find that intranets and the Internet are simultaneously making interactions more global and more local. More global, in that interactions can, and do, routinely flourish over great distances. More local, because online interactions come from deskbound people who may be less apt to engage with the worksite or community around them (Wellman, Garton, & Haythornthwaite, 1997). We also find that CMC is simultaneously making interactions more multi-stranded and more specialized. More multi-stranded, as friends who work together mix work and friendship via computer networks, and as families add CMC to other, more traditional means of communicating; more specialized, as ties are maintained based on a single shared interest among people who will probably never meet.

II   A SOCIAL NETWORK STUDY OF A COMPUTER-SUPPORTED SOCIAL NETWORK

The remainder of this paper describes, in brief, a study of the computer-supported social networks of members of an academic group.[2] The group, which will be referred to by the pseudonym *Cerise*, consisted of faculty, students, and employees in a computer science department of a major Canadian university. These individuals maintained work and community ties through a variety of media, including the telephone, email, fax, and a desktop videoconferencing system that was under development at the time of the study. As well, they had ample opportunities for unscheduled face-to-face encounters, in the hallway or cafeteria, and they met regularly face-to-face in scheduled classes and research meetings. The *Cerise* culture encouraged work sharing and communication in a supportive, collaborative environment. Work was important in *Cerise*, and included the production of computer programs and papers for course work, presentation, and publication.

The rapid growth of email and other forms of CMC has led to questions about the circumstances under which people use these media to support their work and community relations. R&D environments, such as that of *Cerise*, have been of particular interest to CSCW researchers because of the non-standard interactions that support collaboration (see for example, Fish, Kraut, Root & Rice, 1993). Media use debates have been largely dominated by (1) discussions of how a particular medium fits specific kinds of information exchange tasks, such as collaborative work tasks; and (2) discussions of how group norms determine the appropriateness, and the use, of different media in different settings. A social network approach was taken in initiating this research, asking not just what information fits what media, nor just what group

---

[2] Detailed descriptions of this research can be found in Haythornthwaite, Wellman & Mantei, 1995; Haythornthwaite 1996a; Haythornthwaite & Wellman, in press.

norms prevailed, but asking as well, "How do relationships such as work and friendship ties affect who communicates with whom and via what media?"

The first step in this research was to address information exchange and to determine what kinds of information exchange were of importance to the group. Group members were asked to complete a questionnaire asking about a wide variety of work and social activities that required group members to communicate. The questionnaire gathered data not only on what types of information group members exchanged, but also on who they exchanged that information with, via which media. Table 1 provides an example of the question format.

Table 1: *Example of the questionnaire format*

TYPE OF INTERACTION Members:	*Cerise*	1	2	3	...	20
How often have you received instructions (i.e., exact directions on what work to do) from this person?						
in unscheduled face-to-face meetings						
in scheduled face-to-face meetings						
by telephone						
by fax						
by electronic mail						
by videoconferencing						

How often: D for daily W for Weekly M for Monthly Y for Yearly 0 for never
For in between amounts use e.g., 2D for twice a day, 6Y for six times a year.

Respondents were asked to identify the 20 *Cerise* members with whom they communicated most frequently, and to answer each question in relation to each of these 20 correspondents. For each question, respondents recorded "how often" they communicated with each of their 20 correspondents via each of six media. The total *Cerise* population included 35 co-located members, of whom 25 completed the questionnaire (19 of 26 students, 2 of 4 faculty, and 4 of 5 employees). Although respondents were asked to report on 20 correspondents, they actually reported on their communications with from 10 to 20 correspondents, giving a total of 378 respondent-correspondent pairs who communicated at least once a year.

In order to evaluate how work and friendship ties affect communication and media use, respondents were asked to indicate their working and their friendship relations with others in *Cerise*. Reported working relations could be formal, informal or non-working; friendship relations could be *close friend, friend, acquaintance*, or *work with only*.[3] These reports showed that the majority of ties in *Cerise* were working ties, either informal or formal, combined with friendly relations. The array of work and friendship ties provided a picture of the "typical" *Cerise* member's communication

---

[3] There was also a "heard of only" category, but none of these individuals were listed as one of the 20 correspondents.

circle. This egocentric network consists of 15 members of *Cerise* with whom the typical member communicated at least once a year: they were formally tied with 3 others, informally tied with 10, and had a non-working tie with 2 members of their networks. These same 15 also included 2 close friends, 7 friends, 4 acquaintances, and 2 with whom they worked only.

2.1   Defining the types of information exchange

The questionnaire included 24 questions that asked "how often" pairs interacted on different types of activities. Factor analysis revealed six dimensions from these 24 activities (for details, see Haythornthwaite, Wellman & Mantei, 1995), which were named: Receiving Work, Giving Work, Collaborative Writing, Major Emotional Support, Sociability, and Computer Programming (see Figure 1).

These dimensions revealed the following important considerations about information exchange in *Cerise*:
- The separation and importance of Receiving Work and Giving Work highlighted direction of communication as a key distinction in *Cerise* communication patterns.
- Major work tasks and the two major work products of *Cerise* distinguished different communication patterns, i.e., Receiving Work, Giving Work, Collaborative Writing, Computer Programming.
- Information exchange dimensions were distinguished by whether or not they included emotional content: with Sociability, Major Emotional Support, and Receiving Work including affective relations.

Examination of media use at this stage showed that that the use of unscheduled and scheduled face-to-face meetings, and email predominated in *Cerise*. These means of communication fit with the group norms of the group. These *Cerise* members shared office space in the same building, and thus met face-to-face in unscheduled ways. They also participated in group activities and found themselves together in scheduled meetings both for work (e.g., research meetings) and for socializing (e.g., departmental parties). As well, email accounts were provided to all members of *Cerise* and its use was promoted and encouraged by faculty and students.

2.2   Assessing information exchange and media use in *Cerise*

In the second part of the research, the six information exchange dimensions were treated as six social network relations. To provide frequency of communication estimates for each of these relations, the number of communications for each pair for all of the specific activities making up the relation were aggregated. (For example, the frequency of communication for Collaborative Writing was calculated by summing the communications of the pair for written work and for exchanging documents, see Figure 1; to normalize frequency distributions, they were logged.)

These data were examined in several ways relating to social network measures:

- The strength and range of each relation was assessed by examining (1) the frequency of communication between pairs, and (2) the number of pairs communicating regarding each relation. This was examined for overall communication and for communication via each medium.
- The multiplexity of relations was assessed by examining the number of information exchange relations maintained by pairs, showing how single- or multi-stranded ties operated in *Cerise*.
- The multiplexity of media use was assessed by examining the number of media used by pairs, showing how single- or multi-stranded the use of media was in *Cerise*.
- The number and types of information-media combinations maintained by pairs were examined to determine whether each medium was equally capable of supporting each type of information exchange.

These matters were examined first for all pairs, and then by status, reported work tie, and reported friendship tie.

Information exchange
These examinations revealed that the "typical *Cerise* pair" maintained three of the six information exchange relations. Consideration of both the number of pairs maintaining each of the six information exchange relations and the frequency of communication shows that, most commonly, these three relationships were: Sociability, plus the two relationships associated with work allocation, Giving Work and Receiving Work (see Figure 1). These three relations were the heart of the routine day-to-day operations of this research group, comprising the majority of information exchanges. Not only were people giving instructions on what to do or discussing what they had been doing, they were also providing the sociable companionship that supports work relationships.

Looking more closely at communication by pairs shows that those pairs who maintained few relationships (one or two) typically maintained a low frequency Sociability link, i.e., they maintained a weak tie. When two relations were maintained, pairs included a low frequency Receiving Work relation or a Computer Programming relation that was characterized mainly by attendance at demos, both of which are essentially passive relations. Pairs who maintained 3-4 relations show the profile of the "typical pair" with more frequent Sociability, and with the respondent reporting a more collaborative tie with their correspondent that included both Receiving Work and Giving Work. Pairs who maintained nearly all relations (five or six) included relations that involved mutual trust and knowledge, i.e., Collaborative Writing and Major Emotional Support. As pairs maintained more relations, they also communicated more frequently. Thus, *Cerise* social networks are characterized on the one hand by wide-ranging but low frequency connections based on Sociability, and on the other hand by high frequency communication about many different work and social activities among a smaller number of pairs.

Media use

The typical *Cerise* pair used just over two media to communicate, chosen from unscheduled meetings, scheduled meetings or email. But, the choice of media was not random; the media used by pairs conforms to a unidimensional Guttman scale (Guttman coefficient of reproducibility = 0.92) in this order: unscheduled meetings, scheduled meetings, email, and then the "other" media (telephone, fax, videoconference). In *Cerise*, email was not a "poor cousin" as a communication medium: email was used to maintain both sociable and instrumental relations, and was the main choice for communication after face-to-face meetings. This is due in part to the varied time schedules of *Cerise* members. It is also due to the strong culture of email use in *Cerise*.

In the same manner as for information exchange, a high frequency of communication was significantly correlated with use of more media. Thus, a high frequency of contact was associated with both (1) the exchange of many types of information; and (2) the use of many media. Thus, pairs weakly tied in terms of the range of information they exchange are also weakly tied in the channels they use to exchange that information. Pairs with strong ties show frequent, multi-stranded information exchange and multi-channel information exchange.

Information-media combinations

Examining what media pairs used to exchange what types of information provides an opportunity to address one of the major questions in the media debate, i.e., do pairs choose to use one medium over another for different kinds of information exchange? Results from *Cerise* show that, overall, media use differed more in number than in type, with high frequency communicators using more media to communicate about each of the different types of information they exchanged. However, some differences were noticeable across the different relations.

Media use for the work-oriented relations, Receiving Work, Giving Work, Collaborative Writing, and Computer Programming, was characterized by control: more communications between more pairs were accomplished via scheduled meetings and email than via other means (see Figure 1, parts A and B). Note that these are also the media associated with group norms: i.e., scheduled meetings such as classes and research meetings, and the culturally promoted email. Less frequent but more wide-ranging unscheduled meetings also supported these relations.

For the socially-oriented dimensions, Sociability and Major Emotional Support, media use was characterized by spontaneity, with unscheduled meetings predominating. The media use also appeared to follow the interaction pattern of the pair: e.g., unscheduled meetings for close friends; unscheduled and scheduled meetings and email for work-only pairs. Messages appear to "piggy-back" on media used to carry work relations, particularly for pairs who interact primarily for work (e.g., work-only pairs and formally tied work pairs; see Haythornthwaite, 1996).

Figure 1: *Information-media combinations*

A. Percentage of pairs by relationship and medium

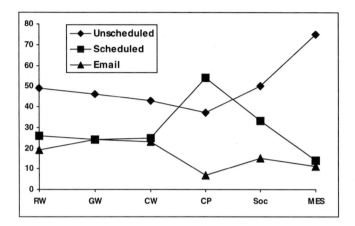

B. Median frequency of communication by relationship and medium

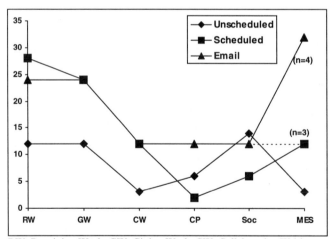

RW: Receiving Work; GW: Giving Work; CW: Collaborative Writing;
CP: Computer Programming; Soc: Sociability; MES; Major Emotional Support
Note: Frequency of communication for MES via email is largely attributable to one pair; without this
pair the median frequency of communication is 12.

Interpersonal ties, information exchange and media use
Each of the communication patterns described above were associated with frequency
of communication: i.e., the more frequent the communication, the more relations
maintained, and the more media used. Who were the frequent communicators in
Cerise? Pairs in a formal work tie, a close friendship tie, and pairs that included a
faculty member as either a respondent or correspondent communicated more

frequently than other pairs and continue the pattern found overall. These pairs maintained more relations than other pairs, used more of all available media to communicate, and used more of all available media to communicate about each relation they maintained.

The type of tie is also associated with an increased frequency of communication and number of media used for types of information that are important for the tie. Pairs in a formal work tie show increased frequency of communication for the work-oriented relations Receiving Work, Giving Work, Collaborative Writing, and Computer Programming. Pairs that included a faculty member show increased frequency of communication for the work allocation relations Receiving Work and Giving Work. Pairs in a close friendship show increased frequency of communication for all the work and social relations and were the most frequent communicators overall (Haythornthwaite, 1996a; Haythornthwaite & Wellman, in press).

III   CONCLUSIONS

This research shows how the social network approach allowed assessment of the types of information exchange and media that were important to the group as a whole, and important to particular pairs. By examining communication from one member to another, without labelling the pairs a priori as belonging to a particular class (e.g., by status), we find communication patterns that describe group interactions and describe subsets of group interactants, e.g., frequent communicators, close friends, and formal work pairs.

In *Cerise*, the type of tie (formal work tie, close friendship, etc.) appears to set the number and types of information the pair exchanges, e.g., formally tied work pairs exchanging work information, and close friends exchanging both work and social information. By following the interactions of pairs, rather than summarizing information exchange and media use across the whole of *Cerise*, we see that the more multi-stranded the information exchanges by pairs, the more multi-stranded their media connections. Thus we can say that strong social network ties are based on high frequency exchange of many different types of information, but also the use of many types of media.

We also find that the types of media used depend on frequency of communication, with the types of media added to a pair's repertoire following a predictable unidimensional scale: from unscheduled face-to-face meeting, to scheduled face-to-face meeting, to email, and then to other means of communication. Both the pair tie and the group norms set this order. Weakly tied pairs communicate infrequently and use few media, staying with face-to-face means of communication. Strongly tied pairs communicate frequently and use many media, adopting first the email, so strongly supported in *Cerise*, and spreading from there to the other media. Thus, group norms may be said to set the order of media used, and within that order, pairs set the number of media they need to use. Instead of finding support for message-medium fit, we find that media use expands to fit the media available, with that expansion progressing in accordance with local norms for media use and with the social network ties maintained by pairs, creating the overall computer-supported social network.

ICTs FOR SMEs: THE SME WINS ON THE INFORMATION HIGHWAY

by Karel UYTTENDAELE

I   INTRODUCTION

During the months of February, March and April of 1997, Fabrimetal and CRIF-WTCM teamed up with the local Belgian Chambers of Commerce and Industry (comprising 35,000 members) to launch an ICT promotion program for the Belgian SMEs, concentrating on Electronic Commerce and on Co-operative Networking between SMEs. It was felt that thanks to Internet technology, ICT was suddenly within the reach of all SMEs, allowing them to make a huge leap toward reaching an ICT penetration on par with or surpassing the big companies. Nevertheless, it was stressed that one should proceed in small steps (E-mail, electronic purchasing, co-operative networking, simple marketing) in order to get acquainted with the new medium, then expand later with an owned Web-site and Commerce Server, then going international.

During 38, 90-minute interactive sessions at 29 different locations, organized between February 14 and April 14, 1997, over 1,600 SME managers were reached with practical demonstrations of Internet-based E-Commerce and Internet-enabled Networking between SMEs. Positive messages illustrated why and how SMEs can prosper in the new global networked economy and how they will stimulate employment and consumption. Ample time was reserved for (lively) question and answer sessions while all technobabble, expensive wording and hypertrendy theories were banned.

Two teams of five people toured the country, carrying with them equipment and software with a value of ECU40,000. The total investment in person-days and depreciation exceeded ECU120,000. Approximately 25 percent of this investment was taken care of by the Chambers of Commerce. Both partners were in charge of *their* investment. Above all there was a strong desire to move fast and to provide *neutral* and clear advice to the participants. Hence it was decided not to apply for public grants nor for commercial sponsoring. All costs were absorbed by the two federations. Only a fraction of the costs incurred were recovered through participation fees.

II   YOUR SME WINS ON THE INFO HIGHWAY

Demo sessions
      Business-to-business E-Commerce
      The virtual giant: SME networking

Discussions
> New ICT within the reach of SMEs
> Dancing with the giants
> New business opportunities on the Info Highway
> Obstacles on the Info Highway

III   CONTENT

During the Roadshow two scenarios were presented.

3.1   Internet-based electronic purchasing (E-commerce)

This scenario demonstrates a stock-keeping system. A company's computer system automatically registers the depletion of warehouse stock and asks the supervisor if an item should be ordered from the supplier; if the answer is yes, the order is automatically placed in the supplier's computer system, etc. This model demonstrates interaction between two companies.

3.2   Internet-enabled networking with complementary SMEs (virtual company)

In this example, known as a virtual company, one company receives an order and decides to hire another company to do part of the design work. The design company in turn needs a mould-maker in order to produce the requested part, thus involving a third company; these companies therefore form a temporary "virtual company." All the communication related to this project is done via the Internet. The *Master of Ceremonies* (MC) talks the audience through these scenarios in a lively, entertaining and non-technical way, while three actors represent the three companies. The scenarios are devised in such a way that all aspects can be shown via a Web browser, projected on a large screen. This enables the presentation to demonstrate clearly and effectively how Electronic Commerce can change the way companies do business. The show is approximately 60 minutes long, but since it always provokes questions, a complete session usually takes around 90 minutes.

During the presentations, the MC gives many practical tips: for instance, he stresses the importance of proceeding in small steps for *quick wins* (i.e., proceeding via E-mail to electronic purchasing, co-operative networking, and perhaps simple electronic marketing), in order to become acquainted with the new medium. Later expansion could include establishing a Web-site, Commerce Server and possibly *going international*.

The essence is to provide positive messages illustrating why and how SMEs can prosper in the new global networked economy and how they can stimulate employment and consumption. The message is kept clear and direct: *technobabble* and trendy *net-head* theories are banned!

IV   POSITIVE MESSAGES

Some positive reflections on the particular position of the SME in the new networked global economy are a stimulus for further discussions among the participants on the roadshow.

4.1   Positive message one: ICT is within the reach of SMEs

Thanks to those two demonstrations, Electronic Materials Management (E-Commerce), and Networking with complementary SMEs, Fabrimetal and CRIF-WTCM hoped to demonstrate that SMEs make a significant leap forward in terms of access to the newest ICT. Thanks to Internet technology, the SME can now dispatch ten proposals to the other side of the world at a cost lower than the cost of one postage stamp.

4.2   Positive message two: The immediate future of E-commerce, or paperless commerce

The share of paperless commerce in the overall business turnover in the US is extremely limited. Over the next two years, the growth between professional partners (between SMEs and their vendors or between SMEs and their professional customers) will be exponential. Remarkably, the expected evolution of interactive home-shopping will only be moderate. Despite massive media attention, this survey rates consumer E-Commerce as small potatoes. We believe this is good news for the future of wholesalers, for the distribution sector as a whole, and even for individual neighbourhood shops.

4.3   Positive message three: There are no more advantages to big business

SMEs often say: "OK, we now have got access to the newest and most powerful ICT. We however have the feeling that the giants of Industry and Services still benefit from many more advantages, e.g., economies of scale." Does this statement still hold?

Peter Drucker remains one of the most astute observers of modern corporate society. He declared in the August 1996 issue of *Wired* magazine:

> In the last 15 years, the world over, there has been practically no growth in big companies. There are a few exceptions – a few information companies. If you adjust for inflation there are very few in the Fortune-1000 companies that have grown. But the medium-sized companies have grown very, very fast over the last 20 years! That is why we have had no rise in unemployment. By and large, there are no more advantages to big business. There are only disadvantages. Big companies had three advantages, and they are all gone. The first was they could get transnational or international money that a medium-sized company could not. Now everybody can. Number two is information. It used to be that nobody had any information. But as you go more international, as the economy becomes global, the access to good information becomes crucial. If you are a medium-

sized company, then the CEO still knows every customer and still knows the industry. You can't know that in the US$10 billion company; you get reports. Reports tell you what your subordinates want you to know. The last and most important factor is that young, educated people do not want to work in the big institutions. That's even true in Japan today. I have an old habit: every September I go into the registrar's office and ask them to give me the folders of my very good students from 10 years back, 8 years back, and then I call them up. They almost all started in a big company for the simple reason that big companies have campus recruiters and training programs. But it used to be that three out of five changed from a big company to another big company. Now more than half have changed from a big company to a small or medium-sized company. They often say, we would really like to have some security, but there ain't no such thing. All of them know that those days are gone. So they say: If there's no security in the big companies, then why should I be bored to death? In the medium-sized company, I don't have the big job, but when somebody has to go to Shanghai to straighten out a distributor, I go. And I have fun.

More reasons that SMEs will benefit most from the Internet revolution are: giants are already well-computerized. During the next two years all the giants will continue to be fully occupied with re-engineering, downsizing, delocalization, the search for core competencies, discussing mergers and acquisitions, discussing innovation strategies, etc.: all activities whereby the management team are not concentrating on their customers nor on their product. In the meantime, SMEs can take further advantage of their built-in flexibility, fast decision making, low cost structure, and 100 percent product and customer dedication.

As the financial threshold to the most modern ICT is low, Peter Drucker sees SMEs from now on dancing with the giants.

4.4   Positive message four: Jobs along the information highway

Will the information society increase net employment? Does this not contradict the popular belief that technology leads to more productivity, however, to fewer jobs and, in the end, to a decrease in the buying power of the masses?

The expectation is that *traditional* SMEs will not only achieve significant productivity increases and become more competitive, but will see hefty increases in their turnover and will need more people. It is obvious that a general implementation of Internet and/or Intranet by two-thirds of all Belgian SMEs will lead to the need for lots of professionals capable of installing the networks, building Web-pages and E-catalogues, acting as consultants, and manning the service provision companies and call centers. It is not unthinkable that more and more young entrepreneurs or even senior managers will take the plunge and start their own businesses. Especially now that the financial threshold for access to this high-tech type of business is rather low. A starter in this type of business does not have to invest in expensive machinery or in large buildings.

Bottom-up stimulation for the implementation of web-commerce servers at the vendors
The SME as a buyer: the bottom-up stimulation by SMEs for the implementation of Web-Commerce Servers, both upstream, at the location of the industrial vendors (the giants), and at the location of the wholesalers. The expectation is that when large numbers of SMEs insist that their vendors place their orders electronically, this demand will lead to significant new and productive capital investments and new jobs! Vendors do benefit significantly from making all ordering information available on-line to their customers, and this goes far beyond savings on the printing costs of paper catalogues.

Top-down stimulation of tele-working, distance learning, home shopping, tele-administration, infotainment and the residential user
SMEs are setting an example for a top-down stimulation in the introduction of multimedia applications for the masses. SMEs and self-employed entrepreneurs operate in close harmony with the residential user. By setting an example they lead the way to a faster introduction of a whole set of multimedia services for the individual consumer: tele-working, distance learning, home shopping, tele-administration, video-on-demand and infotainment. Again, new opportunities for more work.

The export of "broadband" know-how
When it comes to the early use of broadbanded multimedia applications (richly illustrated e-catalogues) Belgium may occupy a particularly strong position: 95 percent of all homes are connected to *the cable*. In the northern part of the country (Flanders Region) venture capitalists have begun to upgrade the existing analogue cable distribution system; within the next three years, 2.2 million residences will be connected to a high-speed two-way digital information highway. To Fabrimetal's knowledge, this is the largest undertaking of its kind in the world. Within the next three years, 6.5 million people will be able to surf at high speed on a broadband Internet.

Belgium must take advantage of a unique situation whereby two capable operators, the incumbent operator Belgacom (with ADSL broadband modems) and a newcomer, TELENET (with cable modems), will fight for the favours of broadband consumers. This will lead to lower prices of bandwidth, and bandwidth is addictive! Belgium may obtain a one-year advantage over other high-tech regions in the use of broadband multimedia solutions like E-Commerce. The know-how derived from an early mass implementation of high-speed multi-media enhanced E-commerce may be exported to other countries and, again, create new jobs.

In summary, Fabrimetal has identified four major levels of opportunity for profitable investments and consumer spending: (1) high-tech starters, (2) traditional SMEs, (3) setting an example through SMEs both for vendors and residential consumers, and finally (4) Belgium as an exporter for broadband know-how. It is not unlikely that these opportunities for extra turnover and spending will eventually help to overcome rather widespread pessimism by leading to new investment and consumer spending, and kicking off a positive spiral of more work, more buying power, more consumption, and so on.

V   CONCLUSIONS

Fabrimetal and CRIF-WTCM hope to have demonstrated that thanks to Internet technology, SMEs and starters are at a turning point in their history. Now they can make a huge leap forward; it is possible to invest in small steps, achieve quick wins, and increase turnover and profits. Examples of such small investments and related productivity increases are the use of E-mail, electronic purchasing, and straightforward networking with colleagues. Fabrimetal and CRIF-WTCM feel SMEs should not wait any longer to jump on the bandwagon of the Information Highway.

5.1   Some observations with respect to the spring 1997 roadshow

1. The average number of participants already using the Internet before attending the roadshow was only 25 percent, despite a stipulation in the invitation letter that some Internet know-how was a prerequisite. It was expected that within the next three months 75 percent of all participants would be on the Net (based on informal discussions after the sessions). The original target, to reach 1,000 SME managers, was surpassed by 60 percent. A positive sign regarding the interest of SMEs in the new medium!

2. The reasons for the success of these seminars: (1) practical applications without hypertrendy theory, (2) the recommendation to get started with small, risk-free steps ("quick wins"), (3) positive messages for SMEs. Eighty percent of all participants evaluated the session as "exceeding expectations" (both on content and on the quality of the presentations). Some positive comments: "enfin du concret," "an impressive, realistic and well-oiled professional show," "thank you for recommending to get started in small steps," "unbelievable that not one single line of code was written for this show," "please give us more of these positive messages," "this event ranks amongst the three most important SME events of the last year."

3. Reactions and comments from the SMEs located in less-favoured economic areas indicate that they are starting to realize that in the new networked global economy, they suddenly have access to the same tools as their big-name colleagues.

4. At the onset: skeptical questions (privacy ...).
    Afterwards: constructive questions (how to...?).

5. The virtual company: a lot of missionary work.

6. Ditto for entrepreneurship.

7. During the first sessions the number of *skeptical* questions was high; as the weeks passed, the number of constructive questions (how to...?) outnumbered the sceptical questions.

8. Much more missionary work will be needed to convince Belgian SMEs to co-operate with complementary colleagues for the creation of *virtual giants*.

9. Ditto for students who need to be motivated at an early stage for more entrepreneurship.

10.   Probably the most important obstacle to the needed accelerated roll-out of Internet access to the 185,000 Belgian SMEs, may be the shortage of IT technicians for the installation and maintenance of all the small networks. Most tasks can be executed by *IT technicians*. For the whole of Belgium only 150 of these have been graduating from *secondary technical schools*; in sharp contrast with a need of 2,000 per year! (This curriculum also prepares for *Industrial Engineering* studies, a degree to be obtained from a technical high school.)

11.   The Belgian federal minister of SMEs called this roadshow an "exemplary effort of networking between professional associations," and promised to take the lead in an interdepartmental effort for the simplification of administrative rules: ("We have to halt the *textual* harassment of SMEs"). The authorities have to move fast with the de-materialization of the paper trade documents as well.

12.   At the end of April, the VRT, the Flemish public TV broadcaster, started a sequel on this roadshow targeted at the same SME audience and illustrated with more E-Commerce and Networking applications.

14.   Another Belgian federation of Small Enterprises, with 80,000 members, has shown initial interest in the transfer of know-how from this ICT promotion package.

15.   All know-how, software, slides, scenarios, scripts and special hardware are easily transferable to any other Belgian or non-Belgian organization interested in pursuing the same goals of promoting ICT for SMEs (Internet, E-Commerce, Networking).

THE CENTRE FOR EDITING EARLY CANADIAN TEXTS (CEECT) AND CYBERSPACE

by Mary Jane EDWARDS

For the last sixteen years the Centre for Editing Early Canadian Texts (CEECT) at Carleton University in Ottawa has been preparing, with the help of computers, scholarly editions of major works of early English-Canadian prose. We have as a result participated actively in the technological revolutions of the past two decades. Despite our use of the electronic highway, Carleton University Press has so far continued to publish our critically edited texts in traditional paperback and casebound versions. With the price of books escalating, however, several of us have contemplated the possibility of mounting our editions on the Internet. In this paper I shall describe what CEECT does, discuss how we use computers, and explain why Cyberspace may not be a suitable medium for editions like ours.

I   CEECT

In the late 1950s, when I was an undergraduate at Trinity College, University of Toronto, Canadian literature did not loom large in our curriculum. In my first year of an Honours BA program in Modern Language and Literature, one of my two obligatory courses in English – I was specializing in English and French – was American literature. This course was to include at its end a brief introduction to the literature of Canada. We never quite got to "Can lit," however, and certainly we were not examined on it. Later, in the final year of my Honours program, I read two or three French-Canadian novels as part of a course on modern French fiction, and in an English course on modern drama and poetry I was supposed to read some Canadian poetry. But the major writers, or those authors like William Butler Yeats and Thomas Stearns Eliot whom we were given to understand were central to the great tradition, took all our time. But even if our professor had elected to cover Canadian authors, we should have had difficulty acquiring the relevant texts, especially those that included early English-Canadian prose.

The situation *vis-à-vis* the teaching of Canadian literature and the availability of moderately priced reprints of Canadian works improved significantly in the 1960s, particularly after 1967, when our centennial celebrations focused the attention of Canadians on our past and created a demand for books about our culture. The first, and most important, of several series of reprints was the New Canadian Library (NCL), which McClelland and Stewart actually began publishing in the late 1950s. Its general editor, Malcolm Ross, aimed to provide a wide variety of Canadian prose and poetry from colonial to contemporary times. Despite his efforts, however, there were relatively few early prose works published in the NCL series, and those that were, through a combination of ignorance, indifference, and the high cost of reprinting small runs of long novels and other prose, were always shortened and often printed from a base text that was itself flawed in various ways. The other series confined themselves almost exclusively to reprints of modern and contemporary authors.

Since the 1960s there have been several attempts to improve the availability of pre-1900 English-Canadian literature. Selections from the prose of our early writers have appeared in several anthologies, including *The Evolution of Canadian Literature in English: Beginnings to 1867* (1973), which I edited, and which, according to George L. Parker, who prepared CEECT's edition of *The Clockmaker, Series One, Two, and Three* (1835-36, 1838, 1840; CEECT 1995), was "the first anthology" to place writers like Haliburton "in a social and cultural context." When one searches for the volumes of these authors, if the early editions are not themselves available, one thinks now primarily of the microfiche collection of "over 70,000 documents" (Bonnelly, 1997) relevant to Canada and mostly published before 1900, prepared by the Canadian Institute for Historical Micro-reproductions (CIHM). But one also remembers the photographic facsimiles in the "Literature of Canada Poetry and Prose in Reprint Series," published by the University of Toronto Press; the "corrected" reprints of earlier editions in the "Maritime Literature Reprint Series," published by the Ralph Pickard Bell Library at Mount Allison University; and such discrete items as Bruce Nesbitt's edition of Thomas Chandler Haliburton's *Recollections of Nova Scotia: The Clockmaker; or The Sayings and Doings of Samuel Slick, of Slickville* (1984), the first series of *The Clockmaker* that appeared in the *Novascotian,* the Halifax newspaper published by Joseph Howe, in 1835-36. None of these enterprises, however, has produced, or was intended to produce, the scholarly editions that at least some of our early prose works so richly deserve and that we so badly need, if we are going to understand as thoroughly as we must our Canadian past.

From the time that we received our first grant from the Social Sciences and Humanities Research Council of Canada in 1981, the mandate of the Centre for Editing Early Canadian Texts has been to prepare such editions. So far, eleven volumes have appeared in the CEECT series. They include Frances Brooke's *The History of Emily Montague* (1769; CEECT 1985), considered to be the earliest Canadian novel; James De Mille's *A Strange Manuscript Found in a Copper Cylinder* (1880; CEECT 1986), a fantastic romance frequently classified as science fiction; Susanna Moodie's *Roughing It in the Bush or Life in Canada* (1852; CEECT 1988), an autobiographical narrative about life in Upper Canada in the 1830s; and John Richardson's *The Canadian Brothers* (1840; CEECT 1992), an historical tale about the War of 1812 based on its author's own experiences as a gentleman volunteer on the northwest frontier in 1812 and 1813. Our most recent publication is Catharine Parr Traill's *The Backwoods of Canada* (1836; CEECT 1997), a series of letters that provides an account of her life in the country north of Peterborough in the years immediately following her emigration from England to Upper Canada in 1832. In preparing these editions we follow more or less the principles and procedures associated with the so-called Greg-Bowers-Tanselle school of Anglo-American editing. Thus, each edition has a critically edited text with such supporting apparatus to document how we established the text as a list of "Emendations in Copy-text," and an "Historical Collation" that records variant readings among the authoritative versions. Because we wish to ground each critically edited text in its British North

American and Canadian contexts, we surround it with an introduction, annotations, and other apparatus that explain the history of its creation and publication and locate its contents in their own time and place.

II   CEECT AND COMPUTERS

One reason why we have been able to make the progress that we have in this ambitious Canadian editorial and cultural project is that from its beginnings we went "hi-tech." We began to plan CEECT in the fall of 1979. I remember the shock that I felt when at one of our meetings in October of that year, a colleague suggested that we really should consider computerizing our as yet unnamed and ill-defined enterprise. From then on, with increasing frequency, at ever greater length, and with progressively more detail, the use of computers in editing in general and in our editing in particular was discussed as we answered the ultimate – and in some ways ultimately revolutionary – question: should we computerize CEECT? At the time the most sensible answer to this question was by no means clear. There were microcomputers that were chiefly programmed for word-processing. There were programs written for mainframe computers that would edit texts in various basic ways, compile concordances, and even run collation programs to compare texts. But systems of programs that would help in the preparation of scholarly editions like ours were few. Even if one did manage to hear about them, furthermore, the language or languages in which the programs were written, the software of which they were a part, and the hardware on which they ran, were frequently incompatible with the languages, software, and hardware available at Carleton.

Still, what had been done and what we were assured could be done by the specialists in Computing Services at the University convinced us that the computer would help us to analyze efficiently the data that we gathered about our works, and to reach the level of accuracy that we desired for our editions. And thus we began the dual process of entering versions of the works that we were editing on the computer so that they could be manipulated electronically, and of inventing the programs with which to manipulate them. By 1987 students in Computer Science at Carleton, whom we employed each summer, had prepared a series of seventy discrete programs that were written in five different languages. These programs, designed to run on Carleton's mainframe computer, not only allowed us to collate our texts in various ways but also to do word searches, prepare parts of the apparatus, and act as our own compositors. Even now, although we have progressed through several generations of microcomputers, personal computers, and laptops, we still use these programs on the mainframe.

III   CEECT AND CYBERSPACE

Inasmuch as these programs have also involved shipping electronic versions of our texts from microcomputer to mainframe to personal computer, we have from the beginning been communicating electronically. We have also used the Internet in various ways. For several years I have taken advantage of the electronic highway to explore the holdings of libraries in various parts of the world and to converse with colleagues in Australia who are involved in a project on Australian literature that is partly modeled on CEECT. A few months before the publication of *The Backwoods of Canada*, when, incidentally, our work on the edition was supposedly complete, a graduate student in History at Carleton, who had been a research assistant for Michael A. Peterman, the editor of the CEECT text, went on the Net to ask for help in identifying the source of a reference in Traill's narrative that we had not found. The answer, Oliver Goldsmith's *The Vicar of Wakefield,* came back almost immediately. I was delighted, but also chagrined, for we should have recognized the allusion ourselves. During the same period, from my office in the Institute of Commonwealth Studies at the University of London, where I spent the fall of 1996, I was able to communicate with Michael on such matters as the location of a letter by Catharine Parr Traill at the Suffolk County Record Office in Ipswich, Suffolk. From London I was also in frequent correspondence via electronic mail with my research assistant and secretary at Carleton.

We have versions of each of our texts, including, most importantly, the CEECT scholarly editions, in electronic form. We have electronic links to people and places around the world. With the increasing cost of our books – the price of our paperbacks, for example, has risen from just over Cdn$5 to just under Cdn$30 in the twelve years that they have been appearing – and the fragility of all University presses, including Carleton University Press, in Canada, we have at least two incentives. Why, then, should we not practice Entrepreneurship, use the most contemporary means of Communication, and send our exempla of Canadian Culture and Identity into Cyberspace? Why not, indeed?

There is one obvious problem: our codes for paragraphs and other features of the text, developed almost fifteen years ago, do not conform to the new standards, insofar as there are standards. We or someone else, therefore, would have to rewrite our works in certain ways. And that would cost more money, personpower, and time than CEECT has. Inevitably it would also involve the inscription of errors into our editions. But even if these difficulties could be overcome, I still have reservations, the first of which follows from the issues of compatibility and portability that I have just raised.

3.1   Obsolescence

Having lived through almost two decades of the electronic revolution, I have not only worked on many generations of hardware, but I have also learned my way through several programs of software. These experiences have been exhilarating, for it is always gratifying to acquire new skills. They have also been costly from the point of view of money and time. Above all they have been wasteful, particularly of data. With every change we have faced three choices with regard to our information. We could transport our data to the new machine; we could abandon our data on the old machine and hope that we could continue to read it for a short time at least; or we could save our data in a different medium, in our case that of print. Over the years we have opted for the last solution. We have hardcopy versions of our data, therefore, but insofar as they only exist electronically on obsolete machines, or disks, or tapes, in obsolete languages, or programs, we have lost our ability to manipulate them. As the generations of computers multiply and the information we store on them explodes, in fact, I have a vision of a labyrinth of dead hardware and dysfunctional software that is so huge and complex that it withstands even our most innovative version of Ariadne's thread, and therefore withholds our now forever unattainable and therefore permanently unknowable information. My other reservations are less apocalyptic.

3.2   Cheapness

One of the arguments that I have heard in support of Cyberspace is that it is cheap. For those of us who teach at universities, especially at universities whose administrators have decided that computers cost less and are far less trouble than colleagues and support staff, our hardware, software, hydro, communication systems, and even ergonomic chairs and tables do come apparently without cost. "Cheap" becomes "expensive," however, when one begins to purchase these items for oneself. And many people, including many of those general readers at whom we partly aimed our editions, choose not to spend their money on what they often consider pretty pricey toys. There are others, however, who for various economic, and social, reasons have no choice about their use of Cyberspace: it is simply not available to them. These people include the poor; they also include more women than men and, one suspects, in Canada at least, more native Canadians than other Canadians and more blacks than whites. Books, in fact, especially if they can be borrowed from public libraries, are still, it seems to me, the pre-eminent democratic medium for the transmission of at least certain aspects of both popular and high culture.

3.3   Availability

Names like the "World-Wide Web" give the impression that material on Cyberspace is universally available. And certainly if one's universe is largely English-speaking and confined to such continents as Australia, Europe, and North America, then one does potentially have world-wide access. But this verity does not hold in other places. In the last few years I have had much to do with the Canadian Studies programs in India, programs that, incidentally, are rather generously supported by the Canadian government. I have as a result talked to, and worked with, many Indian academics both in their country and mine. Their main problem is the acquisition of Canadian material. To those who teach Canadian literature, I have suggested various solutions, including the use of microfilm and microfiche – for early Canadian texts I am constantly recommending the CIHM series, for example. I also enthuse about the value of electronic mail to establish where material on Canada is located in India. To these suggestions I have received one – may I say universal? – response. "But, Madam, you do not understand. We have so many power failures and other technical difficulties that even if we did have these media, we should not be able to get at them." India is a sophisticated country, and it has a thriving computer industry. Still, the best way to disseminate Canadian literature there is through actual copies of books and periodicals. What applies to India is also true for many other countries. At the present time, then,

Cyberspace cannot be used for the transmission of artifacts of Canadian culture to most of the world's population.

3.4   Copyright and copying

The texts that we have edited at CEECT are themselves in the public domain. The editions that we prepare, however, are copyrighted. They thus become subject to all the laws that govern copyright in Canada and elsewhere. These have become quite complex for a variety of reasons, including the photocopying industry that has developed in the last twenty years. In Canada, as a result, we have such organizations as the Public Lending Rights Commission and CANCOPY.

Since the idea of mounting our CEECT editions on the Net was first bruited, I have been trying to imagine how to solve the problems of copyright on, and copying from, the Net. If our editions were available in Cyberspace, should the User pay to read them? If s/he should pay, how much should the payment be? By what means should it be collected? If these editions were available on the Net, should we allow them to be copied? If they could be copied, should they be available for reproduction in their entirety or in part? Finally, given the ease with which, despite smart cards, computer hackers operate, how could the copying of all or part of these editions be controlled anyway? I have no answers to these questions, but it seems to me that these problems must be solved more satisfactorily than they are today if we are really going to send editions like those prepared by CEECT into Cyberspace.

3.5   Canadian culture and identity

So far the reservations that I have discussed are not limited to either a country or a culture. They have been and are being debated in various parts of the world. My thoughts on these subjects were stimulated, for example, by *The Politics of the Electronic Text* (Chernaik {...}, 1993), the proceedings of a one-day conference held at the Centre for English Studies at the University of London in 1993, that explored with a good deal of wit and wisdom the "problems" as well as the "opportunities" of electronic publishing. My final – and most serious – reservation is connected specifically to Canada and Canadian culture. I have spent almost two decades attempting to undo the damage done to early Canadian authors by largely foreign publishers who often stole our prose works, usually revised them to a greater or lesser degree, and always appropriated them culturally by wrenching them out of their original contexts. Having prepared reliable texts of these important early Canadian works, surrounded them with apparatus that help to explain their histories, and enclosed them in paperback covers coloured and illustrated to suggest aspects of their contents, I am, I think, justifiably worried about the preservation of the integrity of our editions in a medium like Cyberspace. This "inquietude," however, is more than that of a mother hen fussing over her chicks – and I certainly worry in this way in regard to these editions. My real concern is that if we do mount these artifacts in Cyberspace, even if we post them with all the guarantees of textual and other integrities of which we can conceive, their new existence in virtual reality will change and shape them in unexpected and at this point, unknown, ways. Some of these transformations may well be neutral or even theoretically and practically desirable. Some of them, however, will surely detach these editions, as they float through electronic space, from their grounding in the historical and contemporary realities from which they came. These works, then, conceived by their authors as contributions to the medium of print, will almost certainly be weakened as witnesses to this culture of newspapers, periodicals, and books. Most importantly for Canadians, however, these foundation texts of our literature will definitely be damaged, perhaps even destroyed, as examples of Canadian culture and identity.

Part Five:
The Role of Government

THE POSITION OF FLANDERS WITH REGARD TO SOME INTERNET-RELATED MATTERS

by Luc VAN FLETEREN

I THE REGULATORY ROLE OF GOVERNMENT

According to a recent Gallup survey, European businesses want government to do more to police the Internet. More than 80 percent of companies surveyed said regulators should do more to prevent fraud on the Internet, 78 percent wanted an increased effort to target pornography and the confidentiality and security of data (*The Wallstreet Journal Interactive Edition*, 1997).

The question is whether this response is due to lack of understanding or fear. It is probably both. The Government of Flanders sees an important but minimalist role for government in regulating the Internet. The danger is that overreaction to some issues like pornography will lead to over-regulation, with too much regulation stifling the potential growth of the Internet. In principle, whatever is illegal on the street should be illegal on the Internet. However, Internet service providers should not be asked to play the role of censor. The most dangerous situation is where Internet providers or telephone companies are asked to play judge on the legality of the content. There are democratic legal systems in existence, including court systems and police. We don't need to create a separate entity for the Internet. The issue of illegal and harmful content over electronic networks needs to be addressed in a manner which is proportional to the problem and which recognizes the importance of the principle of freedom of speech. The identification and implementation of appropriate and effective global solutions requires international co-operation.

The general guiding principle should be twofold: first, using existing laws wherever possible rather than creating new ones; and second, always erring on the side of a limited number of regulations until activities on the Internet assume a clearer shape. Some solutions to apparently intractable Internet problems are likely to emerge from the market itself (*The Economist*, 1997a). These principles are not only true for illegal and harmful content but are also applicable for most of the other hot issues like multimedia content, intellectual property rights, and transaction safeguards: cryptography and the protection of privacy and personal data.

1.1 Bit tax

Globalization and the expansion of business conducted over the Internet will make it harder to track and hence tax transactions. One possible response would be taxing all electronic flows of information, the so-called bit tax. Many European politicians support such a tax, partly because Europe (with high rates of VAT) stands to lose most from untaxed electronic sales. The basic problem with a bit tax is that it is indiscriminate: it taxes not just on-line transactions but all digital communications (*The Economist*, 1997b). It would stunt the growth of that industry. The creation of employment in Flanders is mainly supported by future-oriented service sectors and by some industrial sectors where communication is important. A similar bit tax risks curtailing the development in some promising sectors. Whoever wants to sustain yesterday's employment by levying taxes on tomorrow's, is jeopardizing both.

1.2   Government as catalyst

In some areas, market forces alone will not be sufficient. The role of government consists in creating the optimal climate and conditions for the development and deployment of infrastructure, applications and services and is not limited to the establishment of the appropriate regulatory frameworks and safeguards. Government also has an important role to play as a catalyst for the enhanced use and development of the information society.

Public administration, whether at a national or regional level, is first and foremost an **information service**. Rather than acting as an infrastructure provider, as in the old days, public authorities should concentrate on being a high-value content provider, opening up new market opportunities for private partnerships in the development, distribution and maintenance of new information systems. At the same time, public authorities should ensure that information is understandable and also available in a non-electronic form (European Commission, 1997).

1.3   Universal service and public access

As the information society develops and more elements of the economy, education and entertainment are linked to networks, it is increasingly important that the less advantaged members of society are not excluded or left behind by being unconnected. Setting up public access points in such areas as schools, libraries and community centers is crucial for providing new open gateways to the information society (OECD, 1997a: 10). Subsidies for universal service provision, if necessary, should be transparent. Mechanisms of competitive bidding should be used so as to guarantee that the best and most innovative operators and service providers are awarded. In Europe, most of the state subsidies for Internet-based projects are going to state-owned telephone companies that hold a monopoly grip on Internet infrastructure in Europe.

An important role for government to play in policing the Internet is the application of **competition law** to ensure that telephone companies do not abuse their monopoly positions. According to OECD figures, the penetration of Internet hosts is five times greater in competitive than in monopoly markets. Internet access in countries with telecommunication infrastructure competition has grown six times faster than in monopoly markets. The current trend of rebalancing call tariffs by lowering long-distance charges and raising local charges is increasing the cost of a range of on-line services like the Internet, with users in monopoly markets being worst affected. The additional price paid on average by users in monopoly countries, although already far greater than the average for competitive markets, is growing (OECD, 1997b: 234).

Another major concern of the Government of Flanders is **cultural and linguistic diversity**. Unless new applications are harmonized with custom and cultures, they are unlikely to be developed for a wide spectrum of services. Applications have to be easily understood by the general public. While it is true that the most of the content currently on the Internet is in English, the balance appears to be changing in line with growing access to the Internet throughout the OECD area. According to Digital Equipment Corporation, the operators of the Alta Vista search engine, an estimated 25 percent of all web content is written in languages other than English (OECD, 1997c: 52). One reason for the shifting balance, as noted by the European Ministerial Conference in Bonn, is that the Internet lowers the barriers of entry for the creation and dissemination of content in different languages (Ministerial Conference Bonn, 1997: 33).

Media ownership restrictions or even production quotas in most countries have traditionally involved not only the goal of ensuring a degree of pluralism within the national boundary, but also of protecting national and regional cultures. Such ownership restrictions and production quotas may be expected to come under pressure vis-à-vis their effectiveness in a global information society. But open competitive markets must not be viewed as antagonistic to concepts of cultural and linguistic diversity. On the contrary, in those markets where there is vibrant competition, low prices, and rapid diffusion, domestic industries have an incentive to produce content at a much more rapid rate, and of higher quality, than in closed markets. Cheaper communication may make it easier to set up a channel showing American cartoons, but they will also make it easier to create special television channels devoted to Flemish films. New technologies such as webcasting have opened up a new way to deliver many radio services aimed at international audiences. Through webcasting, *Radio Vlaanderen* can now be heard in English and Dutch all over the world. New channels will be open to disseminate minority cultures, allowing individuals and businesses the chance to create and distribute low-cost content. The first annual report from the Information Society Forum argues that Europe's cultural and linguistic diversity will be strengthened, not threatened, creating new global opportunities for information products that exploit our rich heritage (The Information Society Forum, 1996).

II   THE POLICY OF FLANDERS

I will only go briefly into some initiatives. For a more complete overview, I refer readers to the policy paper about multimedia, which is available in English as well as in Dutch (Van den Brande, 1996: 39). The Government of Flanders has decided to make the Internet accessible to the largest possible public. As of 1997, free access to the Internet will be made available in all Flemish libraries, schools of higher education, and a first group of 150 secondary schools. In the medium term, all primary and secondary schools will be connected.

The most ambitious initiative is *Telenet Flanders*. The goal of *Telenet* is to convert the existing cable networks into an interactive broadband network, which, apart from the existing broadcasting services, also offers telephone, Internet and other multimedia services. The complete regional network overlay will be finished by 2002. *Telenet Flanders* already delivers fast Internet access in some areas, and started with telephony services on January 1, 1998. In converting the cable network, *Telenet Flanders* is one of the world's pioneers. This is easily the most significant cable broadband project in the world. The BEF47 billion (US$1.4 billion) project dwarfs other multimedia-ready cable city projects such as those in Amsterdam, Atlanta, Georgia, and Rochester, New York, none of which covers more than 500,000 homes (*Communications Week*, 1997). Telenet will cover up to 2.2 million households and 11,000 businesses. The more than 95 percent cable penetration, the highest worldwide, is a unique plus for Flanders. The role of the Flemish authorities was confined to gathering the different parties: the "intercommunales" (intermunicipal societies), the operator (US West) and the financial backers. *Telenet* is now a fully private enterprise.

In order to take advantage of this lead in the field of infrastructure, the Flemish authorities will concentrate their efforts on tele-administration, tele-commerce and the use of information technology in education. Government cannot afford to be fixated on offering an excellent infrastructure. The Flemish government is also to pursue a policy that stimulates the development of new services. The uses that people, companies, schools, and authorities presently make of information technology are critical success factors for tomorrow's knowledge society. This multimedia approach has to be realized by way of partnerships where the end users, government, schools and companies divide up tasks according to interest, skill and responsibility.

The tele-administration program provides for guiding and helping implement a limited number of pilot projects in the Ministry of Flanders and the Flemish public institutions. As far as the companies are concerned, they will of course have to be the driving force behind the introduction of tele-commerce. A quick and general introduction of tele-commerce for small and medium-sized businesses will come to revive the SME sector and create new knowledge and new industries. Furthermore SMEs and the self-employed are close to the residential user, and tele-commerce is, by virtue of its model function, an ideal catalyst for the quick introduction of other broadband services like tele-working, tele-learning and tele-shopping. These new services will also create extra jobs. The role of government is confined to developing awareness.

From 1998, an ambitious program was started to stimulate the use of information technology in schools. In the near future, every class in Flanders is to have a sufficient number of computers, and every school in Flanders is to have access to the Internet. In addition, specific training projects will be required in education and continuing education so as to familiarize people with the specific language of multimedia.

QUÉBÉCOIS POLICY AND THE DEVELOPMENT
OF THE INFORMATION HIGHWAY

by Serge PROULX

The purpose of this article is to describe the Québec government's position with regard to the Internet. Right away, I should emphasize that for the moment, despite its sovereigntist project, the Québec government remains a *provincial* government within the Canadian framework. That means that the government of Québec does not control the entire range of legal and regulatory instruments that would permit it to frame – at a national level, at least – the development of a technological network like the Internet. That said, from around 1995 the Québec government has demonstrated a definite interest in this type of technology and in the future prospects that it represents. The following will sketch out the broad directions of forthcoming policy based on the position statements and government actions undertaken in the last two years.

I   MAIN THRUSTS OF QUÉBÉCOIS INFORMATION HIGHWAY POLICY

Following a report submitted to the Premier in July 1995 (*Comité consultatif sur l'autoroute de l'information*, 1995) – generally known as the Berlinguet report, and qualified by most observers as "techno-optimistic" to the point of lacking any critical distance – the government's first significant political act in the information highway sector was the creation, on August 2, 1995, of the *Secrétariat de l'autoroute de l'information* (SAI):

> Its role: to define the government's orientations, elaborate a strategy for implementing the information highway in Québec and coordinate the strategy's execution with public and private partners.[...] The Québec government views as critical the development of the information highways. They contribute to modernizing the public apparatus and to improving the quality of services offered to citizens, to institutions and to businesses. Furthermore, the presence of a critical mass of content in French, useful at work, at school and in leisure, will undoubtedly favour the dissemination of our culture and language (Louise Beaudoin, Minister of Culture and Communications; our translation).

On April 2, 1996, the Secrétariat made public a working paper, entitled "Towards a Strategy for Implementing the Information Highway in Québec" (*Pour une stratégie de mise en oeuvre de l'autoroute de l'information au Québec*). This document presented the basic steps and approach proposed by the Secrétariat to the government of Québec for implementing the information highway:

> The document establishes the objectives targeted, the principles to be respected and the goals to attain in the next three to five years. It also proposes the means

for action and an approach for concretizing the goals retained, with a view to favouring the deployment of the information highway in Québec. The basic orientations (that is to say the objectives targeted, the general principles and the goals retained), as well as the means, have been examined, expanded upon and accepted by the Council of Ministers (*Conseil des ministres*) and the Interministerial Committee on Information Technologies (*Comité interministériel sur les technologies de l'information*). As for the means of action, ministries and public bodies are now invited to evaluate their opportunity and feasibility in the framework of the preparation of their plan of action. They will also proceed to the establishment of other necessary means of action for concretizing the goals that were retained. These, as well as the results of the consultation carried out by the Secrétariat de l'autoroute de l'information, will be integrated into a Québécois strategy for implementing the information highway (*Secrétariat de l'autoroute de l'information*, 1996).

The document defines the special role of government in this area:

The State's objectives with regard to the deployment of the information highway should especially pursue the applications which will allow Québec to maintain its place among advanced, high-performing societies. Social, linguistic and cultural preoccupations and promotion of identity will mark out the path for economic development. In this context, the government will play the role of **catalyst**, of **regulator** and of **partner**. This role will be realized through the following actions:

– The **creation of a favourable environment** for eliminating obstacles, particularly legal and regulatory obstacles in the commercial sectors, and by developing awareness among the public and decision makers of the importance of new information and communication technologies.
– The **coupling of its strategies with those of businesses** providing infrastructures or services, in order to stabilize the rules of the game, to harmonize development, to adapt labour training programs and to reinforce investor confidence.
– An evolution towards a **model user** role, which will contribute to an improvement of productivity as well as to the rapid establishment of a critical mass of services and of an important francophone presence.
– The legal and regulatory interventions necessary to ensure that the deployment of the information highway contributes to **consolidating the gains of the Québécois society** and is **respectful of its fundamental values, of its culture and of its language**.
– **Financial support for particular structural initiatives** which facilitate the deployment of the information highway and accelerate its development and use by individuals, institutions and businesses (*Secrétariat de l'autoroute de l'information*, 1996).

Moreover,

> the government of Québec is looking at six general objectives for the deployment of the information highway:
>
> 1. the economic and regional development of Québec;
> 2. the achievement of productivity gains in the government apparatus;
> 3. the dissemination of Québec and of Québécois expertise abroad;
> 4. better information for citizens, and services which are more user-friendly and better adapted to living and working conditions;
> 5. the improvement of education and social development;
> 6. the promotion of the French language and of the expression of the Québécois culture (*Secrétariat de l'autoroute de l'information*, 1996).

This strategic document lays out a number of steps for action. We may now review the list of 30 proposed targets (*Secrétariat de l'autoroute de l'information*, 1996).

> These *targets* represent the medium-term and long-term results aimed at in the sectors which depend in part or in full on the government and which involve its responsibility. [...] The *areas of government action* with regard to the information highway are grouped together into seven areas:
>
> 1. services to the population;
> 2. business services;
> 3. government services and the modernization of the State apparatus;
> 4. language and culture and the promotion of Québec abroad;
> 5. education;
> 6. health and social services;
> 7. technology and infrastructures and their financing.

1.1   Services to the population

The three targets retained deal with:
   1. access conditions to services;
   2. security and privacy;
   3. regional dynamics.

Access conditions to services: equivalence for everyone, everywhere
Target 1: Equivalent conditions (in terms of availability, of quality and of cost, taking into account the range in carriers) for access to services for all citizens, wherever they may be located within Québec's territory, with the help of a variety of access points adapted to their needs.

Security and privacy: towards a respect for fundamental values
Target 2: The capacity for each citizen to use the information highway without concern as to the protection of her or his private life and personal information, the confidentiality of her or his communications; the security of her or his transactions; and also respecting society's fundamental values as recognized by existing law.

Regional dynamics: remaining close to users
Target 3: The availability of services connected to the information and interests which represent local and regional collectivities.

1.2   Business services

Two targets were retained, dealing with:
1. the availability of adequate services across the entire territory;
2. the visibility of Québec businesses in the global market.

Availability of adequate services across the entire territory: universal, secure and planetary electronic commerce
Target 4: Widely adopted electronic commerce mechanisms, reaching all of Québec's businesses, operating securely and supported by open services, and consistent with international standards ensuring interoperability with foreign markets.

Visibility of Québec businesses in the global market
Québec's businesses should therefore invest in the virtual domain in order to establish new relationships with their customers and providers, to create new products, to open new markets, and to protect existing market share. A service providing research and access to Québec business sites, created as part of a "Québec" showcase, would bring together scattered forces from the ocean of information that is the Internet. Such a showcase could also be promoted by Québec's representatives in foreign countries and be accessible from their offices.
Target 5: The presence of Québec businesses on both international and local networks and their connection to strategic sources of information at the national and international levels.

1.3   Government services and the modernization of the State apparatus

Experiences from abroad reveal that modernizing public management procedures and administrative re-engineering allow better services to be provided with fewer resources. Technology provides viable solutions for policy problems and public finances. That is why organizational and technological modernization has become inseparable from the re-establishment of the State's financial health. Moreover, citizens' needs in the area of access to services have evolved noticeably, given the changes in their living conditions.

The same keywords are always in the background: access from everywhere, need-based scheduling, rapidity and trustworthiness.

Five targets have been retained, dealing with:
1. access to government information;
2. access to government services;
3. user-friendly access on demand;
4. training and awareness development among users;
5. transformation of the public sector into a model user.

Access to government information: anytime, anywhere
Target 6: Accessibility to government information of public interest across the entire territory and at all times (7 days a week, 24 hours a day).

Access to government services: the user's point of view
Target 7: Accessibility to commonly-used government services and the possibility of modulated transactions ranked according to the needs and constraints of users as to the sites, schedules and means of distribution.

User-friendly access on demand: a unified system
Users of government services should not be required to be familiar with the complex administrative apparatus of the State.
Target 8: User-friendly access to information and services, and simplification of exchanges and transactions thanks to a unified system for accessing, locating or transmitting commonly-used information.

Training and awareness development among users: counting on confidence
Users of government services will opt for telecomputing when it offers them direct benefits (increased accessibility) and indirect benefits (reduction of government spending).
Target 9: Generalized use of the services accessible on the information highway through information campaigns and sensitization to associated benefits.

Transformation of the public sector into a model user
Target 10: Transformation and modernization of the public apparatus through its openness to the entire range of electronic networks, the generalization of electronic mail, and the networking of ministries and public bodies, thus providing users of public services with electronic access to government information and to interactive services.

1.4   Language, culture and the promotion of Québec abroad

The information highway ignores linguistic, cultural or national boundaries. It should favour openness to the world and the expression of singular cultures, not the homogenization of content. It is necessary to act so that the information society is indeed diverse, plurilingual, and respectful of the values of Québec society. In the information society, French must take its rightful place.

In this context, the targets retained deal with:
1. French as a language for using the information highway;
2. the creation of original French-language content and the distribution of Québécois culture and artistic works;
3. the promotion of Québec abroad.

French, a language for using the information highway: through a critical mass of services and of content
[...] Globalization seems to give pride of place to English as an international language with a universal vocation. It is necessary to ensure that the deployment of the information highway also favours the presence of French and the flourishing of all languages and cultures.
Target 11: The existence of a critical mass of services and content in the French language.
Target 12: The presence of linguistic plurality on the information highway.

The creation of original French-language content and the distribution of Québécois culture and artistic works
Access to a significant amount of foreign content on the information highway is a boon for culture overall. Québécois culture must take its place on the information highway and contribute fully to the diversity of models and to the many forms of artistic expression. On the information highway as with existing modes of expression, the Québécois mind must not be subjugated to strictly commercial factors [...].

Even as we use communication instruments whose power and versatility would once have been inconceivable, it is necessary to mobilize the intelligence, sensitivity, know-how, creativity, intellectual curiosity and imagination of Québécois.
Target 13: The manifest presence of Québec's artistic and cultural milieus in the creation of multimedia content.
Target 14: Accessibility of Québec's cultural heritage and artistic works on the information highway.

The promotion of Québec abroad: tourism, know-how, Francophonie
Target 15: Worldwide access to information, reservations, transactions relating to tourist activities, attractions and products.
Target 16: Recognition on the international stage of a leading role for Québec on the information highway.
Target 17: Existence of an internal market among francophone countries favouring the creation, distribution and commercialization of French-language content on the information highway.

1.5   Education

The education sector will play a key role over the course of the changes engendered by new information and communication technologies. The State devotes a quarter of its budget to the education sector. Over one million people invest in their education each year.

[...] Pedagogy must therefore be rethought to take advantage of the added value of new technologies and to reach the highest levels of competence and widespread success. To this end, teachers should benefit from a new generation of instructional material, more open and better adapted to the new technological realities.

Decision makers at all levels should find the means to put these tools into the hands of students and their instructors, to ensure that the latter are trained rapidly, and to stimulate the creation of adequate pedagogic material.

[...] In this perspective, the targets will deal with:
1. students mastering the new technologies;
2. teaching personnel mastering the new technologies;
3. accessibility of training;
4. information for the population.

Students mastering the new technologies: equip and train
Target 18: The mastery, by primary and secondary students, of clearly defined competencies in the area of new information and communication technology use.

Teaching personnel mastering the new technologies: mastery, appropriation, integration
Target 19: The mastery and appropriation by teaching personnel of new information technologies and of information highway tools, their integration into the teaching process, and the creation of new pedagogic tools which, while reinforcing the learning process, integrate aspects of the information highway.

In order to attain this goal, teachers and instructors must themselves become model users of new technologies [...].

Accessibility of training: towards telelearning
Telelearning becomes possible with the help of the information highway, at a lower cost than that of traditional training [...].
Target 20: Accessibility for the many possibilities of continuing education and distance learning across the entire territory, especially with the help of tele-learning.

Information for the population: necessary data within easy reach
Youths and adults currently experience difficulties in finding out about the possibilities offered by the educational system. Yet the sums invested [...] to inform the population about services and programs are impressive.
Target 21: Accessibility of information and teleservices useful for the wide range of users and actors in the educational system.

1.6   Health care and social services

The health care and social services sector employs 10 percent of Québec's active workforce. Its Cdn$13 billion budget (1995-1996) represents over 30 percent of government spending. It includes over 750 institutions as well as the many medical clinics and polyclinics and over 2,000 community organizations.

In order to take root in this sector, the information highway must take its particular context into account. Five phenomena should be underlined:

1. the evolution of needs related to an aging population and to new social problematics;
2. the accelerated development of biomedical technology;
3. the coexistence within the same network of underdevelopment in the area of information technology and the presence of carrier projects on customers;
4. cuts in financial resources devoted to this sector;
5. the necessary transformation of the health and social services network.

The targets retained in this sector should contribute to improving the health and welfare of the population, the accessibility and quality of user services, and efficiency in the use of socio-sanitary services, while better controlling program costs.

As a result, four targets have been retained. They deal with:

1. information for the population;
2. information networking;
3. service access mechanisms;
4. telediagnostics, telemedicine and teleservices.

Information for the population: increasing personal autonomy
Target 22: Accessibility of information in order to increase the autonomy of individuals and to improve their decision making related to their own health and welfare and to those of their dependents.

Information networking: better access, better management
Target 23: Information networking between users, health care professionals, institutions, and regional boards, in order to provide better access to services and better management of services.

Mechanisms for access to services: towards a secure health card
Target 24: A secure access mechanism for medical services, health services and social services.

Telediagnostics, telemedicine and teleservices: regional experiences
All citizens, including those who live in remote regions, have a right to the same quality of health and social services. [...] New technologies exist and they offer new avenues for the improvement of diagnostics, treatment, and other distance applications. Use should be made of them.
Target 25: The availability of services through telediagnostics, telemedicine and teleservices.

1.7   Technology, infrastructure and financing

Through its role as catalyst and regulator, the Québec government should contribute to the establishment of infrastructures, to their interconnection and to their optimal use. The government should also ensure the availability of services for everyone, everywhere, and security in communications and transactions. Finally, it should promote the emergence of a business dynamic likely to ensure the financing of the information highway by qualified businesses.

Technologies and infrastructures: availability, universality, security
The impact of the information highway in Québec depends on the speed and quality of its establishment [...].
Target 26: The availability of products, services and technologies able to support the information highway's development and to meet the expectations and needs of the population and specific customers.
Target 27: Networks and services whose standardization facilitates inter-operability (communication among networks), portability of applications (i.e., using a single service on different technologies and equipment), and the export of products and services, while favouring the totality of electronic communications.

The generalization of electronic transactions will make an authentication system necessary to guarantee the confidentiality of communications and integrity of transactions for everyone. Opportunities for putting into place a mechanism attributing an *electronic signature* exclusive to each citizen will therefore need to be examined. This would spare service providers the trouble of developing their own identification systems.

Target 28: The existence of secure and universal access mechanisms to networks and to services for all citizens (avoiding an unnecessary proliferation of cards).

Target 29: An optimal use of infrastructures, present and future, through the generalization of their use, without limiting competition for services.

Financing: an inciting business dynamic

[...] In demonstrating its intention to become a *model user* of the information highway, the government of Québec will encourage investment in the Québec information highway. As a major client, the government will become an essential partner for infrastructure-owning businesses, and will be well positioned to emphasize its concern for universality and for accessibility.

Target 30: The availability of high-performance infrastructures to all Québécois, built, financed and operated by qualified businesses.

The government's role of model user for the information highway will require an **investment of public funds**. This financing will be established on a commercial basis linked to a productivity enhancement perspective. In certain cases, public support will be required, notably in areas related to societal and cultural objectives (*Secrétariat de l'autoroute de l'information*, 1996).

II   COMMENTS ON THE GOVERNMENT'S POSITION AND ACTIONS

Actions taken by the Québec government since the publication of this consultative document demonstrate a certain coherence, even if a number of observers have criticized its bureaucratic tone and overly commercial orientation (Venne, 1997b). The document was presented to the Council of Ministers, which accepted both its basic thrusts and the approach it proposed for the establishment of the information highway. A Decree was then issued in order to confirm the government's willingness to act on this issue. Next, an Information Highway Finance Fund (*Fonds de financement de l'autoroute*) was created to finance various projects corresponding to the goals of the consultation paper for a two-year period. Each ministry and government body has from then on been preparing its own action plan. Elements from some of these plans have already been the object of public debate (for example: the "smart card" [*carte à puce*] of the *Régie de l'assurance-maladie*; the potential regulation of electronic signatures by the Ministry of Justice; the joint involvement of the *Commission de la santé et de la sécurité au travail*, and the *Caisse de dépôt et placement*, in the creation of an electronic commerce network).

We should bear in mind that the Québec government has stuck to three objectives which it considers essential: a) productivity increase in its own ministries and organizations; b) support for private industry to position itself in the world electronic market (the government tends to favour business projects that involve the entire range of the industrial environment, as opposed to those centered exclusively on the development of a particular enterprise); and c) undoubtedly because this is a political consideration intimately linked to the government's sovereigntist project, support for the production and on-line distribution of content and French-language services.

Meeting this last objective recently involved the action of the *Office de la langue française* (a government body whose responsibility it is to ensure the respect of Québec's laws concerning the use of the French language in the public sphere) with regard to an English-language business located on the island of Montréal. The business in question advertised the goods and services it offered on the Internet, but only in the English language, so that francophone consumers may well have been disadvantaged because they could not be served in French. The Office therefore decided to act and notified the enterprise of its responsibility to conform to Québec law. This gesture highlighted a contradiction linked to the transborder nature of the Internet: evidently, any business whose street address is outside of Québec's territory may offer its goods and services to Québécois consumers in English exclusively, and without risk. The *Office de la langue française*'s action therefore raised an outcry in the international web-surfing community (notably within the network associated with the American magazine, *Wired*). This contradiction – between a national policy of cultural protection and the no-holds-barred dissemination of a cross-border technology – is nowhere near resolution.

On the other hand, the achievement of objectives concerning universal access to the net and implantation in the educational sphere are proceeding far more slowly. It is a fact that government reflection on the Internet's possibilities remains strongly coloured by a preoccupation with the development of digital industries, perhaps to the detriment of preoccupations more widely social, ethical and cultural. A public reflection on the stakes represented by cost structures for Internet use, for example, remains to be organized. Even if we are among the most privileged of Western countries at this level, thanks to the flat rate tariffs offered by North American telecommunications enterprises, subscription to servers and the use of a number of on-line services remain subject to a cost structure whose *raisons d'être* are not always clear.

As for the penetration of the Internet in the educational sphere, even if the government has expressed a clear wish to install and connect computers in schools (albeit in restricted numbers), the budgets available for upgrading computer skills among teachers are sadly lacking. We seem to lack the imagination to develop original strategies that would have a spillover effect in the training sector. It is true, of course, that a context of heavy budget cuts to the educational sector is hardly conducive to any sort of new initiative. Finally, investment in distance education and tele-information appears to be inadequate.

Parallel to the government's strategic approach, a Parliamentary Commission (formed by members of parliament from Québec's two major political parties) organized a public consultation on these questions during the fall of 1996. Its report was published at the end of May 1997. This commission's work was closely linked to social and ethical preoccupations, notably in its refusal to take for granted the urgency ascribed by promoters to set up the information highway as rapidly as possible. The members of parliament also took into account the fact that this technology will never be universally accessible as long as important parts of the population remain illiterate or the Internet remains inaccessible to the significant numbers of physically and mentally handicapped citizens. It is important that the apparent explosion of this new technology does not obscure the government's obligation to maintain a diversity of access to government information and services.

> [...] the members of parliament advocate an approach which, while voluntary, is gradual. One which respects the rhythm of individuals, breaks ground with pilot projects, makes sure that children develop a critical sense towards the content they find there, does not listen to those who deny governments the right to combat undesirable content, and reinforces the protection of privacy and the rights of self-employed workers (Venne, 1997b; our translation).

The report is especially pertinent when it recommends that the texts of laws, regulations and other public documents be made freely available on the Internet (Venne, 1997a). In doing so, it takes a step towards a greater democratization that the Internet could help facilitate. It should be said, moreover, that the laws of Canada and those of the United States are already available in this manner. This recommendation also has consequences with regard to another important objective of the Québec government: to increase appreciably the proportion of French-language content on the Internet.

According to editorialist Michel Venne, the commission's report will remain nonetheless at a dead end, on two important dimensions: a) in contributing to a richer reflection on the consequences to democracy of implanting the information highway; and b) on the importance of the government's adopting "an information policy which would define the criteria of diffusion." That is, to try, for example, to distinguish between information which must remain secret and that which should become public, and accessible either free of charge or at cost. These two issues are obviously essential ones in regard to which many governments will sooner or later have to position themselves. In the final analysis, this raises the question of the pertinence of government intervention in the development and management of the Internet. But that is another debate...

III   THE GLOBALIZATION OF MEDIA: TOWARDS NEW CITIZEN IDENTITIES?

A series of major changes in the cultural industries and the media world have occurred at a planetary level. I want to note the following in particular:

a. The technological and economic convergence of the cultural industries of communication, of information and of media entertainment brings with it a hyper-competitivity in the businesses concerned. This competitivity is oriented towards the conquest of the largest markets possible: the apparent diversity of programming conceals a logic of cultural standardization dominated by commercial profitability. There is a hegemony of market logic in the circulation of cultural products at a planetary level.
b. The development of international communication networks transforms the nature of crossborder exchanges (redefine time and space).
c. The political role of the US appears determinant in the promotion of a "globalitarian" ideology. This ideology's shape is *par excellence* the information highway establishment project at planetary level.
d. The growing importance of contradictory crosscultural movements (standardization; affirmation; hybridization of local, regional and national cultures) speeds up tendencies towards indeterminacy regarding the future shape of social and political movements for articulating identities, even for the next decade.

In this context, it seems necessary to answer anew a host of questions in order to better understand the prerequisites for democratic communication at the global level:

a. *National communication policies* are to be redefined in a new context of transnational regulation of global communication networks where the question of *democratization of communication* will become more and more critical.
b. *Personal and collective identities* may be problematized by new cultural practices (mediated or not) that make simultaneous use of multiple poles of identity to create specific forms of social links.
c. These identity shifts will be the source of a rearticulation of relations between the media and the construction of *new citizen identities*. Will we see a redefinition of a global public space from which a *new global public culture* would emerge? Or is this nothing more than a utopic idea?
d. Between market and state logics, is there room for the development of alternative projects tied to the *logic of a global civil society*? Could we develop an alternative, global approach to the collective appropriation of information and communication technologies?

One hypothesis points to new forms of citizen identity and of public space to characterize the range of media practices demonstrated by users and by publics. These are emerging in a new context of global communication as much with the help of old media as with new technological means of information and communication. Marked by use habits linked to old media, confronted at once by multiple poles of identity and by new relations between the local, national and international poles, new citizen identities may form in this globalized mediascape.

The rearticulation between public and private spheres – today increasingly linked with the geopolitical development of communication – is summoned by a series of upheavals in the mediascape at many levels: political, technoeconomic, commercial and sociocultural. It is in this repositioning of *private space* – to what extent should we preserve the privacy of individuals? – versus new *public spaces* – what shapes will citizens' new identities and forms of expression take? – that fundamental issues are raised. Can the globalization of media provoke a flowering of opportunities for the democratization of communications at the planetary level? Or will it, on the contrary, lead to the extinction of democratic virtualities?

ADVANCING CANADA'S INFORMATION HIGHWAY: STRATEGIES FOR THE NEW MILLENNIUM

by David JOHNSTON and Natasha H. FARAQUI

In the 1994 Speech from the Throne, the Government of Canada announced it would develop a Canadian strategy to address the challenges of the Information Highway. Later that year Industry Minister, John Manley, established the Information Highway Advisory Council (IHAC), a 29-member body drawn from private industry, the cultural community and consumer groups, to provide advice on major issues related to that strategy. The Council was guided by three key objectives:

- creating jobs through innovation and investment;
- reinforcing Canadian sovereignty and cultural identity;
- ensuring access at reasonable cost.

At the conclusion of its mandate in September 1997, the Council released its final report, *Preparing Canada for a Digital World*, describing the road to the future. This paper outlines the work of the Information Highway Advisory Council and its vision for the knowledge-based society.

I   THE PROMISE OF A KNOWLEDGE SOCIETY

The Information Highway has profoundly challenged the dynamics of modern society. At the dawn of the new millennium, Canada and the world are in a state of transition. More and more we are moving away from the industrial society that prevailed over most of the 20th century, towards a society in which the management of *information* and *knowledge* has become the key strategic resource that determines the competitiveness of firms and nations.

For the moment the knowledge society is only a vision flowing from the potential opportunities brought by information and communication technologies. There is no doubt, however, that we are rapidly approaching a world where the creation, manipulation, and sharing of information is to become an overriding human imperative. In the knowledge society, distance will no longer pose an obstacle to economic development, social intercourse, learning, business, or participation in society. Information will become increasingly available to everyone and people will be creators – and not simply consumers – of knowledge and content. The results will depend on people who employ their passion, ingenuity, and imagination to shape the development of this society. The potential is limitless but the challenge is real and it is important that Canada respond wisely to issues and challenges that will:

- create a favourable environment for infrastructure development;
- establish strategies for economic growth;
- address the social and cultural dynamics of this new environment.

In its final report, the Information Highway Advisory Council identified four imperatives they believe must shape information policy in Canada. These imperatives include an economic development strategy, a content strategy, an access policy, and a leadership responsibility. Together these imperatives provide the framework needed to build the knowledge society and support the information economy.

II   THE ECONOMIC IMPERATIVE

2.1   Infrastructure development

Just as railroads, highways and airports formed the infrastructure of the industrial society, communication and computer networks form the infrastructure of the knowledge society. The difference between the two is profound. The transportation infrastructure of the industrial society carried people and goods from one place to another. In the knowledge society infrastructure will carry the less-tangible products of the digital age – information, knowledge, and intelligence.

Information technology is the enabling infrastructure of the knowledge society. As such, the future competitiveness of Canadian industry at home and overseas increasingly depends on the availability of high-quality information networks and services in all parts of Canada. The Council believes that the private sector must take the lead in constructing the Information Highway, while government has the responsibility to ensure an attractive policy and regulatory environment for investment. The Council outlined five essential principles of infrastructure development that will strengthen the information infrastructure and allow Canadians to prosper in a global marketplace.

An open, competitive regulatory environment
Only a competitive environment determined by market conditions will drive companies to make necessary investments in infrastructure. This means creating favourable regulatory conditions that encourage private sector investment in innovation. Furthermore, regulations are needed to ensure an open market and the removal of unnecessary barriers to competition.

Technological neutrality
In an environment characterized by converging technologies and markets across the communications and information sector, it is critical that market forces determine what technology is appropriate for the provision of a particular service. However, the policy and regulatory regime cannot favour one technology over another and, to this end, must remain "technology neutral."

Open standards
The true potential of the Information Highway is realized when the infrastructure is interconnected and interoperable, where access to one network means access to all. The development of an interconnected and interoperable network of networks requires the universal adoption of an international open standards policy.

Research and development
The quality of Canada's Information Highway depends on Canada's collective capacity for innovation. The phenomenal growth in computer networking and the Internet has resulted in a need to concentrate research resources on advanced networking and broadband technologies such as Asymmetrical Digital Subscriber Loops (ADSL), cable modems, and Integrated Service Digital Networks (IDSL). Creating a favourable environment for private sector research is essential; however, it is also equally necessary to ensure that public and private research efforts complement and reinforce each other.

Strategic investments
Though the private sector will take the primary role in building the information infrastructure development, government can play a catalytic role through strategic investments that enable public institutions to take advantage of the Information Highway. Future government infrastructure programs need to target investments where the private sector is unlikely to generate sufficient funds. Specific areas include: education, health, research, and community development.

2.2   Economic development

While much emphasis has been focused on infrastructure development, infrastructure alone is not enough to build the knowledge society. The Council firmly believes that *content, applications and services* are the lifeblood of the information economy and a major source of jobs and economic growth. Thus, building infrastructure includes strategies to encourage new information highway-based products and services for a global economy. A key element of such a strategy includes the creation of a policy environment that promotes electronic commerce and economic activity on the Internet.

The Internet and electronic commerce
The Internet has emerged as the central component in the evolution of the Information Highway. Its broad scope, adaptability, and versatility are creating dramatic opportunities for individuals, the economy, and society as a whole. Through the Internet, people have access to many new forms of information and entertainment. The technology also holds the promise of enabling major extensions and improvements in education, health and other public services. As a result, the Internet can significantly contribute to economic growth and job creation.

The Internet is also a powerful and useful tool from which to expand world-wide trade and has the potential to become the driving force behind electronic commerce. Its large market base and the relatively inexpensive cost to transfer huge amounts of data make the Internet an attractive alternative. One cannot tell how the Internet will evolve to generate new markets, goods and services, however.

A number of difficulties prevent firms and consumers from capitalizing on opportunities vested in the Internet as a platform for electronic commerce; this includes security and privacy; consumer protection; authentication and secure modes of payment; and telecommunication tariffs and regulations. These have been major impediments to the rapid development of an electronic marketplace. The Council believes that addressing and overcoming these issues will help ensure the expansion of electronic commerce and realize the potential of the Internet as a venue for broad-based economic activity.

2.3   Sectoral strategies

The Council believes that sectoral areas such as health, education and small business represent significant opportunities for the development of content, applications and services. In each of these sectors the potential benefits of the Information Highway are considerable, and the Council emphasized creating the right environment for these sectors to realize their potential.

Small business enterprises
Small- and medium-sized business enterprises (SMEs) have a dynamic and growing presence in the Canadian economy. The increasing use of information technology is changing the way small business adapts to new markets and commercial opportunities.

The Internet as a means of conducting electronic commerce promises a range of economic benefits to SMEs. Internet technology allows small business as to do new things and organize themselves in different ways. Personal networking can now span a much larger geographic area, making new forms of collaboration possible. Better communication and more timely, precise information represent significant cost-savings to SMEs. Business-to-business on-line commerce is also growing, and will likely allow SMEs to eliminate 90 percent of their transactional operations.

Small businesses are moving rapidly to gain access to the Internet. According to the Canadian Federation of Independent Business (CIFB), 50 percent of SMEs with 50 or more employees used the Internet as of April 1997. These figures are expected to double by next year.

Helping business to use the Internet fully will foster a sophisticated electronic commerce sector in Canada and will help firms expand their capacity to participate on the global stage. This, in turn, will also contribute to domestic economic growth and job creation.

Health
Information technology can transform the health system by providing higher quality care in a cost-effective manner while creating new jobs, markets, products, and services. A

commercial tele-health industry is already emerging in Canada. Meanwhile, global demand is growing for products and services that companies can provide.

Critical to the achievement of these benefits will be the development of a national, integrated, health information network. In *Towards a Canadian Health I-way: Vision, Opportunities and Future Steps*, released in late 1996, Health Canada explored this opportunity and called for specific measures to develop a strategy. Parallel with this effort, Industry Canada is completing a Sector Competitiveness Framework for the tele-health industry. Preliminary work suggests the industry faces significant challenges because of the small Canadian market, strong foreign competition, and a lack of skilled individuals. Yet opportunities also exist. New professional disciplines are emerging in the areas of tele-nursing and health information. Meanwhile, international markets for Canadian expertise are opening up.

To seize these opportunities Canada needs a framework that encourages growth in the health industries, with particular reference to software, information systems, and "intelligent" equipment. Moreover, the growth of these industries depends on wiring health institutions such as hospitals, medical laboratories, research labs, and community clinics.

Technology-assisted learning
From the outset, the Council stressed the importance of lifelong learning as a precondition for developing the human resources needed in the knowledge society, and as a way of ensuring that Canadians qualify for the jobs available in that society. The deployment of technology-assisted learning therefore represents a real commercial opportunity for Canada. The challenge for this new learning industry resides in effectively combining content, hardware, and human talent to create business opportunities and jobs. By defining pedagogical outcomes to include Information Highway technologies, and by converting learning materials into a digital format, Canada can develop new products capable of exploiting the full potential of the technology.

Multimedia technologies are becoming the primary platform for technology-assisted learning. It is expected that the global market for multimedia products will grow 25 percent a year. Both in Canada and abroad, changing skills and knowledge requirements in the private sector are producing a growing corporate market for technology-assisted learning materials and content resources.

There is a real opportunity to develop a multimedia learning industry by taking advantage of the emerging domestic and global training markets. Given the enormous commercial potential of multimedia, the Council encouraged expertise in this area.

2.4   The workplace and human resource development

The way we think of work has changed significantly in the past decade. Canadians now anticipate three or four different careers in their working lives; each position requires increasingly diverse skills; and part-time work, tele-work, contract work, and self-employment are becoming more prevalent. These changes to the workplace require constant learning and adapting. In the knowledge society, learning is no longer limited to formal education, but is a lifelong process. As such, the Council recommended that Canada modernize its labour standards legislation in a way that adequately reflects the changing workplace and new forms of employment. Changes to the labour market and to the nature of work are also creating a pressing need to adequately identify required skills with the anticipated sources of work. The Council strongly urged the government to research the impact of information technology on employment trends, emphasizing that Canada must match skills – especially skills in computer literacy and numeracy – with the labour market realities of the knowledge society.

Helping Canadians secure employment in the new economy also requires the availability of new learning and training opportunities. With advances in technology and computer networking, the effective use of information and communication technologies are essential to support lifelong learning. The Council advised the government to establish a consultation mechanism to resolve policy issues relating to technology and learning.

III   THE CONTENT IMPERATIVE

3.1   Shifting environment for content

Reinforcing Canadian sovereignty and protecting Canada's cultural identity has been a major public policy mandate. Historically, this mandate has included efforts to foster an environment where Canadian cultural expression can be appreciated and preserved. This includes:

- building and sharing common values and experiences among Canadians through cultural expression (television, film, music, books, arts);
- facilitating improved access and support to creators, cultural organizations, industries, and institutions (tax incentives, subsidies, and regulation);
- creating a presence for cultural and linguistic diversity of content by providing Canadian voices and Canadian choices.

Information technology has transformed the meaning of content. There are now new ways to create, produce, market and distribute content; content is being integrated with various types of media formats such as the Internet and multimedia; and the cultural sector is converging with non-cultural industries. New Media is a synthesis of this change. It includes things like the digitization of paintings and books, video on demand, Internet radio, on-line interactive services, and multimedia CD ROMs. The Internet has a special relationship with New Media content. It works well as an extension of traditional media while allowing millions of people worldwide to share information and communicate.

This shifting environment for content is currently challenging traditional approaches to domestic cultural policy and is forcing Canadian cultural industries into a state of transition. The conventional definitions of "culture" (i.e., film, publishing, recording, performing and visual arts) are being radically redefined by the surge of new cultural activities in New Media. These new activities are blurring the distinctions between "broadcasting" and "telecommunications" and creating a dilemma for Canadian cultural policy initiatives.

3.2   Content development strategy

The Council strongly advised the government to develop a stronger, broader, and more integrated Canadian content strategy that not only expands the scope of Canadian cultural policy to encompass new forms of content, but also addresses the plight of traditional media in Canada. As a framework for developing an effective and useful strategy, the Council outlined the following components.

Strong creative base
As production of digital content develops technical sophistication, success depends increasingly on a marriage of creative talent and technical skills. This relationship depends on encouraging content disciplines such as computer graphics, animation, multimedia, and Internet software design. In addition, artists and creators need to work with content providers to develop new production techniques and new forms of content. Artists and technical experts involved with new media content have the potential to transform cultural communication. The Council regards new media as a true opportunity for collaboration between the technical and artistic/cultural communities.

Access to capital
Industry studies reveal that inadequate access to capital substantially restricts a sector's growth potential. If cultural dialogue is to be strengthened, strategies are needed to continue committing public resources through tax incentives, public agencies, as well as direct assistance to private industry. The multimedia industry represents an important growth opportunity. The Council recommended that a Cdn$50 million Canadian multimedia fund be established to support the development, distribution and marketing of Canadian cultural and educational products.

Access to content
Reaching Canadians means ensuring they have access to meaningful content. Traditionally, funding has been focused on the creation and production of content. The Council believes that, despite a range of existing initiatives, marketing and distribution of content has not received adequate emphasis. The Council recommended that funding support not only the production of content but also its effective distribution and marketing.

Export development strategy
All types of Canadian content production will benefit from efforts to expand into foreign markets. The multimedia industry has the potential to become an important source of export revenue. The Council feels it would be beneficial to undertake specific export development initiatives. Under such an initiative, producers of Canadian content in existing and new media would receive increased assistance through existing federal export marketing programs. This would include improved access to market information, inclusion in Team Canada missions, and assistance through Canada's trade development offices and programs.

French-language content
The Information Highway is overwhelmingly an English-language phenomenon, dominated by American content. Though French is the second most important language on the Internet, French-language content represents an estimated three percent of all Internet content. Francophones share with all Canadians the problems of creating indigenous content for a relatively small domestic population. That challenge is greater for a language group that is comparatively small in global terms. In light of these circumstances, the Council urged special measures to strengthen the French language presence, including allocating resources to French language content and helping francophone communities gain access to the Internet.

IV   THE ACCESS IMPERATIVE

Access to the Information Highway is critical to Canada's future as a knowledge society and to our success in the information economy. As the economy becomes more dependent on information, Canadians will increasingly rely on the enabling effects of the Information Highway to succeed economically and remain competitive.

As the Information Highway becomes more pervasive and significant in the economic, social and cultural life of Canadians, so will the scope and complexity of access issues. The Council called for the development of a national access strategy that would address three requirements of public policy:

- ensure affordable access to basic telecommunications and broadcasting services;
- promote access to Information Highway services and networks such as the Internet;
- establish a formal mechanism for defining access and universality.

Access to basic networks
Canada has led the world in providing access to broadcasting services and basic telecommunication services such as telephone. These basic services are also important to Canadians as platforms for access to the Internet. Canada has already achieved universal access to core telecommunication services and has safeguards in place to ensure that Canadians maintain access to these services in a competitive environment. New technologies such as direct-to-home satellites and Local Multipoint Communications (LMCs) are also emerging to provide additional avenues for the distribution of

programming and network services. These steps will benefit consumers with increased choice, affordable rates, and better quality service.

Access to the Internet
The Internet is likely to provide many of the electronic information services that people will want to access. The Internet has the potential to provide significant social, economic and cultural benefits, and is an important avenue for citizen participation. Accordingly, the Council recommended that Canada promote access to the Internet through community networks and electronic public spaces. The Council also supports initiatives for sustainable access to the Internet in all schools and libraries. For rural and remote areas, the Internet is increasingly recognized as a key instrument for economic and social development; however, there is considerable evidence that problems with affordable Internet access will emerge with growing frequency, particularly in areas such as the far North. The Council believes it is imperative that Canada focus its access policies on the Internet and take the steps necessary to accelerate access in all regions of the country.

Definition of essential services
As the Internet begins to provide many of the basic services to which Canadians should be assured access, it is important to consider a process for determining what those basic services might be. Telecommunications policy and regulations have typically addressed the issues of access and universality in terms of network access: broadcast policy and regulations have usually viewed access in relation to broadcast signals and programming services. Neither model is adequate in the new environment. Markets and technologies are evolving rapidly and new approaches are needed to meet critical social, economic and cultural needs.

The Council firmly believes in the need to focus on access issues for the successful transformation, both socially and economically from an industrial to a knowledge society. Access to Information Highway services will become crucial to full participation and, indeed, the exercise of democratic citizenship in a knowledge society. Decisions on what Information Highway services should be considered essential will have far-reaching social, economic and cultural ramifications, and need to be informed by the viewpoints of industry and the community at large.

V   THE LEADERSHIP IMPERATIVE

5.1   Government as a model user

The Council believes that government has a responsibility to take the lead role in developing the knowledge society by positioning itself as a model user of communications and information technology. In doing so, the government would serve as a catalyst in the development and innovative use of the Information Highway, while helping itself to perform more effectively. The ensuing gains in accessibility, responsiveness and affordability are substantial; nevertheless, the key advantage lies in the continued relevance and legitimacy of government in this new environment.

Two important areas where government might use information technology to improve services to the public are committing to electronic commerce as the preferred mode of business, and promoting electronic access to government services. Some ongoing initiatives to accelerate this process include:

- TBS decision to use electronic commerce as the preferred means for government to conduct its business by 1998;
- the Electronic Commerce Secretariat at Justice Canada to determine impediments to electronic filing as a basis for developing legislative options by the year 2000;
- the federal government's electronic authorization and authentication policy. This includes the Public Key Infrastructure (PKI) initiative to support privacy, integrity, and authentication issues by late 1998;
- Industry Canada's *Strategis* Internet site, which allows Canadian business to access and explore 20,000 electronic documents containing strategic business information;
- Industry Canada's SchoolNet and the Community Access Program (CAP), both working to improve Internet availability through public access sites.

The Council feels that it is not enough for the federal government to pursue these initiatives on its own. All governments of Canada (federal, provincial/territorial, and municipal) need to coordinate their activities to provide Canadians with seamless access to single electronic windows on government in Canada. Though most federal Internet sites have direct links to provincial sites, Canadians are still far from having a single window from which to access all levels of government. The closest approximation is the InterGov site, which provides a catalogue of on-line services provided by the federal government and participating provincial/territorial and municipal governments. The Council stressed that government leadership is a necessary and vital objective for promoting and encouraging the benefits of the knowledge society.

VI   MEETING THE CHALLENGE

6.1   The road ahead

Canada has made enormous progress in building the Information Highway in the last decade. While much has been accomplished, more work remains before the full promise of the knowledge society is realized. For the last four years, the Council served as a catalyst for Information Highway initiatives. At the close of its mandate the Council outlined specific areas it felt would require further attention including initiatives in:

- **advanced networks** – infrastructure and applications development encouraging private and public sector partnerships to further the roll-out of advanced networking and related applications development;
- **standards** – promoting the development, diffusion, and adoption of standards for open networks and connectivity and continuously charting the "Standards Roadmap for the Information Highway";

- **performance indicators** – defining and measuring the key economic and social indicators of Canada's progress as an information society, and providing for appropriate benchmarking against international developments;
- **electronic commerce** – realizing the economic benefit of a digital marketplace and establishing a policy framework where electronic commerce can flourish on public networks such as the Internet;
- **lifelong learning** – providing a forum for governments, educators, and the technology community to consider issues where resolutions are necessary to making lifelong learning "a key design element in the Information Highway."

Governments, industry, community groups, and individual Canadians all have a role in making the knowledge society a place that reflects Canadian goals, aspirations, and values. The future is full of opportunities. The innate potential of technology, prudent government action and the unique skills and resources of Canadians, will ensure our successful transition to a knowledge society. The Council's work aims at moving Canada with greater speed and focus in this direction.

ELECTRONIC COMMERCE POLICY AND THE EUROPEAN COMMISSION

by Paul TIMMERS[1]

I   INTRODUCTION

The Internet and electronic commerce currently enjoy enormous interest. Citizens are curious and for many of them e-mail has already become an additional means to communicate with friends and relatives. Business is keen to explore the new opportunities but are still wary of perceived risks. Governments are mobilizing efforts to examine the validity of their legislation for the new electronic forms of business. Hotly debated are the rules for global electronic commerce, which for many today means business over the Internet (although electronic commerce also includes the use of closed networks).

Europe is fully participating in this debate. The European Commission has been especially active in the emerging global discussion. Europe's interest is understandable: as elsewhere in the world, electronic commerce is seen as critical to competitiveness but, moreover, many of Europe's specific characteristics are put in a new light in the open world of global information networks. Can Europe exploit but also protect its rich cultural and linguistic diversity, and a variety of business practices? Can Europe leverage internationally its experience in building an *acquis communautaire* – i.e., the whole body of legislation that together constitutes what the European Union is today, including the Single Market? Will the global information networks become an unparalleled challenge to the industrial and social structure in Europe, where labour rules are at times perceived as rather rigid, while enshrining strong European values like solidarity? Can electronic commerce help to overcome the persistent, structural, high level of unemployment in many countries? And finally, can global information networks facilitate the process of preparing to enlarge the European Union with the inclusion of other Eastern European and Mediterranean countries?

II   ELECTRONIC COMMERCE AND THE EUROPEAN COMMISSION[2]

In 1995 the European Commission hosted the Global Information Society conference in Brussels. On that occasion it was decided to launch 11 global pilot projects. One of those, the G7 project "A Global Marketplace for SMEs,"[3] deals with promoting electronic commerce for small- and medium-sized enterprises (SMEs), and is being led jointly by the US, Japan and the European Commission. At the same time a range of R&D projects, supported by the European Commission, were exploring the Internet

---

[1]The views expressed in this article are those of the author and do not necessarily represent the position of the European Commission.
[2]For general information about electronic commerce and the European Commission, see http://www.ispo.cec.be/ecommerce/
[3]See http://www.ispo.cec.be/ecommerce/g7init.htm.

for business use, addressing basic technology development as well as business organization (e.g., "virtual" or networked forms of enterprise organization). The G7 project, particularly in Europe, organized many consultations between the private and public sectors.

This dialogue, along with feedback from industry in the R&D projects and consultations with industry in the context of regular policy development (e.g., on copyright management, and telecommunications liberalization), clearly identified the critical importance of electronic commerce for Europe's competitiveness in the global marketplace. A consensus has been gradually emerging on key issues, contributing to making the global information society a reality for business and consumers. Awareness building, creating trust and confidence, providing for a clear legal framework, and understanding business "best practice," were and still are among those key issues.

In addition, it became increasingly clear that a coherent policy approach was needed as well as a profound international dialogue. Within the European Commission a catalytic role was played in this thinking by a regular meeting of a core group of relevant competencies. This led to the formulation of the *European Initiative in Electronic Commerce*, a policy paper adopted in April 1997 by the European Commission. In May 1997 a similar policy document was issued by the Japanese Ministry of International Trade and Industry (MITI), and in July 1997 the White House officially published its *Framework for Global Electronic Commerce*, of which drafts had been available a number of months earlier. Finally, also in July 1997, over 30 European countries adopted the Bonn Declaration on the Global Information Networks. Currently, many countries have published or are working on information society/electronic commerce projects (The Netherlands, Italy, United Kingdom, Canada, Mexico, to name a few). This flood of policy work demonstrates that electronic commerce, as the foremost application of the Information Society, has moved high on the political agenda. It also is a good illustration of a growing awareness that electronic commerce is a global phenomenon.[4]

It is interesting to note that there are strong similarities in the principles and observations explicitly or implicitly underlying policy making in Europe, the US and Japan. These are:[5]
- electronic commerce is of critical importance;
- the Internet is causing a major shift;
- urgency to act;

---

[4]The pace of policy discussions and developments has not slowed down. A number of recent key developments, until December 1997, include the Global Standards Conference in October 1997, the Trans-Atlantic Business Dialogue Rome Declaration in November 1997, the OECD Turku Conference "Dismantling the Barriers to Electronic Commerce," also in November 1997, and the EU-US Joint Declaration in Electronic Commerce of December 1997.

[5]Patrick Vittet-Philippe, European Commission, Brussels; Jim Johnson, Global Information Infrastructure Commission, Washington.

- market-driven development;
- global dialogue is essential;
- governments have to ensure a predictable but minimal legal framework;
- governments have a catalyst role to play;
- interplay of technology – legislation – self-regulation/codes of conduct;
- where possible monitor rather than intervene.

Despite the appreciation that this policy work is capturing a moment in time, in a field where things are moving very fast, and today's understanding is necessarily limited, it is generally felt that there is an urgency to act. The European Commission, for example, has taken the year 2000 as its deadline for adapting legislation and other actions (see below). Acting fast matters because of the speed of technological development, the exponential rise in the use of the Internet, the risk of globally incompatible legislation being introduced at the national level, and the perceived dangers of misuse of the new environment.

III   EUROPEAN INITIATIVE IN ELECTRONIC COMMERCE[6]

The aims of the electronic commerce policy adopted by the European Commission are to promote the vigorous growth of electronic commerce in Europe, to increase the competitiveness of industry in Europe, and to ensure that business and consumers benefit from global information networks. To that end, the initiative highlights three interrelated high-level objectives to be addressed within a context of international co-operation and dialogue:

1. ensuring access to the global marketplace;
2. creating a favourable regulatory framework;
3. promoting a favourable business environment.

These three objectives are broken down into specific actions and programs within a range of policy domains. In all objective areas there are three recurrent themes:
- electronic commerce policy development cannot be done in isolation but needs to be compatible with a global approach to doing business;
- building trust and confidence is key to winning over businesses and consumers to electronic commerce;
- policy areas are highly interrelated and technology, legal, and support actions should re-inforce each other.[7]

The first objective, ensuring access to the global marketplace, addresses the relatively high cost of telecommunications and the limited availability of broadband networks

---

[6]See http://www.ispo.cec.be/ecommerce/initiat.htm.
[7]"Building trust and confidence" illustrates the interrelationship: it requires secure and usable technologies, a clear legal framework with protection against inappropriate use (see e.g., http://www.ispo.cec.be/eif/policy/97503toc.html), and "soft" trust-building through the development and recognition of "good practice."

throughout the European Union. Action is proposed at the European level to improve the usability of technology and electronic commerce services for consumers and small companies, and to deliver new forms of competitive advantage through research and development. Interoperability of electronic commerce technology and solutions is identified as a key issue, for which flexible and market-driven approaches will be promoted and developed.

The second objective, creating a favourable regulatory[8] framework, sets out to define principles for the legal framework. Most importantly it opposes "regulation for regulation's sake," indicating that, "any regulation must be based on the Internal Market freedoms" (free movement of goods, persons, capital, services, and freedom of establishment). This expresses, on the other hand, the desire to not constrain the potential of electronic commerce with burdening legislation, and on the other, to take maximum advantage of the assets of the Internal Market in the European Union for this new way of doing business. A response to electronic commerce is necessary for all the steps in business transactions, from the establishment of business to electronic payments, as well as for horizontal issues like security, data protection, taxation, etc. Partial answers already exist and have been or are being implemented, while a review of the current framework is still needed. Issues addressed include:

- electronic payments (July 1997 Recommendation);
- contracts at a distance, contract law;
- copyright (Draft Directive December 1997);
- regulated professions;
- commercial communications;
- accountancy;
- security and encryption;
- data protection and privacy;
- direct and indirect taxation ("no bit-tax");
- public procurement.

The third objective area, promoting a favourable business environment, addresses awareness among consumers and businesses, and establishes confidence through information and recognition of quality in electronic commerce. Enhancing understanding of electronic commerce through the development and promotion of "best practice" is considered key. Public administrations are called to become pro-active users of electronic commerce, to stimulate the take-up, and create confidence. The lack of skills is considered to be a major barrier to the development of the Information Society at large, and to electronic commerce in particular. Finally, a broad and open-minded societal dialogue is strongly advocated, in order to prevent Europe from becoming a fragmented society with information "have-nots" and "want-nots," as

---

[8]For some the word "regulatory" has negative undertones, contrary to "legal." In the current context, however, regulatory framework can be read as legal framework.

there are no certainties as to how electronic commerce will and should develop in Europe.

IV   CONCLUSION

During the last year significant progress has been achieved in mapping out the issues in global electronic commerce, and even in reaching a certain degree of consensus on principles between major players. The challenge is now to take the discussion to a truly global level, involving all parties and interests: that is, countries and regions, as well as businesses, citizens, and public bodies.[9] The road from principles to practical solutions that promote electronic commerce rather than stifle it is still to be discovered on many issues. New ways of doing business and technological innovation require a constant review of policy frameworks. The impact of electronic commerce on our ways of living and working, indeed, on the organization of society at large, is still poorly understood, and will require much more experimentation and study. What is clear already is that electronic commerce, as the first mass application of the Information Society, profoundly affects the way policy making is being done. Beyond new ways of doing business, we therefore also need new policy-making approaches capable of dealing with the interplay of factors and new roles of the players involved: business, governments, and citizens.

---

[9]The Commission recently adopted a policy paper, "Globalization and the Information Society – the need for strengthened international coordination" that addresses this challenge (http://www.ispo.cec.be/eif/).

REFERENCES

Aarts, M.N.C. & Te Molder, H. (1997). Spreken over natuur: een discourse-analytische studie van het debat. In N.E. van de Poll & A. Glasmeier (eds.), *Natuurontwikkeling waarom en hoe? Verslag van een debat.* Working document 59 (pp. 85-110). The Hague: Rathenau Institute.

Bannon, L.J. & Schmidt, K. (1991). CSCW: Four characters in search of a context. In J.M. Bowers & S.D. Benford (eds.), *Studies in Computer Supported Cooperative Work: Theory, Practice, and Design* (pp. 3-16). Amsterdam: Elsevier Science Publishers B.V.

Barendt, E. (1996/1985). *Freedom of Speech.* Oxford: Clarendon Press.

Baym, C. (1997). Interpreting soap operas and creating community: Inside an electronic fan culture. In Kiesler, S. (ed.), *Culture of the Internet* (pp. 103-20). Mahwah, NJ: Lawrence Erlbaum.

Beck, U. (1992). *Risk Society: Towards a New Modernity.* London: Sage Publications.

Becker, T.L. (1981). Teledemocracy: Bringing power back to the people, *Futurist* 15(6): 6-9.

Beelen, J. van (1998). SDU discussie op Internet: Van ons allen, voor ons allen. In L. Hanssen, N.W. Jankowski & J.A.G.M. van Dijk (eds.), *Toegang tot en kwaliteit van het elektronisch debat. Verslag van een studiedag* (pp. 11-4). Utrecht: Stichting Wetenschap en Techniek Nederland.

Bonnelly, C. (1997, September). CIHM on the threshold of the future: A new planning cycle, *Facsimile*: 3.

Bourdieu, P. (1984). Espace social et genèse des "classes", *Recherche en Sciences Sociales* 52/53: 3-16.

Boussen, H. (1998). Digitaal Verkeersplein: Ervaringen met elektronische discussie op een ministerie. In L. Hanssen, N.W. Jankowski & J.A.G.M. van Dijk (eds.), *Toegang tot en kwaliteit van het elektronisch debat. Verslag van een studiedag* (pp. 24-7). Utrecht: Stichting Wetenschap en Techniek Nederland.

Boven, Th. C. van (1982). Distinguishing criteria of human rights. In K.Vasak (ed.), *The International Dimensions of Human Rights* (pp. 43-59). Paris: Unesco.

Brande, L. van den (1996, April). *Multimedia in Flanders: Policy Priorities.* Brussels: Ministry of the Flemish Community.

Buchwald, C. (1997). Canadian universality policy and the information infrastructure: Past lessons, future directions, *Canadian Journal of Communication* 22: 161-93.

Bullinga, M. (1995, July 1). Teledemocratie is nieuwe kans voor burgers en politici, *De Volkskrant*: 18.

Central Computer and Telecommunications Agency (C.C.T.A.) (1996). *Legal Issues and the Internet, Reference Book*. London: HMSO.

Chernaik, W., Davis, C. & Deegan, M. (eds.) (1993). *The Politics of the Electronic Text*. Oxford/London: Office for Humanities Communication/The Centre for English Studies, University of London.

Commission de la culture (1997, May). Inforoute, culture et démocratie: enjeux pour le Québec. Montréal: Rapport final, Assemblée nationale du Québec, Secrétariat des commissions.

Comité consultatif sur l'autoroute de l'information (1995, July). Inforoute Québec. Plan d'action pour la mise en oeuvre de l'autoroute de l'information. Montréal: Rapport au Gouvernement du Québec.

Constant, D., Kiesler, S.B. & Sproull, L.S. (1996). The kindness of strangers: The usefulness of electronic weak ties for technical advice, *Organization Science* 7(2): 119-35.

Crasborn, M. (1998). Digitaal Verkeersplein: Op weg naar een structureel discussieplatform bij Verkeer en Waterstaat. In L. Hanssen, N.W. Jankowski & J.A.G.M. van Dijk (eds.), *Toegang tot en kwaliteit van het elektronisch debat. Verslag van een studiedag* (pp. 21-3). Utrecht: Stichting Wetenschap en Techniek Nederland.

Daft, R.L. & Lengel, R.H. (1986). Organizational information requirements, media richness and structural design, *Management Science* 32(5): 554-71.

Daft, R.L., Lengel, R.H. & Trevino, L.K. (1987). Message equivocality, media selection, and manager performance: Implications for information systems, *MIS Quarterly* 11: 355-66.

d'Haenens, L. (1999). Beyond infrastructure: Europe, the United States, and Canada on the information highway. In J. Downey & J. McGuigan (eds.), *Technocities*. London: Sage Publications.

Dijk, J.A.G.M. van (1991). *De netwerkmaatschappij. Sociale aspecten van nieuwe media*. Houten/Zaventem: Bohn Stafleu Van Loghum.

Dimitrova, D. & Salaff, J. (1998). Telework as social innovation: How do remote employees work together? In P. Jackson & J. Von der Wielen (eds.), *Teleworking: International Perspectives. From Telecommuting to the Virtual Organization* (pp. 261-80). London: Routledge.

The disappearing taxpayer (1997, May 31). *The Economist*: 17-9.

Donk, W.B. van de & Tops, P.W. (1992). Informatisering en democracie: Orwell of Athene. In P.H. Frissen, A.W. Koers & I.T. Snellen (eds.), *Orwell of Athene? Democratie en informatiesamenleving* (pp. 31-74). The Hague: Rathenau Institute.

Drolte, A. (1997). *States looking at electronic signatures appear to favor technology-neutral laws*, BNA's Electronic Information Policy and Law Report, February: 189-90.

Dubrovsky, V., Kiesler, S. & Sethna, B. (1991). The equalization phenomenon: Status effects in computer-mediated and face-to-face decision making groups, *Human Computer Interaction* 6: 119-46.

European Commission (1997). *Communication to the European Parliament, the Council, the Economic and Social Committee and the Committee of the Regions: A European Initiative in Electronic Commerce* 15/04/97, COM(97) 157, par. 51.

European Commission (1997, April). *Final Policy Report of the High Level Group of Experts: Building the European Information Society for Us All*. Brussels.

Europe's Businesses Split over Role of Government (1997, June 4). *The Wall Street Journal* Interactive Edition.

Feldman, D. (1993). *Civil Liberties and Human Rights*. Oxford: Clarendon Press.

Feldman, M. (1987). Electronic mail and weak ties in organizations, *Office: Technology and People* 3: 83-101.

Fernback, J. & Thompson, B. (1995). *Virtual Communities: Abort, Retry, Failure?* Revised version of "Computer-mediated communication and the American collectivity: The dimensions of community within cyberspace" presented at the International Communication Association (ICA) conference, Albuquerque, New Mexico, May.

Fish, R., Kraut, R., Root, R. & Rice, R. (1993). Video as a technology for informal communication, *Communications of the ACM* 36(1): 48-61.

Flos, B. (1996). *Leeswijzer teledemocratie geschriften*. Amsterdam: Instituut voor Publiek en Politiek (Institute for Public and Politics).

Fulk, J., Schmitz, J. & Steinfield, C.W. (1990). A social influence model of technology use. In J. Fulk & C.W. Steinfield (eds.), *Organizations and Communication Technology* (pp. 117-40). Newbury Park/London: Sage Publications.

Fulk, J. & Steinfield, C.W. (1990). *Organizations and Communication Technology*. Newbury Park, CA: Sage Publications.

Garnham, N. (1986). The media and the public sphere. In P. Golding, G. Murdock & P. Schlesinger (eds.), *Communicating Politics: Mass Communications and the Political Process* (pp. 37-53). New York: Leicester University Press.

Garton, L. (1995). *An Empirical Analysis of Desktop Videoconferencing and Other Media in a Spatially-Distributed Work Group*. Laval, Québec: Centre for Information Technology Innovation.

Garton, L., Haythornthwaite, C. & Wellman, B. (June, 1997). Studying online social networks, *Journal of Computer-Mediated Communication* 3(1). http://207.201.161.120/jcmc/vol3/issue1/garton.html

Garton, L. & Wellman, B. (1995). The social implications of electronic mail in organizations: A research review, *Communications Yearbook* 18: 434-53.

Gerard, P. & Willems, V. (1997). Prévention et répression de la criminalité sur Internet. In E. Montero (ed.), *Internet face au droit, Cahiers du Centre de Recherches Informatiques et Droit* (pp. 140-1). Namur: Story-Scientia.

Government of Canada (1995). *Connection Community Content: The Challenge of the Information Highway.* Final Report of the Information Highway Advisory Council. Ottawa: Minister of Supply and Services Canada.

Government of Canada (1996). *Building the Information Society: Moving Canada into the 21st Century.* Ottawa: Minister of Supply and Services Canada.

Government of Canada (1997). *Preparing Canada for a Digital World.* Ottawa: Minister of Supply and Services Canada.

Graham, G. (1993, December 9). Software: the engine of the information age, *Issues For Canada's Future*: 7-10.

Graham, S. (1997). Imagining the real-time city: telecommunications, urban paradigm and the future of cities. In S. Westwood & J. Williams (eds.), *Imagining Cities: Scripts, Signs, Memory* (p. 33). London: Routledge.

Habermas, J. (1981). *Theorie des kommunikativen Handelns*, Band 1 & 2. Frankfurt am Main: Suhrkamp Verlag.

Hamers, M. (1998). De SDU discussie nader bekeken. Of: *much ado about nothing.* In L. Hanssen, N.W. Jankowski & J.A.G.M. van Dijk (eds.), *Toegang tot en kwaliteit van het elektronisch debat. Verslag van een studiedag.* Utrecht: Stichting Wetenschap en Techniek Nederland.

Hands off the Internet (1997, July 5). *The Economist*: 13.

Hanssen, L., Jankowski, N.W. & Etienne, R. (1996). Interactivity from the perspective of communication studies. In N.W. Jankowski & L. Hanssen (eds.), *The Contours of Multimedia: Recent Technological, Theoretical and Empirical Developments* (Academia Research Monograph 19) (pp. 61-73). Luton: University of Luton Press/John Libbey Media.

Hanssen, L., Jankowski, N.W. & van Dijk, J.A.G.M. (eds.) (1998). *Toegang tot en kwaliteit van het elektronisch debat. Verslag van een studiedag.* Utrecht: Stichting Wetenschap en Techniek Nederland.

Haythornthwaite, C. (1996). *Media Use in Support of Communication Networks in an Academic Research Environment*. Unpublished doctoral dissertation. University of Toronto: Toronto.

Haythornthwaite, C. (1996). Social network analysis: An approach and technique for the study of information exchange, *Library and Information Science Research* 18 (4): 323-42.

Haythornthwaite, C. & Wellman, B. (in press). Work, friendship and media use for information exchange in a networked organization, *Journal of the American Society for Information Science*.

Haythornthwaite, C., Wellman, B. & Mantei, M. (1995). Work relationships and media use: A social network analysis, *Group Decisions and Negotiations* 4: 189-207.

Herk, A. van (1990). *Places Far From Ellesmere*. Red Deer College Press: Red Deer, Alberta.

Horning, R.A. (1997). *American Experiments in Digital Signature Legislation*, Symposium Presentation on the European Forum on the Law of Telecommunications, Information Super Highways and Multimedia of the European Lawyers Union, Monaco, April 11.

Hossain, K. (1997). *Promoting Human Rights in the Global Market Place*. Amsterdam: Vrije Universiteit.

Industry Canada (1994). *The Canadian Information Highway: Building Canada's Information and Communication Infrastructure*. Ottawa: Supply and Services Canada.

The Information Society Forum (1996, June). *The Annual Report to the European Commission: Networks for People and their Communities*. Brussels.

International Telecommunications Union (1997). *ITU-T Recommendation X.509 (v.3), Information Technology: Open Systems Interconnection*, The Directory: Authentication Framework.

Inuit Broadcasting Corporation (1995). *Northern Voices on the Information Highway: "Connecting the North" Symposium Final Report*. Ottawa: Inuit Broadcasting Corporation.

Jacobson, R. (1996). "Are they building an off-ramp in my neighborhood?" and other questions concerning public interest in and access to the information superhighway. In L. Strate, R. Jacobson & S.B. Gibson (eds.), *Communication and Cyberspace: Social Interaction in an Electronic Environment* (pp. 143-53). Cress Kill, NJ: Hampton Press.

Jankowski, N.W. (1995). Reflections on the origins and meanings of media access, *The Public/Javnost* 2(4): 7-19.

Jankowski, N.W. (1997). *Virtual Democracy: Reflections on a Recent Initiative*. Paper presented at Jaarcongres Onderzoek in Nieuwe Media, Rotterdam.

Jankowski, N.W., Leeuwis, C., Martin, P. Noordhof, M. & Rossum, J. van (1997). *Teledemocracy in the Province: An Experiment with Public Debate and Opinion Polling Internet-Based Software.* Paper presented at the Media & Politics conference, Brussels, March.

Jankowski, N.W. & Malina, A. (1996). *Community Building in Cyberspace: Theoretical Considerations and Proposals for Empirical Study.* Paper presented at the International Association for Mass Communication Research (IAMCR) conference, Sydney, August.

Jefferson, T. (1969). *The Complete Writings of Thomas Jefferson.* Lunenburg: The Stinehour Press.

Johnston, D. & Handa, S. (eds.) (1995). *Getting Canada Online: Understanding the Information Highway.* Toronto: Stoddart.

Jongman, A.J. & Schmid, A.P. (1994). *Monitoring Human Rights.* Leiden University: PIOOM.

Kiesler, S., Siegel, J. & McGuire, T. (1984). Social psychological aspects of computer-mediated communication, *American Psychologist* 39: 1123-34.

Kiesler, S. & Sproull, L. (1992). Group decision making and communication technology, *Organizational Behavior and Human Decision Processes* 52: 96-123.

Koppenjan, J.F.M., Bruijn, J.A. de & Kickert, W.J.M. (1993). *Netwerkmanagement in het openbaar bestuur: Over de mogelijkheden van overheidssturing in beleidsnetwerken.* The Hague: VUGA B.V.

Kroker, A. (1984). *Technology and the Canadian Mind. Innis/McLuhan/Grant.* Montréal: New World Perspectives.

Landow, G.P. (ed.) (1994). *Hyper/Text/Theory.* Baltimore/London: Johns Hopkins University Press.

Latour, B. (1986). The powers of association. In J. Law (ed.), *Power, Action and Belief: A New Sociology of Knowledge?* (pp. 264-80). Boston: Routledge & Kegan Paul.

Laudon, K. (1986). *The Dossier Society: Comments on Democracy in an Information Society.* New York: Columbia University Press.

Leeuwis, C. (1993). *Of Computers, Myths and Modelling: The Social Construction of Diversity, Knowledge, Information and Communication Technologies in Dutch Horticulture and Agricultural Extension.* Wageningen Studies in Sociology Nr. 36. Wageningen: Wageningen Agricultural University.

Leeuwis, C. (1996). Communication technologies for information-based services: experiences and implications. In N.W. Jankowski & L. Hanssen (eds.), *The Contours of Multimedia. Recent Technological, Theoretical and Empirical Developments*. Academia Research Monograph 19 (pp. 86-102). Luton: University of Luton Press/John Libbey Media.

Leeuwis, C., Jankowski, N., Martin, P., Rossum, J. van & Noordhof, M. (1997). *Besliswijzer beproefd. Een onderzoek naar teledemocratie in de provincie*. Amsterdam: Instituut voor Publiek en Politiek (Institute for Public and Politics).

Leeuwis, C. & Voorburg, R.J.J. (1997). Beleidsvorming en de waarde van elektronische vormen van publiek debat, *Beleidswetenschap* 11(4): 339-59.

Leslie, J. (1996). *The End of the World. The Science and Ethics of Human Extinction*. London: Routledge.

Loader, B.D. (ed.) (1997). *The Governance of Cyberspace*. London: Routledge.

London, S. (1994). *Electronic Democracy: An Annotated Bibliography*. http://www.west.net/~insight/london/bibl.htm

Markus, M.L. (1983). Power, politics & MIS, *Communications of the ACM* 26: 430-44.

Markus, M.L. (1994). Electronic mail as the medium of managerial choice, *Organization Science* 5: 502-27.

McCourt, E. (1965). *The Road Across Canada*. Toronto: Macmillan of Canada.

McGrath, J.E. (1984). *Groups, Interaction and Performance*. Englewood Cliffs, NJ: Prentice-Hall.

McGrath, J.E. (1991). Time, interaction and performance (TIP): A theory of groups, *Small Groups Research* 22: 147-74.

McLuhan, M. (1965). *Understanding Media: The Extensions of Man*. Toronto: McGraw-Hill.

Menzies, H. (1996). *Whose Brave New World? The Information Highway and the New Economy*. Toronto: Between the Lines.

Menzies, H. (1997, June 19). *The Virtual Library: Kiosk or Community?* Speech presented to the Canadian Library Association.

Mickelson, K.D. (1997). Seeking social support: Parents in electronic support groups. In Kiesler, S. (ed.), *Culture of the Internet* (pp. 157-78). Mahwah, NJ: Lawrence Erlbaum.

Ministerial Conference Bonn (1997, July). *Global Information Networks*. Bonn.

Monge, P. & Contractor, N.S. (in press). Emergence of Communication Networks. In F.M. Jablin & L.L. Putnam (eds.), *Handbook of Organizational Communication* (2nd edition). Thousand Oaks, CA: Sage Publications. http://www.tec.spcomm.uiuc.edu/nosh/HOCNets.html

Morley, I.E. & Stephenson, G.M. (1970). Formality in experimental negotiations: A validation study, *British Journal of Psychology* 61: 363-84.

Noble, F. & Newman, M. (1993). Integrated system, autonomous departments: Organizations invalidity and system change in a university, *Journal of Management Studies* 30(2): 195-219.

Nunavut Implementation Commission (1995). *Nunavut Telecommunication Needs: Community Teleservice Centres: A Supplementary Report of the Nunavut Implementation Commission*. Iqaluit: Nunavut Implementation Commission.

Nunavut Implementation Commission (1996). *Social and Economic Benefits and Design Considerations and Costs of Community TeleService Centres in Nunavut: A Supplementary Report of the Nunavut Implementation Commission*. Iqaluit: Nunavut Implementation Commission.

OECD (1997a). *Global Information Infrastructure: Global Information Society, Policy Recommendation for Action*. Paris: OCDE/GD (77)138.

OECD (1997b). *Information Technology Outlook*. Paris.

OECD (1997c). *Webcasting and Convergence: Policy Implications*. Paris: DSTI/ICCP/TISP (97)6.

Oppenheim, C. (1995). *The Legal and Regulatory Environment for Electronic Information*. Wiltshire: Infortics.

Parker, G.L. (ed.) (1995). *Haliburton, Thomas Chandler. The Clockmaker Series One, Two, and Three*. Ottawa: Carleton University Press.

Partsch, K.J. (1981). Freedom of conscience and expression, and political freedoms. In L. Henkin (ed.), *The International Bill of Rights* (pp. 209-45). New York: Columbia University Press.

Pauktuutit Inuit Women's Association (1997, June). *Inuit Women Connect: Telecommunications*. Report from the 1997 Pauktuutit AGM. Draft.

Percy-Smith, J. (1996). Downloading democracy? Information and communication technologies in local politics, *Policy and Politics* 24(1): 43-56.

Perritt, H. (1996). *Law and the Information Superhighway*. New York: Wiley Law Publications.

Postman, N. (1995). *The End of Education*. New York: Alfred A. Knopf.

Powe, B.W. (1993). *A Tremendous Canada of Light*. Toronto: Coach House Press.

Raboy, M. (1990). *Missed Opportunities: The Story of Canada's Broadcasting Policy*. Montréal: McGill-Queen's University Press.

Rafaeli, S. (1988). Interactivity: From new media to communication. In R.P. Hawkins, J. Wiemann & S. Pingree (eds.), *Advancing Communication Science: Merging Mass and Interpersonal Processes* (pp. 110-34). Beverly Hills: Sage Publications.

Rathenau Institute (1994). *Het Rathenau Instituut en het debat. Jaarverslag 1994*. The Hague: Rathenau Institute.

Reddick, A. (1995). *The Information Superhighway: Will Some Canadians Be Left at the Side of the Road?* Ottawa: The Public Interest Advocacy Centre.

Rose, L. (1995). *Netlaw*. Berkeley: Osborne McGraw-Hill.

Salaff, J., Dimitrova, D. & Hardwick, D. (1996). Bureaucratic telework: Hot and cool jobs, *Notiziario del Lavoro: Review of Corporate Organization and Culture* 81: 48-52.

Sanders, D. (1991). Collective rights, *Human Rights Quarterly* 13: 368-86.

Secrétariat de l'autoroute de l'information (1996, April). Pour une stratégie de mise en oeuvre de l'autoroute de l'information au Québec. Montréal: Document de travail et de consultation. Gouvernement du Québec.

Short, J., Williams, E. & Christie, B. (1976). *The Social Psychology of Telecommunications*. London: John Wiley & Sons.

Siegel, J., Dubrovsky, V., Kiesler, S. & McGuire, T. (1986). Group processes in computer-mediated communication, *Organizational Behavior and Human Decision Processes* 37: 157-87.

Smith, G. (ed.) (1996). *Internet, Law and Regulation*. London: FT Law and Tax.

Smith, J. (1995). What does convergence mean for women?, *Intermedia* 23(5): 20-2.

Spears, R., Lea, M. & Lee, S. (1990). De-individuation and group-polarization in computer-mediated communication, *British Journal of Social Psychology* 29: 121-34.

Spears, R. & Lea, M. (1992). Social influence and the influence of the 'social' in computer-mediated communication. In M. Lea (ed.), *Contexts of Computer-Mediated Communication* (pp. 33-65). London: Harvester-Wheatsheaf.

Spears, R. & Lea, M. (1994). Panacea or panopticon? The hidden power in computer-mediated communication, *Communication Research* 21(4): 427-59.

Streeter, T. (1987). The cable fable revisited: Discourse, policy, and the making of cable television, *Critical Studies in Mass Communications* 4: 174-200.

Teitlebaum, S. (1997, November). The call of the wired, *Wired*: 234-86.

Trevino, L.K., Daft, L. & Lengel, R.H. (1990). Understanding managers' media choices: A symbolic interactionist perspective. In J. Fulk & C.W. Steinfield (eds.), *Organizations and Communication Technology* (pp. 71-94). Newbury Park/London: Sage Publications.

Turkle, S. (1995). *Life on the Screen: Identity in the Age of the Internet*. New York: Simon & Schuster.

Van de Poll, N.E. & Glasmeier, A. (eds.) (1997). *Natuurontwikkeling waarom en hoe? Verslag van een debat. Working document 59*. The Hague: Rathenau Institute.

Venders queue for cable windfall (1997, June 30). *Communications Week*. London: 27.

Venne, M. (1997a, May 28). Pour un accès gratuit aux lois sur Internet, *Le Devoir*.

Venne, M. (1997b, May 29). L'inforoute et la démocratie, *Le Devoir*.

Vimbert, C. (1994). L'ordre public dans la jurisprudence du Conseil constitutionnel, *Revue du Droit Public*: 701.

Wasserman, S. & Faust, K. (1994). *Social Network Analysis*. Cambridge, MA: Cambridge University Press.

Wellman, B. (1997). An electronic group is virtually a social network. In Kiesler, S. (ed.), *Culture of the Internet* (pp. 179-205). Mahwah, NJ: Lawrence Erlbaum.

Wellman, B. & Berkowitz, S.D. (eds.) (1988). *Social Structures: A Network Approach*. Cambridge: Cambridge University Press.

Wellman, B., Carrington, P. & Hall, A. (1988). Networks as personal communities. In B. Wellman & S.D. Berkowitz (eds.), *Social Structures: A Network Approach* (pp. 130-84). Cambridge: Cambridge University Press.

Wellman, B., Garton, L. & Haythornthwaite, C. (1997, May). *Confronting Global Mythologies: What We Can Learn From Intranets*. Paper presented at the International Communication Association, Montréal, Québec.

Wellman, B., Salaff, J., Dimitrova, D., Garton, L., Gulia, M. & Haythornthwaite, C. (1996). Computer networks as social networks: Collaborative work, telework, and virtual community, *Annual Review of Sociology* 22: 213-38.

Wilby, T.W. (1913). *A Motor Tour Through Canada*. London: John Lane.

Winsbury, R. (1995). Who stands at the gateway to the Information Superhighway?, *Intermedia* 23(2): 8-10.

Woerkum, C.M.J. van (1997). *Communicatie en interactieve beleidsvorming*. Houten/Diegem: Bohn Stafleu Van Loghum.

ABSTRACTS

The Trans-Canada Highway vs The Information Highway: The Road Less Traveled?

Irwin Shubert

The information highway, the information superhighway, the infobahn, the freeway, digital intersection, fiber optic routes... You can't find any of these in your dog-eared atlas of Canada, but these metaphors for telecommunications technologies are rapidly changing our attitudes towards more traditional aspects of travel. The web of intersecting roads and thoroughfares criss-crossing the globe, are now criss-crossing in cyberspace – the web is now the *Web*. The Trans-Canada highway is the longest national highway in the world. It is my intention in this paper to trace the spatial history of this national icon and compare its development to that of the burgeoning development of the information highway. This will begin as a travelogue of a trip taken across the Trans-Canada 26 years ago, a revisitation of sites once vital, now seen as *quaint*, in our so-called *global village*. Will the Trans-Canada highway become the road less traveled? Or, more in keeping with Robert Frost's poem, will it simply become the *road not taken*?

On the (Information) Highway: So Is This a Journey or What?

Robert Kroetsch

The metaphor announced in the expression *information highway* suggests travel and travelers. The delivery of bits of information in sequence further reinforces the sense that we are involved in a narrative pattern. If we are traveling, what are our assumed meta-narratives? Are we re-imagining traditional journeys or quests? What are the landscapes we visit?... In the past the great Dutch landscape painters did much to shape our understanding of space and place. In more recent times highways have reshaped what we call landscape and travel. What changes are we now entering into under the rubric, cyberspace?... I will try to explore (itself a version of travel) the questions (not the answers) by looking at two of Aritha van Herk's most challenging texts: her novel, *No fixed Address*, and her geografictione, *Places Far From Ellesmere*.

Human Rights in Cyberspace

Cees J. Hamelink

This essay explores the application of the international human rights regime to the governance of cyberspace. The proliferation of cyberspace technologies inevitably implies a confrontation with moral issues on different levels. These relate to – among others – choices about the way the technology will be designed; choices among possible applications and the responsibility for certain applications; choices about the introduction and the use of applications. They also address issues such as the unequal distribution of harm and benefit of applications among social actors; the control over technology and its administration; and the uncertainty about the future impacts of technology. The specific question that concerns me here is whether the current international human rights regime can provide us with meaningful moral and legal guidance in addressing these moral choices.

Internet and Public Order
Stylianos Garipis

If we accept, as we should, that the use of the Internet is related to the recognition of several constitutional rights and liberties (right of expression, communication, publication, advertisement, and so on), we are then obliged to search for the legitimate regulatory institution in this domain. Should this regulatory institution be found on a national or international level? The answer to this crucial question is strongly related to the impact of Internet use on public order. If certain uses – or abuses – are not compatible with the national public order, can the national institutions legitimately limit such uses? Then, of course, we should answer the following questions: can the notion of national public order justify *de facto* restrictions imposed on citizens of other States?

The Legal Aspects of Digital Signatures
Patrick van Eecke

In its recently adopted Communication, *A European Initiative in Electronic Commerce* (European Commission, Communication to the European Parliament, the Council, the Economic and Social Committee and the Committee of the regions, 15.04.97, COM(97) 157: 13), the European Commission announced its intention to come forward with a specific initiative on Digital Signatures. This initiative will aim at ensuring a common legal framework encompassing the legal recognition of Digital Signatures in the Single Market, the setting up of minimum criteria for Certification Authorities, as well as pursuing worldwide agreements. Also, the European Parliament has invited the Commission to prepare as soon as possible legal provisions concerning information security and digital identifications (European Parliament Resolution A4-244-96 of 10.09.96, OJ320:164 of 28.10.96). The paper first wants to describe the need for secure authentication in cyberspace. Second it wants to analyze the legal situation in the different EU member states regarding the use, the implementation, and the legal acceptance of Digital Signatures and Certification Authorities. Finally, the keynote wants to compare the European vision with the Canadian legal and technical state of the art. The Canadian government is, indeed, currently developing guidelines for the introduction of digital signatures in Canada.

How Comfortably Does the Internet Sit on Canada's Tundra? Reflections on Public Access to the Information Highway in the North
Lorna Roth

Much of the recent discourse in Canadian communication studies has focused on the development of the information highway, the Internet, and the ways in which minority constituency groups may gain equitable access to its common routes. One of the assumptions underlying current discussions it that everyone would automatically want to be linked to the information highway in order not to be *left behind*. Using case study materials from Canada's North, this paper will examine several ways in which First Peoples have intervened in the broader Canadian debates to examine their own cultural, political, and economic objectives and goals in an effort to construct an infrastructure reflecting their unique information needs. First, it will focus on the ground-breaking teleconference, *Connecting the North*, which took place in 1994 to discuss Northern priorities and services. Second, I shall look at the more recent pilot projects and plans for the extension of the information highway into the North. Evidence from the Northern planning process supports a more deliberative decision making approach consistent with those like Harold Innis (1951) and Heather Menzies (1996), both of whom argue for a slowing down period in which to contemplate long-term technical priorities and policy strategies, as well as the information highway's possible implications for (cross)cultural communication patterns in the future.

Policy-Making and the Value of Electronic Forms of Public Debate: Underpinning, Assumptions and First Experiences

Cees Leeuwis

This paper investigates the potential value of electronic forms of debate in governmental policy processes. For this purpose, some strengths and weaknesses of conventional forms of political debate are discussed. On the basis of insights derived from communication science and social psychology, a number of preliminary assumptions are generated. These assumptions address the way in which electronic forms of debate may compare with conventional forms of debate, keeping in mind the strengths and weaknesses of the latter. It emerges that – under specific conditions – electronic forms of debate may have various advantages over conventional forms of debate. These potential advantages are, amongst others: (a) a larger number and variety of participants; (b) less occurrence of time pressure; (c) more egalitarian participation; (d) more extensive articulation of arguments; (e) more flexible information provision during the debate; (f) better opportunities for in-depth debate along a greater diversity of discussion lines; and (g) greater freedom and openness during the debate. A major weakness of electronic forms of debate may lie in their limited capacity to facilitate a group identity, thereby having counterproductive effects on consensus formation and conflict resolution. On the basis of some initial research experiences, the paper sets out to critically reflect on the extent to which the assumed advantages and disadvantages have materialized in actual practice.

Two Canadian Models of Communities on the Net: SchoolNet and Community Access

Alan L. Cobb

This paper outlines recent experience in Canada with two national initiatives: *SchoolNet* and the *Community Access Program*. Launched in 1993, SchoolNet is surpassing all expectations and is considered to have been an outstanding success. SchoolNet connected 300 schools by 1994. All 16,500 schools are connected as of 1999. In addition, 400 of the 450 First Nations schools and 2,100 of the 3,400 libraries are connected as of 1998. As of the end of 1998 all libraries and First Nations schools were connected. Each month SchoolNet receives 2.5 million "hits." Every day, on average, someone signs on to SchoolNet over 83,000 times. Launched in 1995, and an offshoot of SchoolNet, the Community Access Program is an equally outstanding success to date. Beyond the use of computers, the purpose of Community Access is to provide Canada's rural communities with affordable public access to the Information Highway and to familiarize rural Canadians with how the Information Highway can be used for economic and community development, particularly the creation of jobs and growth. The Program provides assistance of up to Cdn$30,000 to help cover the start-up costs of establishing a community site, including equipment, Internet connections, staff, training and technical support. A site is usually situated in a community center, library, school or other public facility. Average program costs to date (i.e., the 50 percent share) is some Cdn$20,000. Starting with 20 sites in 1994, there are now over 1,200. While the current target is to establish sites in 5,000 remote communities by year 2000, there is a proposal to increase that target to 10,000 communities in the same timeframe.

Teledemocracy in the Province: An Experiment with Internet-based Software and Public Debate

Nicholas Jankowski, Cees Leeuwis, Peter Martin, Margreet Noordhof and Jeffrey van Rossum

In November 1996 a month-long experiment was held with teledemocracy in the Dutch province of North Brabant. During that experiment, some 100 residents and representatives of organizations in the province were invited to debate aspects of land use for the province. This public debate took place with the aid of an Internet-based software program which allowed for moderated discussion, periodic polling of participants, and voting. A research report of this experiment was completed in May 1997 and this paper – based on that report and academic theses subsequently prepared – provides an overview and assessment of this experiment with teledemocracy. Data are presented on the participants and their reflections on the experiment. Attention is also paid to the role of the provincial government in this initiative with *on-line democracy*. These findings are related to two of the central theoretical perspectives which guided the work – Rogers's and Kincaid's convergence model of communication and Habermas's notion of public sphere. The paper ends with a summary of the main findings from the experiment along with consideration of a number of central issues valuable for future research around initiatives with teledemocracy.

Work and Community in Networked Organizations

Caroline Haythornthwaite

When computer networks link people as well as machines, they become social networks. Such computer-supported social networks (CSSNs) are becoming important bases of virtual communities, computer-supported co-operative work, and telework. We review our Toronto-based Virtually Social Research Group's analysis of scholarly networks and on-line workgroups. We find that CSSNs sustain strong, intermediate and weak ties that provide information and social support in both specialized and broadly-based relationships. CSSNs foster sociable and work communities that are usually partial and narrowly focused, although some relationships do grow to become encompassing and broadly based. CSSNs accomplish a wide variety of co-operative work, connecting workers within and between sites that are often physically dispersed. Although many relationships function off-line as well as on-line, CSSNs have developed their own norms and structures. The nature of on-line media both constrains and facilitates social controls. Thus CSSNs have strong societal implications, fostering situations that combine global connectivity, the fragmentation of solidarities, the de-emphasis of local organizations, and the increased importance of home bases. For our case study, we report in detail about our social network study of *Cerise*, an English-Canadian university computer science research group, to understand how 25 scholars' work and friendship relationships were associated with the kinds of media they used for different kinds of information exchange. The use of electronic mail, unscheduled face-to-face encounters and scheduled face-to-face meetings predominate for the exchange of six basic kinds of information: Receiving Work, Giving Work, Collaborative Writing, Computer Programming, Sociability, and Major Emotional Support. Face-to-face contact is the medium of choice for pairs with weaker ties, i.e., those who exchange only one or two types of information. Those pairs with stronger ties supplement face-to-face contact with e-mail, but few use synchronous, intrusive desktop videoconferencing or telephoning. The intensity of work and friendship relationships are each independently associated with greater frequency of communication, the exchange of more and different types of information, and the use of e-mail as well as face-to-face contact.

ICTs for SMEs: The SME Wins on the Information Highway

Karel Uyttendaele

In a blitz co-operative effort, Fabrimetal and CRIF-WTCM, along with the Belgian Chambers of Commerce and Industry, reached 1,600 SME managers with a promotion campaign concentrating on Internet and on E-Commerce. Fabrimetal is convinced that SMEs should not wait any longer to get acquainted with the Internet. The G7 and the EC believe that the accelerated introduction of Information and Communications Technologies (ICTs) at SMEs can stimulate new economic growth. A second series of "roadshows," aiming at Internet-enabled innovation and manufacturing, took place in November and December 1997 at 25 locations, in 35 sessions, using 4 ISDN lines per location. Central aims of the initiative were the promotion of Internet-based Electronic Purchasing (E-Commerce) and Internet-enabled networking along with complementary SMEs (E-messaging), as initial steps for a full informatization of the 185,000 Belgian SMEs. Fabrimetal is the Belgian federation (with 1,200 members) of industries in the "metal" sector (machinery, transport, electroconstructions, electronics, telecommunications, IT), and CRIF-WTCM is its associated joint research arm. With this initiative, Belgium operates at the forefront of the diffusion of ICTs for SMEs.

The Centre for Editing Early Canadian Texts (CEECT) and Cyberspace
Mary Jane Edwards
For the last sixteen years the Centre for Editing Early Canadian Texts (CEECT) at Carleton University has been preparing, with the help of computers, scholarly editions of major works of early English-Canadian prose. We have thus participated in the revolutions in both textual theory and technology that have occurred in the past two decades. We have, nevertheless, continued to publish our critically edited texts in paperback and casebound copies. With the price of books escalating and the medium itself threatened with obsolescence, however, we are now contemplating the advantages and disadvantages of mounting our editions on the Internet. This paper describes briefly the scholarly editions prepared by CEECT, discusses succinctly its use of computers, and analyzes some challenges posed by cyberspace for scholars who wish to protect both the integrity of their authors' work and the reliability of their editions, but who, at the same time, still hope to have their publications distributed cheaply, conveniently, and widely.

The Position of Flanders with Regard to Some Internet-Related Matters
Luc Van Fleteren
The Government of Flanders has decided to make the Internet accessible to the largest possible public. As of 1997 free access to the Internet was made available in all Flemish libraries, schools of higher education and a first group of 150 secondary schools. In the medium term all primary and secondary schools will be connected. The most ambitious initiative is *Telenet Flanders*. The goal of *Telenet* is to convert the existing cable networks into an interactive broadband network which, apart from the existing broadcasting services, also offers telephone, Internet and other multimedia services. The complete regional network overlay will be finished by 2002. *Telenet Flanders* already delivers fast Internet access in some areas, and started with telephony services after January 1, 1998. The Government of Flanders sees an important but minimalist role for government in regulating the Internet. The general guiding principles should be twofold: first, using existing laws wherever possible, rather than creating new ones; and second, always erring on the side of a limited number of regulations until activities on the Internet assume a clearer shape.

Québécois Policy and the Development of the Information Highway
Serge Proulx

The Québec Government takes very seriously the development of the information highway. Its policy orientation aims at six general objectives: (1) economic and regional development of Québec; (2) achieving productivity gains in Government; (3) internationalization of Québec and Québécois expertise abroad; (4) better citizen information, with services that are more adapted to people's living and working conditions; (5) improving education and social development; and (6) promoting the French language and the expression of Québec culture. The Québec Government intends to assiduously pursue three essential objectives: (1) growing productivity within its own ministries and organisms; (2) supporting that part of the private sector interested in positioning itself on the world market for electronics (the Government favours projects with payoffs in the industrial environment as a whole over supporting projects that are aimed at the development of one particular firm); and (3) supporting the production and on-line dissemination of contents and services in the French language (undoubtedly to be understood as an element of the Government's sovereignist project). However, the objectives concerning universal access and its integration into educational contexts seem to be long in coming. In conclusion, the author reminds us of the current globalization context. This context is characterized by a series of major transformations in cultural industries including the media sector, and this on a planetary level.

Advancing Canada's Information Highway: Strategies for the New Millennium
David Johnston and Natasha H. Faraqui

Canada has made enormous progress in building the Information Highway in the last decade. While much has been accomplished, more work remains before the full promise of the knowledge society is realized. At the close of its mandate (September 1997), the Information Highway Advisory Council (IHAC) outlined specific areas it felt would require further attention including initiatives in advanced networks, standards, performance indicators, electronic commerce, and lifelong learning. The IHAC believes that:
1. government has a responsibility to take the lead role in developing the knowledge society by positioning itself as a model user of information and communications technology;
2. access to the Information Highway is critical to Canada's future, as the economy becomes more dependent on information;
3. reinforcing Canadian sovereignty and protecting Canada's cultural identity continues to be a major public policy mandate. Thanks to information technology, there are now new ways to create, produce, market and distribute content;
4. sectoral areas such as health, education and small business represent significant opportunities for the development of content, applications and services. In each of these sectors, the potential benefits of the Information Highway are considerable.

Electronic Commerce Policy and the European Commission

Paul Timmers

Electronic commerce has become an important policy area for the European Commission over the past few years, within the context of the promotion of the Information Society. Recent developments in policy making related to the European Commission and their international dimension are presented in this overview.

ABOUT THE AUTHORS

Alan L. Cobb held several senior executive positions in the Government of Canada over a thirty-year period. He is currently a Management Consultant based in Ottawa offering executive management services to industry and governments in Canada. E-mail: alcobb@ibm.net

Mary Jane Edwards is Professor of English and Director of the Centre for Editing Early Canadian Texts, Carleton University, Ottawa, Canada. E-mail: mjedward@ccs.carleton.ca

Patrick van Eecke is Lecturer at the Interdisciplinary Centre for Law and IT, University of Leuven, Belgium. E-mail: patrick.vaneecke@law.kuleuven.ac.be

Natasha H. Faraqui is a Policy Analyst on information highway matters at the Ministry of Industry, Ottawa, Canada. E-mail: faraqui.natasha@ic.gc.ca

Stylianos Garipis holds a Master's Degree in Law Theory (LL.M.) from the Université Libre de Bruxelles and is currently an independent attorney in Thessaloniki, Greece.

Leen d'Haenens is Associate Professor at the Department of Communication, University of Nijmegen, The Netherlands. E-mail: l.dhaenens@maw.kun.nl

Cees J. Hamelink is Professor at the Department of Communication, University of Amsterdam, The Netherlands. E-mail: hamelink@pscw.uva.nl

Caroline Haythornthwaite is Assistant Professor at the Graduate School of Library and Information Science, University of Illinois at Urbana-Champaign, US. E-mail: haythorn@alexia.lis.uiuc.edu

Nicholas Jankowski is Associate Professor at the Department of Communication, University of Nijmegen, The Netherlands. E-mail: n.jankowski@maw.kun.nl

David Johnston is Professor at the Centre for Medecine, Ethics and Law, McGill University, Montréal and served as chair of the Information Highway Advisory Council, Ottawa, from 1994 to 1997. He presently chairs the Canadian Institute for Advanced Research, and is Special Advisor to the Minister of Industry on information highway matters.

Robert Kroetsch is a writer, an editor and a teacher. He taught at the universities of Calgary and Manitoba in the late 1970s. He is a prominent figure in the Canadian literary scene with a special interest in the Canadian Prairies.

Cees Leeuwis is Lecturer and Senior Researcher at the Department of Communication and Innovation Studies, University of Wageningen, The Netherlands. E-mail: cees.leeuwis@alg.vlk.wau.nl

Peter Martin holds a Master's Degree in Communication Science (University of Nijmegen, The Netherlands) and is currently employed as a Customer Support Specialist at Solvay Pharmaceuticals, Weesp, The Netherlands. E-mail: pema@dds.nl

Margreet Noordhof holds a Master's Degree in Communication Science (University of Nijmegen, The Netherlands). E-mail: mnoordhof@prvgron.nl

Serge Proulx is Professor at the Département de Communications, Université du Québec à Montréal, Québec, Canada. E-mail: proulx.serge@uqam.ca

Jeffrey van Rossum holds a Master's Degree in Communication Science (University of Nijmegen, The Netherlands) and is currently employed as an IT-specialist at IBM Global Services, The Netherlands. E-mail: j_vanrossum@ibmmail.nl

Lorna Roth is Associate Professor at the Department of Communication Studies, Concordia University, Montréal, Canada. E-mail: roth@pop.microtec.net

Irwin Shubert is Lecturer at the Centre for Canadian Studies, Simon Fraser University, Burnaby, British Columbia, Canada. E-mail: ishubert@sfu.ca

Paul Timmers is Head of Electronic Commerce Sector, European Commission, Directorate General III, Brussels, Belgium. E-mail: paul.timmers@dg3.cec.be

Karel Uyttendaele is Manager of Fabit Information Technologies, Fabrimetal, Brussels, Belgium. E-mail: karel.uyttendaele@fabrimetal.be

Luc Van Fleteren is Technology Advisor of the Minister President of the Flemish Government, Brussels, Belgium. E-mail: luc.vanfleteren@vlaanderen.be